Praise for *The Fat Girl's Guid*

"Fun y, f   e St   ou,   lfilling."
—F   ns   ho   l   A   logu

"This send-up of the thin-is-in mentality is funny enough to make even diehard dieters consider replacing their baby carrots with Krispy Kremes . . . Irreverent, refreshing and human. Anyone who has ever tried to lose a pound will gain confidence and a sense of humor from Shanker's story."—*Publishers Weekly*

"Thank heavens for Wendy Shanker: She's written a manifesto for all of us who are sick of obsessing over our bodies. Armed with hilarious wit, she covers everything . . . all as though you're having a 3 A.M. dorm room chat. You just want to say to her, 'Oh sister . . . I've been there too!' "—*Seventeen*

"Wendy Shanker's terrific book proves that size does matter. Luckily for us she has huge talent, wit, and insight."—Susan Shapiro, author of *Five Men Who Broke My Heart*

"Put on your seat belt and enjoy the fun-filled, wacky ride!"—Emme, supermodel host of E!'s *Fashion Emergency* and author of *True Beauty*

"An enjoyable rant by a 'fat' woman who has chosen to be herself." —*Chicago Tribune*

"Shanker's humor hits its mark."—*Bust* magazine

"Brutally honest, occasionally conflicted, wryly funny and sadly poignant . . . worth a read for any woman, regardless of her size." —*Detroit Metro Times*

What Real Women Say About *The Fat Girl's Guide to Life*

"My self-image is not perfect, but now when I look in the mirror or think something self-loathing, there is a little Wendy in my mind that tells me, 'Enough of that. You are fine the way you are.' Thank you for being the angel on my shoulder. We have such better things to do than worry about our abs! Let's change the world!"—Dena

"I've wasted so much of my adult life fighting my weight and being afraid of life because of it. I hope your book reaches the coming generations. I hope my daughters, when I have them, don't go through what I've been put through. Thank you so much! You're the Fat Girls' champion."—Hope

"Your book has really changed my life—in little things I say and do, and in ways I think about myself. Because of the ways in which you tell your story, rather than preaching about what people should and should not do, I was able to relate and learn."—Iris

"I just finished *The Fat Girl's Guide to Life* and it was great! It gives women the strength to love their bodies and the truth about the forces working against us . . . We are smart, sassy, beautiful women and we cannot let weight hold us back."—Andrea

"Thank you for writing the story of my life!"—Banji

"Your book should be required reading for every teenage girl out there. It would save so much heartache and improve their self-esteem immensely."—Julie

"*Yes*, there are people under size 12 who are reading your book—me and my fifteen-year-old daughter, for two. This is for *every* girl, not just fat or Fat girls . . . I'm forty-one and am finally going to just enjoy myself; my body image issues are cured!"—Sally

"I, like every woman out there, have hated my body almost since I started living in it. No matter how many admirers appreciated my boobs, hips, and belly, I didn't get it. I loved your funny, understanding look at our struggles."—Kathleen

"Reading your perspective on 'fatness' has made me want to try harder to treat myself better and be more accepting of myself at this moment in time. Thanks for the inspiration."—Stacy

"I found *The Fat Girl's Guide to Life* to be refreshing, enlightening, honest, and laugh-out-loud funny (really, I laughed out loud). Thanks for writing a book that no one else has had the guts to write."—Svetlana

"Please continue to spread this truthful and refreshing message to people. If all women could embrace themselves a little more and not focus so much on weight, we could accomplish amazing things."—Beth

"Thanks for validating the creed that I live by—which is that you can be fat and fabulous. It's wonderful to know that I'm not the only one who believes that."—Amanda

"While I was reading your book I realized that I'm not the only one who felt like this. Suddenly, I feel almost normal. I just wanted to thank you, Wendy Shanker, for giving my life a new perspective and for understanding me without even knowing me. Thank you for writing your book and thank you for being a Fat Girl."—Norana

The Fat Girl's Guide to Life

WENDY SHANKER

BLOOMSBURY

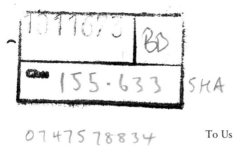
To Us

Author's note:
Some names have been changed

First published in Great Britain 2006

Bloomsbury Publishing Plc, 36 Soho Square, London W1D 3QY

A CIP catalogue record for this book is available from the British Library

ISBN 0 7475 7883 4
9780747578833

10 9 8 7 6 5 4 3 2

Typeset by Hewer Text Ltd, Edinburgh
Printed in Great Britain by Clays Ltd, St Ives plc

www.bloomsbury.com/wendyshanker
www.wendyshanker.com

Table of Contents

Make your choice. Are you ready to be strong?
*   —Buffy the Vampire Slayer*

Introduction

I went on a sixteen-year odyssey of self-loathing and self-doubt. Instead of a Cyclops, I faced off against Jenny Craig. Instead of Sirens, vast quantities of chocolate-chip banana muffins attempted to lure me from my true path. The odyssey's over now. The monsters, both the ones I discovered and the ones I created, have been vanquished. Now I know that there's nothing wrong with me mentally or physically. I'm just fat, that's all.

I didn't win by epiphany, or a life-changing conversation; nor was I shot by a magic bullet. This was a war of attrition; I simply decided I'd had enough. Enough of looking in the mirror and cursing myself out before I'd even brushed my teeth. Enough of punishing myself and my body by reading Danielle Steel in the shade while everyone else was swimming in the pool. Enough of looking up at mirrored ceilings in elevators to assure myself that I was pretty. Enough of squeezing into nylon undergarments that cut off my circulation and left red welts in my skin. Enough of giving away my hard-earned cash to undo a situation that steadily got less undoable.

Honestly, given the choice between being fat or putting myself through the drama of trying to be thin, I'd rather be fat.

It's not that I've "given up on myself" or "let myself go." I don't sit around in my jammies eating bonbons all day. I go to the gym four or five times a week. I count up my proteins and carbohydrates, and usually record what I eat in a little notebook at the end of the day. I follow the latest medical news and research new ideas. I go to the doctor to stay on top of my blood pressure, cholesterol, and triglycerides. I haven't stopped trying to finesse my body into a shape that would make life easier for me and simpler for society to accept.

But I've certainly changed my standards. And I've changed my attitude.

I encourage you to diet and exercise and liposuck and Ab-Roll if that's really what you want, and if you're convinced that you have to change your body to make yourself happy.

But if it's not . . .

If it's really what you think your husband wants . . .

If it's really what you think your mother wants . . .

If it's really what you think Cameron Diaz wants . . .

If it's what you think you've been doing for just about forever and it isn't working and some days you just hope a car will run you over but you're pretty sure that you're so fat that the speeding vehicle will simply bounce off of you . . .

. . . then it's time to stop and reevaluate.

It's time to change our attitudes about this whole body-image business. It *is* a business. It *is* an image. But it is *YOUR* body, which contains *YOUR* mind, which can be a whole lot easier to change than the width of your thighs or the shape of your ass.

We should be able to laugh at an issue as silly as cellulite, but we don't. Can we at least try to evaluate beauty on our own terms instead of the terms we've decided to accept from *Vogue* and Hollywood and your aunt Gertrude and the girl who won "Best Booty" in high school? Shouldn't we teach men to lust for something other than women with little-girl bodies and Play-boy Bunny breasts? And can't we figure out a better way to spend our time and money while we're in the process?

I'm not a doctor. I'm not a therapist. I don't have a degree in health education. I'm just a professional ex-dieter with a chip on my shoulder and a mission on my mind. There are too many women just like me who know more information about fat grams than about foreign policy, who spend more time count-ing calories than communicating with friends. That ain't right.

I'm going to take a good hard look at the weight loss industry, the government, media and celebrities, family and friends, feelings, fashion, and feminism. All of these things affect the way I think about myself and my body and the strategies I've used to come to terms with the skin I'm in. It's been a long, uphill battle.

Now I champion anti-dieting with the best of 'em, but I have to admit I still have my good days and my bad days. I swear off calorie counting, but secretly hope that someday I'll come up with the resolve to ban bagels from my life. I've pretty much resolved that I'll never mold a bicep out of my bat wings, but I still lift weights at the gym. I'm not one hundred percent self-satisfied, but I'm trying; I'm closer. I'm not pushing for com-plete self-acceptance; self-tolerance is a perfectly reasonable place to begin. I'm not in touch with my Goddess Power, I don't think I have a fabulous body, and I'm certainly not about to chant some New Agey "just love yourself" mantra. I don't look in the mirror and see a beautiful, bountiful me with a sunset on the horizon and doves flitting around in the air. But I no longer apologize for who I am or how I look. I have more important things to do.

So do you. You have a career to pursue, you have creativity

to develop, you have a family to raise, and you have friends to love. You live in a society in the midst of major transition that needs your attention and your help. In light of what's happening to women across the globe—rape, poverty, lack of health care, lack of legal rights, and civil war on a daily basis—our obsession with calorie counting seems ridiculous.

We are ready, willing, and able to change the way the world sees us. But to do that, we start by changing the way we see ourselves. Friends won't stop making helpful yet asinine suggestions about corn oil and couscous until you tell them that their suggestions are asinine, not helpful. Bullies won't stop making fun of you until you stand up to them. Magazines won't start putting fat girls in their pages until you start buying magazines that already feature fat girls in their pages. Manufacturers won't stop making fattening fat-free food until you stop eating it. And don't expect Brad Pitt to make out with Camryn Manheim in his next movie, or the captain of the football team to push aside the head cheerleader so he can get some face time with the chubby yet sweet yearbook editor until you are ready to accept those changes yourself.

The good news is that the wheels are already in motion. We have fat girls starring on Broadway and in prime-time TV shows. We are heroines in best-selling novels, and our faces (and bodies) are finally showing up in mainstream women's magazines. We are going to win this battle. After all, we are bigger than they are. There are more of Us than there are of Them (68 percent of the American female population wear a size 12 or larger). So why are we scared to fight back? Why do we shoulder the responsibility of failure ("I have no willpower"/"I'm not trying hard enough"/"I'm a loser"/"It's because of my period") instead of challenging the system? Has it occurred to you that if you can't reach your goal weight at Diet Center then maybe something is wrong with the goal weight and *not* wrong with you? If you suck down Slim-Fast shakes, feel hungry and irritable, do the plan to the letter, and still don't lose weight, have you considered that it's not the piece of cinnamon toast you ate last Tuesday that messed you up? If you work out like a triathlete and still have flab hanging from your arms, did you ever think that maybe those are just the arms you've got and even if you hired Jennifer Aniston's trainer to kick you into gear you still wouldn't feel comfy in a tube top?

The truth is, women who wear a size 2 often feel just crappy about themselves and think they look as big as houses. So go ahead and feel fat. Or, if the f-word doesn't apply to you, substitute "zitty." Or "curly-haired." Or "short." Whatever. If you have a physical attribute that's going to keep you from getting a $20 million paycheck from a Hollywood studio, then we have a lot in common.

Maybe you'll relate to body changes that are beyond your control (say, from illness or accident or pregnancy), or body changes that you regret to this day (like Cheetos overload, or sitting on your couch all day watching *Ricki Lake* reruns, or breaking the seal on Baskin-Robbins Jamoca Almond Fudge for the first time). You may be thinking about those five elusive pounds you want to lose, or the fifty-five, or the hundred and five.

I suggest that you take it a step further. Think about how much time you've spent thinking about that poundage, and the time you've spent punishing yourself about that poundage. Then I'd like you to imagine NOT doing that. Instead, imagine the relief you'd feel if you could walk past a plate-glass window without cursing your reflection. Imagine not sucking it in when your office crush object strolls by. Imagine walking around on a windy day without holding your shirt out in front of you so it doesn't brush your belly.

Now imagine if we all did it. The Fat Girls and the Skinny Chicks. The Beauty Queens and the Dowdy Spinsters, the Flaming Queens and the Butch Rodeo Riders. The Movie Stars and the PR Agents, the Senators and the Interns, the Personal Shoppers and the Supermarket Clerks. The Soccer Moms and the CEOs. Mmm . . . all that free time on our minds that we aren't using to rip ourselves to shreds. All that money in our wallets that we're not going to spend on fat-free, sugar-free, taste-free sorbet. That's a lot of minutes and a lot of money from a lot of women who have a lot of brain power.

This book is for you, whether you feel fat or look fat or act fat or none of the above. I hope that by the end of it you'll understand the difference between being fat and being FAT. You are going to take all the time and energy you've been wasting thinking about your body and work on the stuff that really matters to you as an individual. You just may find that the thing you thought you wanted—a thin body—isn't really what you need the most.

I figure: If we can't take it off, then we might as well just take it on.

CHAPTER 1

From ''fat'' to ''Fat''

Wendy is a fat girl's name.
—Monica (Courteney Cox Arquette) on *Friends*

I start by telling the friend or coworker or acquaintance that I'm writing a book called *The Fat Girl's Guide to Life*. He or she usually looks me over from head to toe before choosing words carefully. "But Wendy, I don't think of you as—" this generally takes a second, because it's hard to say the word— "fat."

I know, sweetie, because you think fat is something really awful. You think fat means "loserish" and "lame" and "disgusting" and "hopeless." None of those words describe me. But I'm here to tell you that "fat" is a word. It's an adjective. Like "tall" or "brunette" or "female" or "Jewish" or "smart," which are other adjectives that describe me. By any standard you can find—societal norms, a doctor's chart, a clothing rack, my own personal ideals—I am most definitely fat. So go ahead and start thinking of me that way.

The F-Word

"Fat."

If you ever want to make people visibly uncomfortable, just say the f-word out loud.

You can refer to yourself as fat ("Hi, I'm fat!") or acknowledge that someone else is fat ("She's pretty, but she sure is fat!"), but either way, you're pretty much guaranteed to freak someone out.

"Fat" is the word I use to describe my physical stature. I use it without apology. The more I use it, the more comfortable I feel with it, and the less power it has to hurt me when someone else uses it as an insult. When I describe myself to someone else, I like to say I'm fat, but it usually scares the hell out of 'em. I don't know what they picture—maybe one of those people Richard Simmons has to suck out of a house with a forklift. By now I've said the word so many times that it really doesn't bother me anymore. I don't mind the word; it's the associations I can do without. What's the worst thing someone can say to me? "You're fat!"? No duh. I just told you that.

"Fat" literally means "containing or full of fat; oily; greasy . . . said of meat." It also means "prosperous; profitable; lucrative; valuable." Screw the dictionary definitions; in our society, "fat" means bad. Unless you're on one of those high-fat, no-carb diets, that is. In that case, set yourself up with a slab of bacon and some eggs Benedict on the side—without the English muffin, of course.

"But Wendy," says my poor innocent friend/relative/victim, "since 'fat' is such a loaded word, isn't there a different one you can use?"

Sure. I could use "overweight," or "plus size," or "curvaceous," or any of a million others, and I do. But why not call it like I see it? The word that I like the most, and the one that I think aptly describes my body, is "fat." The opposite of thin. I like it. It's short, it's sweet, it's surprisingly compact.

But why do I call myself a fat girl instead of a fat woman? Personally, using the word "girl" conjures up the energy of "girl power," aka the fun side of feminism. "Fat girl" is also one of those phrases in our collective unconscious—like "the fat kid"—that's desperately in need of a mental makeover. One night—and this is recently—I was on a packed subway train minding my own business. As the train pulled into my stop I said "Excuse me," so I could start weaving my way through a knot of people. Right behind me, this teenage girl who had been making out with her boyfriend the whole ride said in a really loud voice, "FAT GIRL COMING THROUGH!" I can't begin to tell you how surprised I was, how humiliated I felt. I didn't get my composure back until I was off the train and it was too late to say something in response. I mean, I'm ME. Fantastic ME. I'm the thirty-one-year-old you-go-girl, writing the book you are reading this very minute, but that little phrase cut me to the quick. I don't know why she said it. I'm pretty sure that it was about her and not me—maybe she wanted to impress her boyfriend, maybe she needed to let him know that she would never get fat (like me), maybe I reminded her of her mother or sister or friend or ex-friend or some girl at school she hates. Maybe she was pissed that my big fat ass was taking up valuable subway seat space and I had been too lost in my own thoughts to notice.

And what was I supposed to say to her? I know what I would have asked her if I had the moment back again. I'd calmly ask her why. "Why say that? What are you trying to accomplish? I'm not going to be mean to you, like you were to me, I just want to know why." It's not my job to defend myself against this girl. It's her job not to attack me.

Still, it's hard to be called "fat" and just roll with it. I think of poor Fergie. You know, Sarah Ferguson, flame-haired duchess and current spokesmodel for Weight Watchers. British tabloids regularly referred to her as "the Duchess of Pork." Journalists printed a story that said 82 percent of men would rather sleep with a goat than Fergie. But a recent news story from Reuters revealed that Fergie "recently came face to face with the author of the 'Duchess of Pork' headline that most haunted her, only to find that her enemy was a jovial, balding, middle-aged man who had no idea of the years of distress he had caused. Before long she was joking with him, realizing suddenly that the writer bore her no malice and never had. 'He was paid to be clever, end of story. It occurred to me that we survive our critics by knowing that their agendas, at heart, may have little to do with us,' she said." Kind of like my little lady on the subway. Props to Fergie for calling her tormentor out, but what a shame that she had to hurt for so many years. Can you relate?

Words are just a bunch of letters in a row. A word isn't negative, it's our connotation that is. The words can stay the same; it's our attitudes about them that have to change. You've seen this evolution happen in the gay community with the word "queer." Once reviled, the word "queer" now demands respect and pride. Only a few years ago, would you have thought that a show called *Queer Eye for the Straight Guy* would be a hit on network television? Could *The Fat Pick on the Skinny Chick* be far behind?

Like gay men have, we need to reappropriate "fat" and take back the power of the word. But just because I'm opening the floodgates on "fat" doesn't mean that someone outside the fold is allowed to take it too far. Yes, I am a Fat Girl. And I am coming through. But to the rest of you riding the train with me, I hope this is what will come through loud and clear: Keep your insults to yourself.

Are You Fat Enough to Read This Book?

Let's say the attitude does change, and we can say the word "fat" as comfortably as we can say the word "thin." Now you're saying it a lot and I'm saying it a lot and at first we're scaring people but the more we say it the less freaky it sounds and eventually the shock wears off and we can all go about our business—except for one very important thing: What if you're not fat?

After all, when my friend in her size 8 pants complains that she looks like a _____ (fill in large animal here: hippo? cow? pig? elephant?), I snort to myself, "Oh, as if she knows what she's talking about. Ha. She's fat? Ha." Then again, I know there are size 26 women out there who think, "Oh my goodness, Wendy's a peanut—as if she knows how hard it is to be fat!" Fine, fine. There are a few different ways we can go about determining who is actually fat and who is just having a kinda bloaty day.

1. Assume We Are All Fat
Almost every woman I know thinks she is fat, or at least not thin enough. Whether or not we can actually grab handfuls of flesh on our bodies (I can—and I give my tummy frequent grab-

'n'-tugs), we say, "Oh my God, I'm so fat." Or we finish a big meal and say, "Uck, I'm gonna get so fat." Or we call our friends and say, "I feel so fat today." Or we go with the old classic, "Do I look fat in this?"

My answer to that last question is usually, "It doesn't matter what I think." Chances are I think you look great in this. I probably think you look less fat in this than I'd look in this. Technically, because I am fat, I look fat in everything. I'm more likely to ask, "Is this flattering on me?" or "Does this color complement me?" or "Is this outfit appropriate to wear on this occasion?"

Most of us walk around in fear, strapped into our minimizer bras and control-top panty hose, sweaters looped around our butts, afraid that someone somewhere is going to call us fat. I saw a girl at the gym the other day, hopping up and down like a madwoman on the Precor step machine, with a jacket tied around her butt. I mean, what is that? Woman, you are at the gym working out. Why are you trying to hide that butt? I'm hardly worried about your tremendous ass working its way into my personal space, especially when your ass is anti-tremendous.

It may be true that we all *FEEL* fat, but statistics show that not all of us *ARE* fat. So a new realization comes to light: The body-image anxiety we put ourselves through is mostly a crock. If even Britney Spears feels fat sometimes, doesn't that make you want to throw in the towel?

Nope, the "assume we are all fat" theory does not work for me. What it proves is that someone has really managed to run a trip on us, or we have run one on ourselves, and we're sucking it up lock, stock, and Cracker Barrel.

2. Use Subjective Standards to Determine Inherent Fatness

Maybe we can use totally subjective standards to decide if we're actually fat or not, like:

- Can I tuck?
- Does my stomach stick out?
- Is my flesh smooth like plastic, or puckered like a . . . human's?
- Does the size of my clothes include a double digit or the letter X?
- Have I worn a bathing suit in public since puberty?
- Do I still hope to fit into the jeans I wore senior year of high school?
- Did I make an effort to move my body this week?
- Did I eat candy today?

Uh-oh. The problem with subjective standards is that they are truly subjective. And they change minute to minute. No, we're going to have to go with something more hard-core.

3. Use Objective Standards to Determine Inherent Fatness

We could use a physical standard to assess our girth, such as:

- Body mass index (BMI)
- Fat clippers
- Waist circumference
- Doctor's orders
- The face your mother makes when she looks at you in a dressing room (oops, sorry, that goes on the subjective list)

This is a logical way to determine how fat you are. There's only one problem: Most of these parameters are scientifically unproven and unfound. I'll be addressing that in chapter 7.

Most objective standards involve numerical statistics, but I've never been a big fan of numbers as an accurate representation of who I am. We get so locked into the weight we're supposed to be, the size we have to be, the lowest size we ever were. I'm 5'7", and I'm supposed to weigh 135. Granted, I haven't seen that number on the scale since the early eighties, but I know that's my correct weight/height formula. You know the one I'm talking about: To figure out your ideal weight, add five to one hundred pounds for every inch over five feet. According to this purely unscientific measurement, a 5'6" woman should weight about 130. I scoff at thee! The day I see 135 pounds, I will know that someone chopped off all my limbs and my head. It's simply not going to happen—no matter how many 5'9", 114-pound celebrities I read about in *People* magazine.

Weight is one of the few numerical situations where less is more. We want more money, more food, more clothes, more room, more muscles. We suffer from loss; we lose games, money, friends, parents. Loss is bad everywhere, except on a scale. When it comes to our bodies, we try and try and try to win the numbers racket. We want to best the averages, to beat the odds. But at 5'4" and 152 pounds, even the average woman is less than ideal—she should be 5'4", 120 pounds according to the formula above. This is one numbers game we can't win.

Getting "Over" Weight

Ding-ding-ding! See, it's one thing to be fat and feel miserable. And it's a total waste to be thin but feel fat and miserable. But to be physically fat and feel normal? To take yourself out of the mindset of "I'm fat, I gotta lose weight . . ."? It does take weight off: weight off your shoulders, weight off your mind. It's like spending your whole life feeling guilty that you didn't go to law school and finally understanding that you're not going to go to law school and that's okay. Or thinking you've got to make fifty thousand a year, you've simply got to, but then realizing you can do just fine on forty thousand. The burden lifts, and the focus shifts toward changing the stuff that's more in your control.

I don't *feel* fat anymore (where fat = ugly, bad, worthless, lazy). Now I *am* fat (where fat = the opposite of thin), but I feel . . . Fat. It's like, fat girls are embarrassed when they can't find their size; but Fat Girls go up to the salesperson and ask for it. Or, fat girls hide their bodies in big, drapey, shapeless clothes; but Fat Girls show off their cleavage and draw attention to their curves. Fat Girls question statistics and ask for more research; Fat Girls tell mean people to mind their own business. Fat Girls fight back.

Now, feeling Fat will freak people out even more than saying the word "fat" out loud a couple of times. It's just assumed that if you're overweight, you must be doing whatever you can *not* to be. Very few people, especially the Indignant Thin, understand that NO ONE WANTS TO BE FAT.

To decide or announce that you're just going to stay overweight (not necessarily unhealthy or unfit, just overweight) is a rebellious move. The person you are talking to will have to wonder why she is struggling so hard with this same issue. She will get mad at you. She will think you're being defensive. She will think you are being irresponsible. I say, it doesn't matter what she thinks. It matters what *you* think. Because fat is a state of body—but Fat is a state of mind.

I have to say, there is a sense of loss when you actually give up on the fantasy that you've been nurturing for so long—the one where you wake up one day and you are thin and life is great and you burn all of your fat clothes and fat pictures and take the shot where you're standing in your fat jeans with your thin body. Oh, to let that go . . . the idea that you're going to be the one they admire at PTA meetings, the one they whisper approvingly of in the locker room at the club. That's okay. Now you have the opportunity to come up with a whole new goal for yourself—maybe one that's actually in the realm of possibility.

Please note: As I mentioned in my introduction, you don't have to be fat to be Fat. I have a friend who spent her entire adolescence flat as a board. No boobs at all. They didn't show up till she was twenty years old. She estimates that she did fifty thousand "you must increase your bust" push-ups, all for naught. She was convinced that her entire high school was staring at her thinking, "Can't believe she didn't get tits yet!" Convinced she was so homely and unwomanly that no man would ever be attracted to her. Of course a man was—more than one man. When she was in college, her boobs finally showed up. One breast was a little bigger than the other, but she liked 'em well enough, and she understood that she was smart and funny and beautiful, and that was that.

The point is, my friend is thin, but she's Fat. She realized that she'd wasted a lot of time and energy on something that was out of her control, something that her body would or wouldn't change when the time was right.

People take your cue on how to behave around you. If you act ashamed of yourself, they will be ashamed of you. If you act proud—even if it's just an act—people will kowtow. Get over it. Dress well. Own it. Fake it long enough and you just may start believing it yourself. As for those who freak about the f-word or the f-body, just try to shine some love on those poor fools. Then go ahead and take up space.

CHAPTER 2

The Story of My Body

*Can't you see what a good job God did here? Can't you
see how beautiful he made you?*
— from the film *Big Eden*

Everybody has a story. Every body does, too.

My body's story starts a couple hundred years ago, with my
ancestors in the Old Country. I come from fat people. We
probably inherited all of this fat because we were Ashkenazi
Jews, and we landed in the harsh terrain of the Russian Pale of
Settlement, where you had to defend yourself against brutal
winters with lots of insulation, like a big layer of fat. Someone
who was *shtark,* or big and fat and strong, signaled a good
mate who would live a long life (that is, if the Cossacks didn't
get you first). So you'd eat to survive, the more fat the better.
The food Jews eat is all brown, fatty, and fried; it really hasn't
evolved in about six thousand years. We're talking meat and
bread and stuffing and more bread and some guts and a little
chicken fat and an extra serving of liver for good measure. Not
a veggie for miles. Not exactly haute Lean Cuisine. I have a
feeling that biblical manna tasted like Krispy Kremes.

Pretty much everyone in my extended family is fat. If they

aren't fat, then they are generally struggling with it. I had cousins on my mother's side who were morbidly obese and died at a young age; I'm named after one of them. My paternal grandfather didn't get lean until he got diabetes in his forties. My maternal grandfather was so fat that his stomach looked big and round like a pregnant woman's, but felt hard like a rock. Didn't matter to me what they looked like; I was crazy about both of them.

Every family event, every rite of passage, is celebrated with food. If you're a Jew, it's celebrated with deli trays and trips to the bakery. Births, deaths, and everything in between are well-deserved reasons to eat, eat, eat. In the Jewish faith, you're really screwed size-wise if you're a woman. Our gene pool is made up of almost all fat women and, like, two skinny girls who stay skinny come hell or high water. We Jewesses may start off slender, but postnatally you gotta watch out. This is not specific to Jewish culture, of course. If you've seen *My Big Fat Greek Wedding, The Godfather, Big Night,* or *Eat Drink Man Woman,* you know it's the same in every culture. Except for those poor Scandinavians. They're the people who need body fat the most to survive the weather, and they seem to eat the least. Have you ever seen a Bergman film with a deli tray in it?

Weight, Loss

My weight is some combination of genetics and environment and taste buds and yo-yo dieting, and a binge or twelve. My diet history started when I was a bun fresh out of the oven, and my mom started counting my calories for me. Oh, poor body-conscious moms of the seventies. Sometimes I think Medea's kids had it easy.

I was on a diet before I knew how to walk. Worried about her extra pounds, my mother feared that I would inherit her weight problem. So family lore has it that instead of formula—all those empty calories!—she switched me and my little brother, Josh, to skim milk. Meanwhile, my mother wore a size 12. Perfectly average.

Her stay-thin-and-win! plan worked out well during my childhood. I never knew about all the treats that I was missing. Ironically, my dad was a gourmet-food distributor. Consumer appetite for chocolates and cookies and olives and fancy teas and coffees put a roof over our heads and well-balanced meals on our dining-room table. But sweet treats and rich delicacies were not on our menu. We also never had sugar cereals or sodas in the house, like our friends did. We weren't rewarded with sweets (my mom got Mallomar cookies for walking across a room when she was a toddler). Sure, we had birthday cakes, and treats on special occasions. But we ate meals sanctioned by the holy food pyramid, and played outside after school. We were normal, average-size kids.

Unfortunately, as we only acknowledge once it's too late, how we look is the least important thing about our physical selves. At the age of thirty-five, my mom died of leukemia, leaving behind a forty-year-old husband, a ten-year-old daughter, and an eight-year-old son. The whole world collapsed on top of us. Her death was as shocking as a car accident, as my parents had decided to keep her illness a secret from the family, including Joshie and me. They figured since she wasn't showing any symptoms of illness, there was no reason to worry anyone until they had to. Well, she went from fine . . . to having a cold . . . to dying in just a week.

At a funeral packed with hundreds of family members,

neighbors, and friends, people had all sorts of things to say about my mom. They said she was kind, and smart, a good friend and wife and mom and daughter, a great entertainer with a beautiful smile. And guess what? No one said, "It's too bad she couldn't lose those twenty pounds." Or "If only she would've done step aerobics, she could have had real power hamstrings." No one checked to see what size skirt she was wearing in her coffin.

I stopped eating. It wasn't a conscious hunger strike; I just didn't feel like eating. But in a Jewish family—especially a Jewish family in mourning—there is no greater sin or cause for alarm than someone who skips a meal. After a couple of days, my anxious aunts gathered around me to make sure I put something down my gullet—in this case, some dry toast. Once I started eating, I couldn't stop. Especially when we finally had tasty treats around the house.

Our house was filled with food from the funeral on. Well-meaning neighbors sent over trays of chicken and cold cuts. Aunts and uncles invited us over for dinner every night. It all tasted so good. In this case, food was definitely love. When my dad remarried—a wonderful woman named Myrna—a year later, we celebrated with another round of community-wide dinners and desserts. Luckily, even as I entered puberty, no one was on my case about my weight. Except me.

Getting Schooled

I was a high-school freshman when I first started paying money to lose weight. Before that I'd picked up little diet tips from teen magazines, but never given dieting too much thought. But when I was in the ninth grade my next-door locker mate told me she weighed 129 pounds. I don't remember what I weighed, but I knew it was more than that, and it gave me pause. Pause, but not outrageous concern. So I started with the classic: Weight Watchers. I felt grateful to be on the teen program, because it meant extra bread and milk exchanges each day. After a series of mild losses and gains and restarts on Weight Watchers, I switched to Quick Weight Loss Center, buying little pudding packages to supplement my proteins and vegetables. That's when the process began in earnest. Losing weight, then gaining it back, plus. Losing, and gaining back, plus. Plus, plus.

By the time I was sixteen, I weighed 186 pounds. I couldn't shop for clothes with my friends. My stepmom, Myrna, took me to the one decent plus-size women's clothing store in town, where the clothes were super-expensive and the clientele's taste more sophisticated than mine. Thankfully, Myrn never made me feel bad or guilty about my special shopping needs. I began to formulate the sense of style that I still have today—lots of basic black, a few gem-tone accents, big jewelry, and bold red lipstick. Call it Fat Girl Fabulousness.

The summer before my junior year of high school, I found a letter in our mailbox from the William Beaumont Hospital Weight Control Clinic. My parents had contacted them to see if I was a viable candidate for their obesity program; apparently they were pretty concerned about my weight after all. When I saw the word "obesity" I went through the roof. Obese? Me? No way! Maybe a little overweight, but certainly not obese. Not even f . . . f . . . you know, the f-word, fat! I knew I had to battle my body a bit, and I could sure stand to curb that sweet tooth of mine. But I was certain that I'd never look as gross as the fat women at the mall—the ones draped in polyester who wore too-tight jeans that revealed this yucky pouch hanging below their belly buttons. *They* were fat. *They* were obese. Not me. I fended off my folks and signed up for Weight Watchers again.

I went to school, I went to dances, and I kept buying my big clothes. My driver's license gave me access to a car, which gave me access to buy cookies that I would eat by the boxful, and bread that I would eat by the loaf. I became an expert at hiding my binges and disposing of the evidence, but never asked myself why I was compulsively eating in the first place. Like the rest of my girlfriends, I'd diet and go to aerobics class and count exchanges and pretend that everything was perfectly normal. At least I wasn't a druggie or a burnout, or 'rexing out, or eating lite yogurt and puking it up in the girls' bathroom during study hall like some of my classmates.

By the time I graduated high school, I was as thin as I'd ever be in my adult life. In my black dress with my dream date at the high-school prom, in my white dress delivering the commencement address at my high-school graduation, I wore a size 12 and weighed 164 pounds. Okay, so Heidi Klum would faint if she saw that number on the scale, but it was a big accomplishment for me.

The Freshman Fifty

I zipped off to the University of Michigan. Ah, college, land of the famous Freshman Fifteen. Only for me it was more like the Freshman Fifty. Picture this: I'm hunched over on a beanbag chair with one hand in the mini-fridge and the other shoving a piece of my roommate's leftover birthday cake in my mouth. Couple of problems with this situation: First of all, I hate my roommate from the moment she tapes her Andy Warhol

Marilyn Monroe poster on the wall (then again, I had "Monet at Giverny," so let's call a spade a spade). We live in a kind of angry détente, and she has not given me permission to eat her cake. It just so happens that this particular hunk of cake has been torturing me for almost twenty-four hours, calling to me in a voice that apparently only I can hear, begging me to free it from its chilly prison and suck it down my gullet. How could I resist that kind of begging? I didn't logically think this one through—there was no way I was going to be able to cover up for the missing cake when my witchy roommate discovered it. I didn't know who bought the cake or where, so I couldn't pull a switcheroo. I could try to blame it on our third roommate, but she'd never believe me. Maybe I could just clear out of the room for a couple of days, then by the time the cake theft was discovered I could play dumb . . .

Wait—what's that noise?

Ah, I forgot to the lock the door. And now, my roommate, the one without a sensitive bone in her freshman-fifteenless body, has caught me in the act. She doesn't have to say a word. I don't have to hear the f-word fly out of her mouth as she stands in the doorway, her mouth agape (mine, of course, is covered with frosting). I can see the accusation of "fat" in her eyes. I can see myself as she sees me, and I am completely disgusted.

In any other go-getter's life, that's the moment when she tells you that the stars aligned for her, and she started training for a marathon, never ate French fries again, and lived happily ever after. Not me. Once I, Frosting Face, understood that I was not a good person, but a super-gross fatty, I began to believe that I had all of the attributes that were associated with fat people. I was bad. I was helpless. I had no will power. I was lazy. I didn't care about myself. I wanted food more than I wanted love. Something was wrong with my body. Something was wrong with me.

Any shred of self-love left in me hit the road when I found an essay in *Allure* written by arch British writer Fay Weldon, author of *The Life and Loves of a She-Devil*. Weldon explicated every inch of my self-loathing:

> Fat is depression. Fat is wanting minor pleasure now instead of major pleasure later. Fat is not believing in a future, which is why you want the minor pleasure now. (A candy in the hand is better than true love around the corner.) Fat is also honoring the pleasures of the day: living now, not later. Fat is one long party. Fat is rolling flavor and delights around the tongue. Fat is heart attacks, bad knees, and a self-perpetuating low self-image. Fat is all kinds of things, but one thing it's not is thin. Another thing it's not is beautiful. Fat is disgusting. Fat is a dulling wall between you and the pain of reality; fat is a comfort, an excuse, and an escape from sex. Fat is yours to control. Fat is transformation; fat hurts and humiliates. Fat is how you lose the little girl in the fullness of the woman . . . Lucky the thin, because the sun of society's approval shines on them. Weak and unlucky the fat, because they refuse to see it, will go on trying forever to change the world rather than themselves, crying "It isn't fair" all the way to their extra-large coffins.

The perfect rant of self-hate. It suited me to a T—an XXL T. I knew I was miserable, and the food was connected to the misery. I couldn't figure out what was wrong, and I couldn't stop. But I could finally interpret the disdainful message coming at me from all angles. From guys. From my female peers. On TV, on the movie screen, and on the pages of magazines. The more I denied it, the worse I felt, and the easier it became to blame my body. Hiding in my college apartment at night, downing quarts of ice cream and feeling lonely, I finally understood. The guy I had a crush on liked me only as a friend because I was fat. I didn't get the internship I wanted because I was fat. My grades were mediocre because I was fat. I didn't get the part in the play because I was fat. So I started therapy because I was fat. The therapist and I spent a lot of time talking about my mother's death and my family's response to it, but she couldn't help me get my eating under control.

When I hit 215 pounds, I dug up that letter from the obesity clinic at Beaumont Hospital and started on Optifast (the first round of it, at least). Sophomore year, while my pals were eating fries and drinking beer, I was swallowing protein packets, drinking Metamucil and bouillon, and feeling pretty left out. I actually brought a protein shake to a bar once. I remember being proud enough to admire myself in the mirror when I dropped down to 196 pounds. (Oh, to see 196 again—I'd be practically skinny!). That four-month Optifest eventually helped me lose about fourty pounds before I started to make the transition into real food again.

When I think that I went for months without actually eating anything—just packets of powder and mountains of Metamucil—I'm astounded. I literally starved myself. For someone who spends as much time thinking about eating as I do, fasting is actually a weirdly pleasurable reprieve. Once you get past the first four or five days of nerve-screaming hunger, you sort of go numb. It's a relief to never think about food, to never wonder what you're going to make for dinner, to never break out cash you weren't planning on spending. Watching the pounds drop away is a nice bonus prize, but deep in your fiber you know they'll be back. Your life gets very quiet without business lunches and dinner parties. Your kitchen stays very clean without chicken broiling and oatmeal boiling. But eventually, you have to eat again.

That time had come. I was starting to integrate a fruit here, a veggie there, moving forward in tiny, tenuous steps. One night I went to a concert with some friends and was going to stay at my parents' house instead of my college apartment in Ann Arbor for the first time since I'd gotten on Opti. No one was going to be there but me. An alarm went off in the recesses of my mind— trouble ahead. I knew I would have a tough time in my parents' house, the one where I'd gotten fat in the first place—with that fridge—by myself. I begged a friend to sleep over, but I wasn't honest with her. Didn't tell her what the problem was. She opted to stay at her boyfriend's instead. I stayed with my significant other, my abusive boyfriend, Mr. Frigidaire.

There I was. Me versus Fridge. Let's just say Fridge won, and kept on winning for years. Packed that forty back on in no time, plus an additional twenty-pound bonus just for playing.

Body of Work

After graduation I moved to New York City. Away from home and family and the University of Michigan, I made new friends, danced at wild clubs, and experimented (as much as a nice Jewish girl from the Midwest could) with drugs and sex. I started working with a new therapist. I took film classes at NYU and got an internship at MTV. I saw a life beyond

Michigan's horizons and society's expectations, and I started to find myself.

I remember getting ready for a party one night when I was twenty-five. I looked in the mirror and decided that I liked what I saw there. My entire dieting life, everyone had always told me to get my weight under control before I was an adult, because "it only gets harder and harder!" (I always thought they meant it as a man-catching statement; Pulitzer Prize–winning science writer Natalie Angier, author of the book *Woman: An Intimate Geography,* says that twenty-five "is the age at which the body's various organs are thought to be at their peak size and performance and its metabolic set point is well-established. The weight that you are at age twenty-five is the weight at which your body is most likely to feel at home. It is the weight that your metabolism strives to attain, adjusting itself up or down if you can or drop a few pounds, which is why dieters have such a vicious time of maintenance.") But I looked at my twenty-five-year-old body and face in the mirror, and I'll be damned if I didn't think I looked pretty! So I go to this party, feeling like the bee's knees. That night, every man in the room completely ignored me. I came home and stared at my reflection again. How foolish I'd been to think I was good enough. How foolish I'd been to give myself a stamp of approval. It was too late for true happiness. And I knew why.

Beauty was the ticket to success and jobs and love, but beauty meant thinness, and I couldn't get thin. I was fine in the brains department, but I didn't have what it took to be truly successful in our society: a body that was going places. At the office, I'd see dumb girls with great legs climb up the ladder past me. At night in the bars, guys would laugh at my jokes, but leave with the chick wearing the lowriders and the high heels (nasty combo, by the way).

So I rejoined Weight Watchers for the eleventy-thousandth time. I spent my tiny income on nutritionists and personal trainers and stacks of diet books. I brought cabbage soup to work in Tupperware and farted all the way home. I joined a gym but changed clothes in the bathroom stall, feeling unentitled to strip down in the locker room next to other, more obviously fit women. I got bitter, I got fatter, and I got desperate. Here's how low I went: I put my life on the line. Insert dramatic music sting here.

Okay, it's not that dramatic. My doctor offered me a prescription for a drug combination called fenfluramine phentermine, otherwise known as fen-phen. Fen-phen alters the way the body metabolizes serotonin, a chemical messenger that modulates mood, emotion, sleep, and appetite. I loved that medicine; it shut down the little voice in my head that was always telling me to "Eat, eat, eat." I finally understood that I wasn't evil, or lazy, or willpower-free; I was just wired differently when it came to appetite. I still had to eat a balanced diet and exercise to lose weight. But for the first time in as long as I could remember, I stopped torturing myself. I lost weight. I looked great.

Unfortunately, fen-phen started killing people—twenty-four reported cases of primary pulmonary hypertension were reported among millions of people taking the drug. The FDA pulled it off the market. I panicked. My EKG was fine, and I was still willing to take the risk. I tried to get the meds on the black market, convinced that without them I'd go supersize again. I knew the medical facts, but I was happy to trade heart-valve failure for a boyfriend and a pair of pleather pants. (By the way, I never joined a fen-phen lawsuit. I loved the peace of mind it gave me and I'd take it again without hesitation. I had a perfect EKG, so I stand by it.) I tried alternatives: Phentermine alone didn't work. Prozac didn't work. It was back to the old "binge-not-purge, work out, and reward with Reese's Peanut Butter Cups" plan. Eventually, I got too tired to fight the weight gain, and too exhausted to pretend that I didn't care.

Fed Up

Then the strangest thing happened: I began to benefit from my weight. An agent asked me if I was interested in being a plus-size model. I wrote magazine articles about body image and stopped putting a happy face on a miserable situation. I'd get letters from people who read my articles. They'd write, "I thought the same thing!" I performed at comedy clubs. Scared that someone would heckle me for being fat, I'd beat 'em to the punch with my material. Fat women would come up to me after shows and thank me. It got to the point where I actually began to believe my own BS. Why wouldn't men prefer sex with a fat girl to sex with a skinny girl? Why shouldn't I eat what I wanted to if my heart was healthy and my blood tests were perfect? I'd conned myself into thinking I had it all figured out.

That was the upswing; so you know the kick in the pants couldn't be far behind. I got sick. I was diagnosed with a rare, incurable autoimmune disease called Wegener's granulomatosis. It had nothing to do with my weight; it was just one of those things. To get it under control, I had to take a lot of steroids. I gained forty pounds in about four months. When I finally looked in the mirror, I was horrified at what I saw. I was twenty-eight years old. I weighed 257 pounds. To add insult to injury, I had an awful haircut (why did I go for a shag when I knew I was a bob girl?). I was in a state of utter misery.

It was back to another round of doctor-supervised Optifast to get the weight off—forty pounds, AGAIN, which I've fended off for almost three years. Still, the world looked at me and didn't see forty pounds less. It saw eighty pounds left to lose.

The Saga Continues

By my calculations, I've spent sixteen years trying to lose weight. I've lost and gained hundreds of pounds. I've eaten thousands of bagels, hundreds of pints of frozen yogurt, and have yet to retire my search for the perfect chocolate-chip cookie. I've tried to throw up, I've downed laxatives that look like delicious little Hershey bars, and I've pressed different pressure points in my feet to try to stave off my appetite. I've met with seven weight-loss specialists, worked with three nutritionists and three personal trainers, tried a dozen weight-loss programs, taken thousands of pills, joined six gyms, read thirty-one books, and spent enough money on weight loss to buy myself an Ivy League degree. Approximately zero days have gone by since the age of fourteen that I haven't reflected on all of this.

I'm not exactly sure, because I don't weigh myself every day, but as of this morning I believe I weigh around 220 pounds. Wow. Up until this minute, no one else knew that number (except for my doctor), because I'm embarrassed by it. Hmm, do you think my friends will like me less now that they know how much I weigh? Will my parents disown me now? I don't think so.

My stepmom, Myrna, is in her fifties and struggles with the same body issues that affect so many women her age—hormonal shifts, metabolic changes, self-image debates. It's been hard for her to find clothes that fit well, even when she's willing to pay top dollar. I give her all the credit in the world for being a supportive friend when it comes to issues about weight loss and body image. I wish all the other Fat Girls could be so lucky.

Now that I'm in my thirties, my father and I have come to some sort of fragile détente about my weight. But it hasn't been easy. We have at times gone for months without speaking to each other due to something that he's said about my weight. We had an outburst in a restaurant about the kind of salad dressing I'd ordered that sent me running to the restroom in tears. But the more vocal I became about my own priorities and goals, the more my dad had to concede to my feelings. Today we can carefully, objectively discuss dieting and exercise without me feeling like I'm under the gun.

I try to be a role model for my parents and their health. I make sure to exercise when we're together. Still, when we go to restaurants, I order exactly what I'd order if they weren't with me. I pay for any weight-management efforts without their financial assistance (gym memberships, medication, etc.), so that I am fully responsible and have total control. I often wish that my dad would manage his health in a different way. I worry about his weight and other risk factors. But I can't tell him what to do. How would I feel if he did that to me? His concerns for me are the same as mine for him: We both want each other to live long, healthy, happy lives. If he won't change his weight—because of physical limitations or personal frustrations or disinterest or laziness or private reasons of his own—there is little I can do to motivate him. We are responsible for our own decisions about our bodies.

It Ain't Over

Who's to say what would have happened if my mom hadn't died? Maybe I would have revolted against her and become anorexic. Maybe my weight never would have been an issue. Maybe I would be writing a book about how hard life is when you're thin and beautiful and no one takes you seriously because you're only seen as a sex object. I have a feeling the story of my body would still play out the same way, because most folks in my family are fat, and disinclined to play a lot of sports, and genetics have an awful lot to do with our physical destiny. (My brother, Josh, in his sweetest moment, apologized to me for having a more efficient metabolism than I had.) I know that the story of my body isn't over; I've just stopped trying to rewrite the ending.

CHAPTER 3

Mind Your Own Business

I have lived my life in a culture that hates fat people. From magazine covers to late-night talk show hosts. From would-be employers to would-be lovers. I have felt the judgmental scorn of society's contempt for people like me. It is against all odds that I've managed to arrive in my mid-thirties with any self-respect and self-worth. It's a miracle that I laugh every day and walk through my life with pride and confidence, because our culture is unrelenting when it comes to fat people. I don't understand it and I doubt I ever will. We hurt nobody. We're just fat.
— Camryn Manheim, *Wake Up, I'm Fat!*

The question I come back to again and again is "WHY DO YOU CARE IF I'M FAT?" It's *my* body. I know full well what I'm doing to it. I'm not blowing secondhand smoke on you. I'm not drunk-driving into you. I'm not taking food out of your mouth. Unless you're crawling around in my skin, it doesn't affect you in a direct way. So, assuming that you're a relatively healthy human being, why is everyone (your next-door neighbor, your cousin Beverly, the editor of *Cosmo*) so damned invested in making you thin?

Thin Logic

Everyone Is Jealous of You.

What? Jealous of *you*? No one in her right mind wants to be stuffed into your Lane Bryant capris. How could anyone possibly be jealous of you?

Well, Thin Logic (a theory purveyed by Skinny Chicks everywhere) assumes that if you are overweight, you pretty much just sit around on your keester all day long, chowing down sleevefuls of Oreo Double Stuffs and throwing all caution about good health to the wind. Fat Girls have our bad days, but we know this is generally not the case.

I know where Thin Logic comes from. When I'm on a diet, and I see someone eating something I want to eat but can't eat, I get super-jealous of that person (especially if they say things like, "God, I just keep eating and eating and never gain weight." Uck). Usually just watching them pound down something as innocuous as a Special K waffle that's two too many breads turns me green with envy. Of course, I'd feel slightly less jealous after a waffle binge six hours later, but still . . .

Imagine that all across America, diet-conscious men and women are watching you jiggle down the block (that's your worst nightmare anyway, right?). Now, imagine that they are thinking, "I bet that fat lady eats all the Ben & Jerry's New York Super Fudge Chunk she wants. I wish I could eat Ben & Jerry's New York Super Fudge Chunk but I can't because I'm following some sort of rule book that really doesn't make any medical or common sense. This is so frustrating. I have to take out my frustration somewhere. Hmm . . . how 'bout I take it out on that fatty who can't stop stuffing her face the way I'd like to stuff mine?"

What follows? Crude jokes, dirty looks, the fodder that keeps seventh graders busy for weeks on end and is spread by the media into adulthood. Insecurity festers, and voilà, a diet industry is born.

Strangely, Skinny Chicks need to have fat girls around. The Fat Girl has a very important place in social strata—she's the best friend. The wacky best friend. The ingenue's sidekick. No one wants you to change. You're not competition. You enhance without stealing the spotlight. They need to have you around for comic relief, and to move the plot of everyone else's life ahead. If you actually did lose weight, you'd become even more threatening—yet another competitor. As Natalie Angier acknowledges, "It's a sad business when women indict other women for their take on life, for their choice of reproductive and emotional strategy. It may be understandable, given the role of female-female competition in recent human history, but I argue that it is maladaptive for women to continue on this course of she said/she said, the yowling and mud wrestling. We need each other now."

The next time your cubicle mate points out that you ordered fries, but she waited for a baked potato, remember that she's not worried about you. She's stressed about herself. If she clicks her tongue when she says she's going to the gym but you say you're going to the movies, don't take it on. That's her drama. You just go ahead to the multiplex. And bring her back some M&M's.

The Contract

Okay, let's take this a step further. Not only are Skinny Chicks mad or jealous because they wish they could eat what they assume you are eating, but they are mad at you because you are boldly defying The Contract. You know, The Contract that you entered by virtue of being an American female in the twenty-first century? You don't have to sign the contract; you enter into it just by being born.

The Contract silently states that as a woman, you are supposed to make yourself attractive to men. This is born of biological necessity. Female humans need to mate with male humans in order to preserve the future of the race. Ducks quack, peacocks throw open their feathers, and women buy Frizz-Ease and get collagen injections.

When you break The Contract by doing something that is not considered attractive by the opposite sex—say, gaining weight, getting old, or making more money than men do—men become frustrated. They have a mission, and you are preventing them from accomplishing it. Now they'll have to have sex with you even if you have arms that flap in the wind or gray roots or a really intimidating bank account. So they get pissed. Instead of examining the root of this frustration or even fighting it, they grunt along with Craig Kilborn when he makes cracks about Monica Lewinsky. Heaven forbid they are still attracted to you even if you are fat or old or rich—then they'll have a lot of explaining to do to their brethren. But we'll get back to that later.

The other half (and, I would argue, the more potent half) of The Contract is the Silent Agreement Between Women. See, there are a lot of women who work really hard to keep up their end of the Silent Agreement with Men. They spend their free time at the gym, they deny themselves the food they want to eat, they wear shoes that hurt their feet and clothes that restrict their body movement.

Then you come along: jiggle-jiggle-jiggle. Damn you, don't you understand that just by your very fat existence you are breaking all the rules! You are like someone who has cut into the line at the movies. *Here's everyone in line behaving them-selves, and you just took cuts, and you got in before me! How dare you? I've been waiting for twenty minutes! I might not get a seat! I demand revenge!*

The worst part of The Contract is that fat and old and successful women sometimes beat the odds and still get men and friends and careers, and that's *sooooo* not fair! The Skinny Brain races with antagonism. *I'm working so hard, and for what? Why am I busting my ass when she's sitting there eating rice pudding—which has sugar AND fat AND carbs?!*

I know that feeling. Every time I see a woman with breast implants, I roll my eyes on the outside but feel a jealous twinge inside. She's taking cuts in line. She got fake boobs. She cheated! *Now she's going to get a mate before I do! I know, I'll crack a joke or call her a whore behind her back, and that'll show everyone.*

But maybe she's the smart one. After all, I could get implants if I wanted to. Or lipo, for that matter.

I yearn to tell the skinny chicks, "You won!" And get them off my case. After all, Darwinian evolutionary theory would suggest that the fatter we are, the more the Thin have to gain (ha ha). The Thin have a better shot at getting a sex partner than the Fat. The Thin get paid more than the Fat. So to ensure their own chances of evolutionary success, why won't they leave us and our Pepperidge Farm Mint Milanos well enough alone?

My Big Fat Conspiracy Theory

There's a Big, Fat, *Matrix*-size conspiracy behind making Fat Girls into Skinny Chicks. It's not an alien invasion, but a corporate and political invasion. I don't think I'm being overly paranoid when I say there are an awful lot of people who make an awful lot of money trying to make you thin. I'm not only talking about weight-loss companies—we'll get to those later. For now, think about food substitutes and supplements like Slim-Fast, Healthy Choice, Dexatrim, Jell-O, Sweet'N Low, and Diet Coke. Think about late-night pitches for Suzanne Somers's Ab Roller and Marilu Henner's cookbooks. Think about control-top panty hose, minimizer bras, Nancy Ganz Bodyslimmers. Think about every women's magazine, every gym, every fat-free product, every sugar-free product ever (unless of course you're diabetic), and all those creepy ads in the backs of magazines.

These entities make money if you're fat. They make money if you think you're fat. They make money even if you're not fat. There is no motivation for anyone listed above to say, "You know what? Forget it. You look great, you feel great, that's good enough for me!" The only person who has any motivation to stop the faulty fat-burning machine is you. I'm not saying these folks are evil or ill-intentioned (well, not all of them). But your hopeful dollars have bought the people behind these products a lot of Jaguars and trips to Antigua and Harry Winston diamond earrings and earned you nothing but heartache.

"Mass" Hysteria

How is the "correct" weight determined in the first place? The Surgeon General and the National Institutes of Health tell Americans to use the body mass index (BMI) chart to find their ideal weight. BMI is a measure of body fat based on height and weight. The formula is: $BMI = \left(\frac{\text{Weight in Pounds}}{\text{(Height in inches)} \times \text{(Height in inches)}}\right) \times 703$. The numbers were developed from the Second National Health and Nutrition Examination Survey (NHANES II) that extended from 1976 to 1980. Overweight, according to BMI, used to correlate with the eighty-fifth percentile of height and weight on that survey—around a 27. Then, on June 3, 2003, 30 million Americans who went to bed average woke up fat, when the National Heart, Lung, and Blood Institute—an arm of the National Institutes of Health—shifted the numbers. Now, anyone with a BMI of 25 to 29.9 is considered overweight, while those with a BMI of 30 or more are considered obese. (I'm a 34.5!)

BMI is often used by doctors to determine whether or not you are overweight, and by insurance companies to see if you're eligible for insurance. (Remember, as much as our government chastises us for being overweight, very few weight-loss programs are covered by insurance. So you're damned if you eat and you're damned if you diet.) But BMI doesn't factor in your age. It doesn't factor in whether you are male or female. It doesn't factor in bone density, or family history. It doesn't factor in if you are an Olympic athlete or a nursing mother. But it's the government standard. According to NHLBI's standard nearly two thirds of adults twenty to seventy-four years old are classified as overweight, and about three in ten adults are classified as obese.

Most doctors weigh you, check your BMI, and tell you to lose weight. If you're really lucky, you'll get a seventeenth-generation copy of a piece of paper that lists a suggested diet for a day; grapefruit here, cottage cheese there. No Chubby Hubby, then, Doc? "Not really. And oh, you should work out." Ya think?

BMI is a handy-dandy guideline for white coats who need to make quick assessments, but even the National Heart, Lung, and Blood Institute, which developed the BMI statistics, refers to the numbers as "somewhat arbitrary." My BMI will never be at a level that satisfies the chart. Physically impossible. If I got there, I couldn't maintain it. But I exercise, my cholesterol is normal, my blood pressure is normal, I am not diabetic, and my family history is relatively clear of heart disease. I work out four or five times a week and I eat a bountiful balanced diet. I consider myself healthy. So go hassle the skinny chick who eats Twinkies for lunch and hangs her dry cleaning on her dusty stationary bike, not me.

Shockingly, the *Wall Street Journal* revealed that half of Hollywood is overweight, according to BMI. "Several muscular Hollywood hunks and star athletes could be considered overweight or obese according to height and weight statistics posted on various celebrity and sports Web sites," including Mel Gibson, Michael Jordan, George Clooney, Brad Pitt, Bruce Willis, and Harrison Ford (no doubt crushing Calista in the sack). "Meanwhile, many of their female counterparts are . . . underweight, according to these statistics." That includes Julia Roberts, Hilary Swank, Nicole Kidman, Gwyneth Paltrow, and Madonna. No shocker there.

If so many people rank off the BMI charts—I mean, George Clooney!—has anyone considered that maybe the BMI needs to be adjusted, not you and me? That maybe the standards we use to evaluate healthy weight aren't realistic in an industrialized nation of the twenty-first century? No, because too many people make money from the BMI's all-but-impossible standards.

Researchers in the medical journal *Science* suggested that there is a more accurate measure of risk factors for high blood pressure, heart disease, and diabetes than BMI. A test of metabolic fitness, for example, would measure cholesterol, triglyceride, glucose, and insulin levels in the blood, blood pressure, and the way the body handles glucose. So ask your doctor to give you a blood test that will measure these things. Discuss with your doctor how to assess a healthy weight for you. Take into account your age, your family medical history. Take into account your diet and your exercise habits. Don't pick an arbitrary number off a chart and decide that's what you have to weigh. In his book *Big Fat Lies,* professor of exercise physiology and faculty advisor to the Cardiovascular Health and Fitness Program at the University of Virginia Dr. Glenn A. Gaesser suggests that "you are probably at your ideal weight when you are not trying to do anything to control your weight, but are eating a relatively low-fat, fiber-rich diet abundant in fruits, vegetables, and whole grains, and being physically active." Remember, it's like the beautiful woman in the commercial with the high cholesterol. Sometimes the most important factors about your health are the ones that you can't see.

Political Pounds

What about our government—could the White House be in on this conspiracy? Every day, government agencies—Food and

Drug Administration, National Institutes of Health, and the Centers for Disease Control—issue different recommendations about what we're supposed to eat and not eat. One day it's lots of carbohydrates, the next day it's no carbohydrates. All fat, then no fat. The government suggests a short walk one day, then says you have to do hard-core cardio for an hour a day, seven days a week to expect any sort of weight loss. According to the *New York Times*, "Americans need to exercise more—at least an hour a day, twice as much as previously recommended—to maintain their health and a normal body weight, according to new guidelines issued yesterday by the Institute of Medicine, the medical division of the National Academies . . . Dr. Marion Nestle, chairwoman of the Department of Nutrition and Food Studies at New York University, called the exercise recommendation 'amazing but impractical,' given that 60 percent of the population is now totally sedentary."

With every news bulletin, you spend money and someone pockets it. Every time the government tells you to eat less fat, a new rash of fat-free products is created. Factories are built, people are employed, the economy improves, and the president gets re-elected. Or, a fat-fighting drug is invented. Investors invest, the stock market booms, drug companies sell prescriptions, and everybody is happy—until we find out how it's going to kill us.

The media explodes every day with stories about how fat we all are—61 percent of us overweight or obese, according to the U.S. Surgeon General. It's worth taking another look at the numbers. This is what the *Wall Street Journal* reported about the oft-repeated statistic that two thirds of Americans are overweight or obese: "Those numbers, based on a sample of only 1,446 people conducted over seven months in 1999, are the standard most experts use when talking about the nation's current weight woes . . . What's more, the most recent CDC statistics, oft cited by the Surgeon General, doctors, and others—come from a survey that even the CDC says is too small to be conclusive." Rinse and repeat: That horror-inducing statistic is based on a sample of only 1,446 people, less than .0005 percent of the population. I'm no statistician, but even the CDC doesn't think that's a large enough sample to make an accurate assessment about 280 million people.

Paul Campos, a professor of law at the University of Colorado/Boulder, points out that weight-loss companies pay for much of the obesity research done in this country. He compares weight-loss-industry hype to the recent stock scandals on Wall Street, when analysts recommended stocks sold by their banks' own investment divisions, causing demand to dramatically rise. Campos also wonders if we need a separation of weight and state, as he found that former U.S. Surgeon General C. Everett Koop funded his Shape Up America campaign with more than $2 million from Weight Watchers and Jenny Craig.

Even the American Obesity Organization, a well-intentioned nonprofit that lobbies Congress for changes in public policy about obesity, is funded by corporate partners including Abbott Laboratories (makers of Meridia), Roche Laboratories (makers of Xenical [orlistat]), and Weight Watchers International, Inc. Everyone is ready to make a buck off of you. You're the only one fighting for yourself. Don't depend on Uncle Sam to slim you down; you are your only advocate.

Government agencies moan about the girth Americans have gained in the last fifty years. But even if you diet to the letter—eating your dry-broiled chicken breast and half cup of broccoli for dinner—it's not the same quality chicken breast that you ate in 1950. It's filled with hormones and preservatives and mystery meat. "Raising meat in America has become such an exact science that, through genetic selection and better knowledge of nutrition, researchers have been able to alter the physical composition of most of the animals we eat. Poultry companies, for example, have reduced the time it takes a chicken to reach its final four-to-five-pound weight from seventeen weeks, in the nineteen-fifties, to six weeks today," revealed the *New Yorker*. If a chicken is altered to gain weight at superspeeds, and we eat that chicken, might we gain weight too? McDonald's is taking strides to use fewer antibiotics in animals to speed growth, since "the routine use of antibiotics in animal production [is] a practice that is diminishing the effectiveness of antibiotics in humans." No need for antibacterial soap; apparently you are what you eat. Let's say you skip meat and go vegetarian. Even the healthy stuff, like fruits and veggies, are biologically altered to make them bigger and crunchier and more colorful. You can go organic, but it's too expensive. We can't afford it.

The government is a big business with a capitalist agenda. If the truth about losing weight came to light—that it's not about putting some food you can't find in nature in your mouth, it's actually about taking a walk around the block—then no one makes any money.

Get With the Programs?

Weight loss is one of the only products or services we buy into where we blame the failure of the product on ourselves. When you order a hamburger in a restaurant that doesn't taste good, you don't blame your taste buds. When you buy nail polish that chips, you don't blame your fingernails. When you buy a light bulb that doesn't illuminate the room, you don't blame your hands for screwing it in wrong (unless, of course, you did screw it in wrong).

Paying for a weight-loss program is like gambling at a casino in Vegas. The odds of the house are against you. Once in a blue moon someone randomly hits the jackpot—just often enough to make us think that we can win, too. But if you don't hit the jackpot, you can't logically blame yourself. The system is designed for the house to win. (Hmm . . . maybe some sort of gaming commission should supervise these programs?) Really, giving your hard-earned dollars to a weight-loss program is essentially the same as dumping your quarters into a slot machine.

But if that's how you want to spend it, you're not the only one. Americans spend $35 billion a year on weight-loss plans and products. Weight Watchers had record worldwide attendance in 2001, with approximately 47 million people counting up their points (23.4 million in the U.S. alone). Weight Watchers' total sales in 2001 added up to $623.9 million.

The weight-loss industry is spending $39.8 billion annually to draw you in. Weight Watchers spends more than $30 million each year to advertise to you. (In second place, Jenny Craig spends just $20 million.) How can your individual will possibly compete with a $30 million budget? Weight Watchers seems to be spending the big bucks, until you discover that Wendy's spends $270.2 million a year to get you to eat up Biggie Fries. McDonald's spends $537.6 million annually in advertising to give you the ultimate Happy Meal. That means McDonald's is spending over two dollars on every man, woman, and child in this country to get them to pass through the Golden Arches. No wonder twenty million Americans eat at Mickey D's every day.

Aside from advertising, don't overlook how weight-loss companies have been planting their tentacles into your everyday life. Ford, Pepsi, and General Mills are all launching programs to fight obesity in the workforce by putting healthier options in vending machines and opening up stairwells for people to use instead of elevators. The thinking is that these companies will lower their insurance costs if they have healthier employees. Not a bad idea, but it's worth questioning how much of a say your employer has about the shape and size of your body. On CNN's *In the Money,* Jack Cafferty interviewed Helen Darling from The Washington Business Group on Health, a nonprofit lobbyist organization that advises large employers on health-care issues. Cafferty asked hypothetically, "If I habitually violate company safety rules and thereby put my fellow workers at risk, the company has every right to fire me. If I refuse to lose weight and thereby I'm one of those who incur exaggerated health-care costs putting the financial security of my fellow employees at risk, why shouldn't the company be able to fire me after a certain period of time if I refuse to lose the weight?"

Geez, Jack, that's Thin Logic if I ever did hear it. First of all, I'd love to find someone in the world who actually "refuses" to lose weight. That would be interesting. Then there's the question of how fat my ass would have to be—a measurement, I suppose, of how intense my "refusal" to lose weight is—to actually put a company at financial risk. And there is that pesky old "antidiscrimination in employee hiring practices" law. I mean, look at Bob over there in the wheelchair. He "refuses" to start walking, I guess! If only Bob would try a little harder, then maybe the whole company won't go down the sinkhole!

Luckily, Darling responded by saying that her intent was not to fire all fat people, but to provide employees with information and options that could help them improve their health and lifestyle.

It's not just employers that need to stay out of my body's business; I don't want my coworkers mucking around in there either. "Weight Watchers at Work" will set up meetings at your office, so you don't even need to leave your workplace to do the plan. Sure, it makes attempting weight loss more convenient. But I worry about an invasion of my privacy. Does Sharon in accounts payable really need to know how many points I threw back at the beach last weekend? Should my boss be privy to that information? As there is a separation between church and state, I'd prefer to see a separation between body and business.

A Case Study: Weight Watchers

Yes, my Big Fat Conspiracy Theory includes even holier-than-holy Weight Watchers, which most of us would agree is the world's pre-eminent, moderate, affordable weight-loss program. I've spent quite a chunk of change at Weight Watchers. As far as I can tell, they keep coming out with new booklets, but the gist of the thing doesn't change. Like the clientele. It's mostly average-size women wearing their 12's and 14's, who've been told their whole lives that they're "big-boned." There's always one three-hundred-pound woman with a midwestern accent, who is there with her equally large mom. And of course there's always one overweight man who will lose his sixty pounds in about three weeks.

The leaders are truly inspiring people who've somehow followed the Weight Watchers plan and made it a lifestyle. Most have reached their goal weights, and maintained them.

Except this one guy who used to lead the group I went to in downtown Manhattan who used to say, "When we talk about one bread exchange, we mean half a Lender's Bagel. Not a big Pick-A-Bagel. You know the big ones that weigh about half a pound? Hmm, I love an everything bagel at Pick-A-Bagel. Toasted, with veggie cream cheese . . . Really? You like H&H?" And suddenly the meeting would devolve into Carbo-loaders Anonymous. This guy hadn't seen his goal weight for at least twenty-five or thirty pounds, but he always left me hankering for a bagel with a schmear.

Someone at a Weight Watchers meeting, like the midwestern lady, always asks this kind of question: "If I eat three tomatoes instead of two tomatoes, how do I account for those points? Should I use some of my optional calories, or . . . ?" Now, points are confusing. But you and I know that the problem is probably excess Pop Tarts, not excess tomatoes. Very few of us end up at Weight Watchers because we overdid it on the fruits and veggies.

However, MAJOR WEIGHT-LOSS PROGRAMS WOULD NOT BE SUCCESSFUL BUSINESS MODELS IF THEY HELPED YOU LOSE WEIGHT AND MAINTAIN THAT LOSS. Think about it. If you joined one of these programs the first time, lost the weight, and kept it off, you would not have to keep giving them money and going back again and again to try to get down and down and down. Think about that first question they ask at the beginning of a Weight Watchers meeting: "How many of you have been to Weight Watchers before?" Have you ever been to a meeting where not one hand goes up in the air? I haven't. Fronting a British organization called AnyBody, Professor Susie Orbach, author of *Fat Is a Feminist Issue* and a sociologist at the London School of

Economics and Political Science, "plans to take a 'class action suit'" against a major international weight-loss organization, just as many U.S. tobacco companies have come under fire. "'We want to show that that organization knows a huge proportion of diets fail—its profits depend upon that, and the recidivism rate is absolutely crucial to them.'"

If the plan is so doable, and so logical, and so easy, and it makes so much sense, then why aren't we able to do it successfully? We buy homes. We have jobs. We raise children. And yet, we can't become Lifetime Members of Weight Watchers? We assume it's because we did something wrong. We didn't follow the program. We didn't tally up the points. It's our fault. But with such a low success rate, maybe the failure is not in you but in the program. Even the success stories on Weight Watchers' Web site have a legal disclaimer that says "results not typical." Even their spokeswoman's results are atypical. As it says on the latest WW pamphlet I received (unsolicited) in the mail, "Sarah, Duchess of York. At goal weight since 1997. Results not typical." Hello! Wouldn't you prefer to sign up for a program where losing weight and keeping it off is a typical thing to do? A recent study revealed that people who did Weight Watchers for two years lost an average of only six pounds.

I discussed these frustrations with my friend Carrie, who had done Weight Watchers several times. She was convinced that she had failed at the program because she didn't write down her menu at the end of the day. Now, this girl can do anything. She wrote, produced, directed, and edited a feature film. She renovated a house. She got married and is raising a fabulous child. And she's telling me that because she was too lazy/stupid/careless/self-hating/forgetful to scribble down her points on a little chart she couldn't succeed at Weight Watchers?

Of course there is a mental connection between wanting to lose weight and losing weight. I've read a zillion before-and-after stories where people say, "One day I just decided to do it, and I did it." But if weight loss is a matter of decision making, then what are you paying Weight Watchers to do? Use the money for therapy, or new clothes, or a trip to a spa. Weight Watchers can motivate you, but it can't fix you. Weight Watchers is math. The Zone is math. There are 3,500 calories in a pound, and you have to burn 3,500 calories to lose a pound. So if you don't, it surely is not because you didn't write something down. A two-hundred-pound person burns only twenty-one calories in ten minutes of writing, so you'd have to write in your frickin' food diary for about twenty-eight hours straight to actually burn off a pound of fat. There's either a flaw in the math of the program or a flaw in the information we have about weight loss that keeps you putting money in other people's pockets while you keep putting on pounds.

I don't think Weight Watchers is out to get you. I don't think they're trying to make you fat. I do think they are trying to make money off of a human fault. Sure, Weight Watchers can help if you're looking to lose moderate amounts of weight or eat a balanced diet. The fine print on their advertising copy contains a legal disclaimer which reads, "The Weight Watchers program is designed to achieve a weight loss of no more than 2 lbs. a week. For many dieters, weight loss is temporary. Weight Watchers makes no claim that these results are representative of all participants in the Weight Watchers program." If you're going to spend all that money, don't you want more than that?

Exactly how much time and money are you giving to Weight Watchers International? Try this exercise. Let's say you are going to join Weight Watchers for six months and you live in New York City.

Registration Fee: $15.00

Weekly Fee: $11.95 a week for twenty-six weeks

That adds up to $325.70, not including any Weight Watchers food or special calculators or magazines or scales or other riffraff. What could you do with $325.70? Buy a new summer wardrobe? Half a dozen pairs of sneakers? Twenty-one MAC lipsticks? A desk for the study? Enroll in a course at the community college?

Let's try it timewise. You plan to join Weight Watchers for six months. Just meeting time alone (no tallying, no transportation, no measuring, and no meal planning) adds up to twenty-six hours. What could you do with that time? Help your daughter with her algebra homework? Try out that recipe you saw on *Nigella Bites*? Let Calgon take you away? Read the book that's been sitting on your nightstand covered with dust since the day you joined Weight Watchers six months ago? I myself would use it to watch a *Buffy the Vampire Slayer* marathon, and you're welcome to join me. By the way, if we go back to the study that showed the average person loses only six pounds on weight watcher in two years, then at the going rate of $11.95 per week, that's $1,242.80, or just over $207.13 per pound (I'll be generous and toss in free registration). It would take you just over seventeen weeks—almost four months—to lose each of those six pounds. Not to mention the 104 hours of your life that you could spend a different way. The "especially diligent" WW winners—or shall I say losers?—took off an average of eleven pounds over two years. Most people would say that losing is better than gaining and Weight Watchers can help you lose weight. However, I would ask, what do you have to lose to win?

Free Thinking

Businesses can take our money if we want to give it to them; that's the joy of capitalism. But when you are a happy, satisfied person, no one makes any money. Cash registers only ring when your brain clicks into "I want" mode. We need to be kept in a perpetual cycle of want, of desire, of things out of reach in order for a capitalistic society to succeed. The no-fee "Eat your veggies and go outside and play" plan that Laura Fraser recommends in *Losing It: America's Obsession with Weight and the Industry That Feeds On It* seems to work just as well. Remember that any diet plan that you pay for would be a business flop if it actually worked.

Could you have used the money you spent on failed diets to fund a campaign to elect a woman to Congress? Could you have used the time to write a letter to your local school board demanding computers in your child's school? Give it to charity? Could that time or money have been used to improve your life or the life of someone you care about instead of lining someone else's pocket? Yes. But that someone with the full pockets—or the guy in the three-piece suit strolling the corridors of Washington, D.C.—that guy doesn't want you thinking too hard, or feeling empowered, or working too hard to change things. Think of it as a subtle but powerful form of brainwashing that you have the power to stop just by putting your wallet away.

And you thought you just had an uncontrollable urge to eat Rice Krispie Treats.

CHAPTER 4

Further Adventures in Diet Land

The year I lost 60 pounds, strangers on the street would come up to me and say, "Are you all right? What happened to you?" I was tempted to write a personal memoir entitled I'd Rather Be Fat.

—Wendy Wasserstein,
"New Year New Outlook," *Harper's Bazaar*

Fat isn't just in your head; the drive to eat is all around us. Some environmental influences on your individual weight, according to recent studies? Corn surpluses that led to cheap production of the high-fructose corn syrup used in soft drinks. Cheap palm oil imports. New technologies. Employment, education, and income. Giant portions sold at extremely low prices; surround-sound advertising; a wide availability of food at every given moment; and an endless variety of choices.

I don't blame myself for getting sucked into diet mania, because dieting—not baseball—is our true national pastime. But do I take responsibility for my body and my actions? You betcha, every single day.

Lose Weight—or Die

I stopped going to Weight Watchers for three reasons. First, I thought the program wasn't tough enough for a hard-core Fat Girl like me. Ha. Then I developed my Big Fat Conspiracy Theory, and that became reason number two. The third reason has nothing to do with Weight Watchers directly, but spooked me nonetheless.

One night I went to my weekly meeting in a hotel conference center on the Upper West Side of Manhattan. I was in line, waiting to be weighed in, when I heard a crash.

I turned around to find a guy standing there. He was wearing a ski mask and pointing a gun at me. Another masked man lurched out from behind the desk, clutching a poor Weight Watchers clerk by the neck and holding a gun to her temple. For a moment I was confused, thinking this had to be some sort of dramatic new scare tactic—like, "Weight Watchers: Lose Weight or Die!" Then, horrified, I understood that we were being held up.

The masked men forced all of us (including the ever-present Midwest Tomato Lady and the Fat Guy Who Loses Weight in No Time) to lie down on the floor in the conference room. Part of me longed to do a quick roll, kick one criminal in the balls, grab his gun, and somersault over to crack the other guy across the skull. But because I'm not exactly La Femme Nikita, and because I was terrified, I stayed put. I tried to do whatever I could to shelter myself from the reality of the situation and distract myself from the panicked whispers of the other members around me.

Facedown in hotel carpeting with my hands clasped behind my head, my heart racing a mile a minute, I thought, Why us?

Why threaten a group of nice, moderately fat people who were already humiliated enough by having to show up at Weight Watchers? They probably assumed that we were dumb and slow and weighed down by the Ding Dongs in our pockets. I imagined the cops bursting in, taking the thieves by surprise. The cops would shout, "Put down the fat-free Smart Snacks, you bastards! I will give you to the count of three to put down the Smart Snacks!" The criminals would declare, "We will give up the hostages in exchange for one box of Berries 'n' Cream Mousse Bars, two *Get It Moving* exercise tapes, and a year's supply of Smart Ones frozen dinners!" Then the cops would come back with "Will you accept a case of Handy Ham 'n' Cheese Omelets and a complimentary subscription to *Weight Watchers* magazine instead?" The crooks would confer and say, "Yes, we will!" We'd all jump up and cheer, and someone would pop some air-popped popcorn with no salt or butter (3 points), and we'd all go to a spinning class together at Crunch.

But that's not what went down.

I prayed for safety as the crooks came around and stripped us of our jewelry and the contents of our purses and wallets. When they finished making their rounds, they told us that if we moved they'd kill us. After a couple of silent, scary minutes, the Weight Watchers leader courageously got up and called the police. We all checked in with each other as we shook off the fear. The cops arrived moments later.

I called my folks in Michigan to explain what happened. Here's a helpful hint: Don't ever call your folks in Michigan and tell them that you were just the victim of an armed robbery at a Weight Watchers meeting in New York City. They will want you to move home to Michigan immediately.

As a cop took my statement, he noticed that he was standing

next to a scale. He asked me, "And then what happened? Did you hear anything?" Then, thinking I wouldn't notice, *HE GOT ON THE SCALE AND WEIGHED HIMSELF.* This cop wasn't fat or thin. He was just a regular thirtysomething white dude with a crew cut and a badge, but that scale was calling out to him. He gave himself a little nod of approval and stepped back down to continue our conversation. If I didn't understand before, that cop on the scale proved to me that we live in a society that is obsessed with fat. In that moment, how could a cop be more curious about his weight than about my safety?

I left, thinking about the headlines on the next day's *Post,* like SCARED THIN! I was happy and lucky to be alive. I stopped by the ATM to refill my wallet and bought a box of Entenmanns's chocolate-chip cookies to celebrate my longevity.

I went back to my Weight Watchers meeting the following week, determined not to let some petty crooks make me live my life in fear. A security guard was posted by the door. Aside from the leader, I was the only person who returned. That was the last time I went to Weight Watchers.

One of the perps was caught the following week, trying to trade our jewelry for crack. I wanted to get him in a room and slap him across the face. "You jerk!" I'd scream. "As if we didn't feel pathetic enough at a Weight Watchers meeting, paying people to give us stamps and stickers that are supposed to help us lose weight. You had to humiliate us even more? Scare us? So you could buy crack, you stupid asshole?" At least I felt like I was part of a cool writers' club when I read *Heartburn* and found out that Nora Ephron had gotten ripped off by muggers who broke into her group therapy session.

The way I see it, being held up at Weight Watchers is pretty much a sign from God that I should be happy with myself the way I am.

More Than a Fad

I've sworn off dieting, but I'll admit that the urge to keep doing it is strong. I read the before-and-after stories in *Shape* and *Self*. I watch the successes of friends who hire personal trainers and refuse to eat rice, and sometimes I start to think I've got this down-with-diets thing wrong. But when I'm around dieters enough, my resolve to be myself in my body grows strong again.

Sure, no-carb aficionados lose weight like crazy, but at what cost? Is it worth being thin if your cholesterol shoots sky-high? Wouldn't you rather risk heart disease from a bread basket than from a platter of red meat? Bread is the staff of life. Plus, it's so boring to say no all the time. Why live a life full of "no"? I have no patience for people who won't eat this and won't eat that—"No bread please," "No fat please," "No gluten please," "No sugar please," "I'm allergic to this," "I can't have that," no no no. Three cheers for discipline, but, like, stay home and eat. When you're out and about, go with the flow, and deal with your personal eating drama behind closed doors later. And I don't want to hear how much you ate or didn't eat or comments about what I ate or didn't eat or what's going to happen when you weigh in next Tuesday. I'm not looking at your plate. I'm not counting. Keep it to yourself.

The most successful low-carb plan, the Atkins Diet, seems to lean toward overindulgence. Eat as much cheese as you want! Gorge yourself on bacon bits, but God forbid you eat a nectarine! Isn't that antithetical to the discipline of weight loss? It seems so off to me. Think of the damage it must do to your kidneys. Imagine the effect of the toxins that linger in your system when you don't take a crap for two weeks because you have no roughage in your system . . . it's like cement for your bowels. P.S.—Those Atkins people get so mean! I think they're angry at the world because they can't crap and they won't eat pizza.

How are we supposed to pick through all the diets on the market right now, anyway? Every day a new one comes out that invalidates the one before. Which one is right? Which one is right for me? How many of these best-sellers are gathering dust on your bookshelf:

Eat More, Weigh Less by Dean Ornish, M.D.

Get with the Program! by Bob Greene

The pH Miracle by Robert O. Young, Ph.D., and Shelley Redford Young

Eat Right 4 Your Type by Peter D'Adamo, N.D.

8 Minutes in the Morning by Jorge Cruise

The Peanut Butter Diet by Holly McCord, R.D.

The Zone by Barry Sears

Body for Life by Bill Phillips

The Fat Flush Plan by Ann Louise Gittleman, C.N.S.

The Insulin-Resistance Diet by Cheryle Hart, M.D., and Mary Kay Grossman, R.D.

The Omega Diet by Artemis P. Simopoulos, M.D., and Jo Robinson

Sugar Busters! by H. Leighton Steward; Sam S. Andrews, M.D.; Morrison C. Bethea, M.D.; and Luis A. Balart, M.D.

The Schwarzbein Principle II by Diana Schwarzbein, M.D.

Dr. Atkins' New Diet Revolution by Robert Atkins, M.D.

Protein Power by Michael Eades, M.D., and Mary Dan
Eades, M.D.

Picture Perfect Weight Loss, by Howard M. Shapiro,
M.D.

Lot of M.D.'s on that list—how could they lead you wrong? *Dr.
Atkins' New Diet Revolution* alone has sold 15 million copies.
And don't forget the Raw Foods Diet, the Perricone Prescrip-
tion, Life Choice, or macrobiotic dieting. You can do the South
Beach Diet, the Grapefruit Diet, the Bran Diet, the Chocolate
Chip Cookie Diet, or the All-Candy Diet. In her delightful book
Stuffed: Adventures of a Restaurant Family, writer and lifelong
dieter Patricia Volk remembers the many diets she and her sister
tried, more or less unsuccessfully: "The Nine-Egg-A-Day, the
Grapefruit, the Beverly Hills, the Atkins, the Modified Atkins,
the Ornish, the Pineapple, the Scarsdale, the Sauerkraut, the
Red Soup, the Mayo Clinic, the Duke Rice Diet, the Vanderbilt
Rotation Diet, the Hilton Head Metabolism Diet, the Substitu-
tion Diet, Weight Watchers, Weight Watchers Quick Start, the
Watermelon, the Lorna Linda, Fit For Life, Sugar Busters!, Dr.
Hervert's Famous Diet, the Chew Everything 30 Times Diet, the
Blood-Type Diet, the Bloomindale's Eat Healthy Diet, Dr.
Berger's Immune Power Diet, Dr. McDougall's 12-Day Diet
Meal Plan, the Carbohydrate Addict's Diet, the Hollywood 48-
Hour Miracle Diet (ten pounds in one weekend), the Cyberdiet,
the Stillman, Optifast, Dexfenfluramine HCI, the Nutri/System
Diet Plan, the Zone Diet, Medifast, Metrecal, Slim-Fast, Ultra
Slim-Fast, Richard Simmons Deal-A-Meal, the 8-Glasses-of-
Water-a-Day, the Pritikin Diet, HMV, Horse Hoof Protein,
the Liquid Protein." I've tried nearly all of them.

Why not let Jesus give you a hand at the Weigh Down Workshop, "a twelve-week program of videotapes and prayer meetings designed, in the words of workshop leader Kate Burford, as a 'spiritual, even radical, Christ-centered way to lose weight,'" . . . observed Alexandra Lange in *New York* magazine in 1997, noting also that Tennessee dietician Gwen Shamblin's *The Weigh Down Diet* was the year's second-best-selling book in the Christian market. Then there's *What Would Jesus Eat? The Ultimate Program for Eating Well, Feeling Great, and Living Longer*. You eat what Jesus ate according the Bible, including fruits and vegetables, fish, kosher meat, olive oil, red wine, and lots of water (I assume you don't walk on it, but drink it). While you're at it, read *Step Forward: A Christian 12-Step Program to Lose Weight and Keep It Off*, and ask God for help AA-style. Don't forget *The Prayer Diet: The Unique Physical, Mental, and Spiritual Approach to Healthy Weight Loss*. The theory is that neglecting your spiritual side makes you fat, because you're using food to compensate for spiritual starvation.

Older men who might be embarrassed to try the trendy methods listed above may want to follow in the footsteps of fashion designer Karl Lagerfeld. "German designer Karl Lagerfeld put a new spin on Tuesday on shrink-to-fit clothes, suggesting that Chanel customers lose weight to squeeze into his tiny creations . . . Lagerfeld has been obsessed with size since he went on a diet and lost 93 pounds." Karl plans to publish his diet of cacti, fish, and horsemeat (!!!) in an upcoming book. Or why not try London literary agent Ed Victor's Obvious Diet. It's so . . . obvious!

My personal favorite is the NeanderThin Diet, crowing the virtues of caveman cuisine—food you can "find on the ground, pluck off a bush, or kill with a stick." I guess life would be better if we just ate what cavemen ate: all meat and the occasional berry. Cavemen had it going on. Society would be a lot less complicated if we just grunted at each other and dragged women around by the hair. Unfortunately, times change and the world evolves and bread was invented and we'll just have to deal with it. I'd prefer to see people miss out on a processed tube of Pringles than a nice gorgeous rye.

As all dieters have heard relentlessly, from the time we were cavemen we never knew when the next meal was coming, so our bodies learned to store up fat and not let it go. That's several zillion years of evolution, which can't compare with the last eighty or so (if we're starting with the flappers of the twenties when a slender silhouette came into vogue as mirrors and magazines grew abundant). I'm tired of leaning on the caveman defense, also known as Famine Theory, to defend our food choices, by the way. We evolved far enough to be able to lift our heads up and not be covered with hair, so let's just assume that evolution may have kicked in elsewhere, too.

Faking It

I have total disdain for dieting shortcuts. Like, if you're on a diet, is it better to eat four SnackWell's or one real chocolate-chip cookie? If you're trying to get over dessert, should you be making fat-free chocolate mousse with Equal instead of sugar, or just eat a frickin' strawberry? Is it better to compromise or to just say no?

I've always felt that one of science's great creations is Tasti D-Lite, one of the many nonfat, nondairy frozen desserts you can buy. It's rich and creamy, comes in a zillion flavors, and has hardly any calories. Could be women's perfect food—they're the gender lined up around the block at my local Tasti store. But as much as I love it, I suspect that fake, calorie-free food may not be good for you. Plus, you never really know what you're eating. One of my favorite food studies comes from *New York* magazine. Samples of low-cal frozen dairy desserts and muffins were taken to a lab to test their actual fat and calories versus claimed fat and calories. A sugar-free, low-fat, low-cholesterol deli muffin claimed to have 140 calories. The lab revealed it contained 574 calories and 21.6 grams of fat. A fat-free, sugar-free diet corn muffin that claimed to have 85 calories really had 654 calories, with 22.7 grams of fat. Then they tested the faux fro-yo. Ten fluid ounces of Alpha 1 claimed to have 47 calories—but actually had 323. As for fat grams, it claimed none, but actually had 12.5. Colombo nonfat frozen yogurt? A hundred calories claimed, 233 actual. Zero fat claimed, 4 grams actual. No wonder this study was later turned into a *Seinfeld* episode.

In late 2002, the *New York Times* went for another round of testing. Tasti D-Lite advertised a small vanilla (4 fluid ounces) at 40 calories. The actual small ran from 4.8 ounces and 143 calories to 6.7 ounces and 224. The competition, CremaLita, advertised a small vanilla (4 ounces) as having 60 calories. The actual small ran from 3.9 ounces with 98 calories to 5.9 ounces with 143. I love Tasti D-Lite, but there's a moral of the story to me. Eat real food, not faux food.

I'm so grossed out by what passes for food today, especially when it comes to kids. Lunchables Fun Fuel, a processed food tray for kids, is advertised as "a balanced lunch with good stuff from four of the food groups." What's in that balanced lunch? Two ham bagels, yogurt "Jammers," Fun Fuel 100 percent juice. All prepackaged, probably filled with sodium and sugar. And that's advertised as a "healthy" lunch. Uck. What about Jell-O Chips Ahoy! No-Bake? Feel free to bake dessert—without Jell-O and Chips Ahoy! in it. And what's with the sudden surge of mini-food now? Mini Milanos. Mini Reese's. Mini M&M's. The smaller they make it, the fatter we get.

The problem with fake food is that it's generally processed, made with lots of chemical preservatives that improve taste and make it last on shelves for a long time. These are products like cookies and snacks and chips, things you throw in a lunchbox or grab from a vending machine. Even the low-calorie options tend to be packed with trans fats like hydrogenated oil that go straight to artery-clogging the minute they're in your system. On July 9, 2003, the Food and Drug Administration finally insisted that food makers will have to list levels of trans-fatty acids on their labels by 2006.

In a preemptive move meant to avoid lawsuits akin to those in the tobacco industry, food makers are making signs of changing their ways. "Kraft Foods, the nation's largest food company . . . plans to reduce the portion size, fat, and calories of many of its foods," *USA Today* reported in July 2003. "McDonald's . . . will test an option to replace the wildly popular—but fat-filled—French fries with a bag of fresh, sliced fruit. Frito-Lay is within weeks of eliminating all artery-clogging trans fatty acids from its chips and snacks . . . Kellogg recently bought Kashi, whose cereals have no highly refined sugars or preservatives. Analysts say the food giants haven't suddenly become food pyramid angels looking out for the nutritional well-being of America's youth. Rather, they're increasingly concerned about lawsuits, legislation, and profits." At the same time, snack food companies are still making soups and salads that adults can drink out of a cup or guzzle down in their cars so they never even have to tilt their heads to eat. Now we're deluged with stories that keep coming out about acrylamides and how they may cause cancer. FYI, it's not just fries and chips that contain acrylamides—they're in "vitamin-packed breakfast cereals, toast, and coffee," too. I no longer eat margarine. I'd rather have a little butter than a lot of mystery spread.

In April 2002, a woman named Meredith Berkman launched a $50 million class-action lawsuit against Robert's American Gourmet, the maker of Veggie Booty, claiming "emotional distress" and nutritional damage when she discovered that the "healthy" snack she was feeding to her kids allegedly wasn't healthy at all. Berkman says that she didn't file the suit to make money; she did it to make a point about what she considered false food labeling. "[A] lab found that Veggie Booty, a high-in-vitamin spinach and kale coated rice puff that was a favorite among moms whose kids wouldn't eat their greens, had 10 grams of fat—the same as a candy bar." *Good Housekeeping* hired an independent laboratory where "chemists ground up samples, bathed them in acid until only the soluble fat was left, then dried and weighed the fat. They found 8 grams of fat and 147 calories—a far cry from the 2.5 grams of fat and 128 calories the package claimed." (It's not the first time that company has been slapped on the wrist by the FDA, by the way.) I've inhaled an entire bag of Veggie Booty solo. I'm so annoyed with myself. Too good to be true? Every time.

Some parents can't help indulging their children. Maybe they try to replace attention or love with food. Hey, if a Happy Meal keeps kids satisfied, why complain? That's not exactly an ironic name for dinner. My mom took me and my brother to

McDonald's once a week on the way back from my ballet class. Josh and I each got a burger and split a small fries. Mom would eat the crusty ones from the bottom of the bag that we didn't want. Now I know those little crunchers soaked in beef tallow were the best-tasting fries in the bag.

A friend of mine told me about getting stuck in traffic with her two-year-old daughter, who began to lose it in the car. Against her better judgment, she pulled off the highway and took the little girl to McDonald's for the very first time. It was one of the stores with the big playgrounds inside, and her daughter was wide-eyed at the sight of all the manic kids running around. The mom ordered Chicken McNuggets and a bag of fries. She remembers looking up at her daughter, holding a nugget in one hand and a fry in the other. The little girl began to shake and quiver. "Are you all right?" my friend asked, her concern growing with the second. "Honey, what's wrong?" she begged, as her daughter continued to quake. Then, with a giant exhalation of breath, the girl cried out, "HAPPY!" An adult could not have captured the McDonald's experience more completely.

Some parents could stand to be a little more focused, as seen in the lawsuit filed by obese teens against McDonald's. The teens' parents (whether or not they are telling the truth) claim that they didn't realize that Mickey D's would plump up their kids like Shrinky Dinks from McCheese Land. Even the best-intentioned parents keep shoveling faux food into their kids' mouths; playgrounds are filled with remnants of Goldfish and Cheerios and Booty meant to keep our children quiet and content. Of course, for every suburban matron who has her children on strict diets of soy cheese and rice milk and gluten-free salad dressing, you've got moms in the barrio shaking their heads over obesity concerns that they don't understand as they deep-fry dinner. Obesity rates have soared most in poor Hispanic communities. In his essay "Let Them Eat Fat: The Heavy Truths about American Obesity" and his recent book *Fat Land,* Greg Critser delineates the clear connection between poverty, race, obesity, and class. He shows how fast-food companies specifically target growth in poor communities that need cheap, fast food the most.

I say, if you're going to eat a cookie, buy it in a bakery instead of a cardboard box. If you want a piece of cheese, slice it off a block in the dairy department instead of spraying it out of a can. When it comes to fake food and fad diets, it's time to get real.

CHAPTER 5

My Name Is Wendy, and I'm a Compulsive Eater . . . I Think

I have not become fat because I am angry. I am angry because being fat means countless assaults on my body and soul no matter who I am or to whom I speak.
                    —Jane Stern, "The Big Fat Lie," *Allure*

People say to fat folks, "I don't understand. You don't seem to eat that much more than I do." That's true. There are plenty of fat people who are fat simply because of math: They take in more calories than they put out. No drama, no excitement, a little blind spot plus some blissful ignorance when it comes to exercise and you end up with more than an inch to pinch. A lot of the guys I met at the Duke Diet & Fitness Center—more about that later—were middle-aged men who just needed to switch their potato from mashed to baked and take a walk around the block every once in a while. That's, like, 1 per cent of the population.

Then there's the other 99 percent of us. The *Oprah* watchers, the magazine readers, the brides, the girlfriends, the middle schoolers, the divorcees, the career women, the baby-sitters, and the moms. Usually we're good to go. But sometimes, when the door is shut and the lights are low, we go to town. Some of us need a midnight snack; some of us get up at 4 a.m. for a little late-night nosh. Some can't start their day without "a little something," and some people crash and burn without a late-day perk from the vending machine. Some of us need a petite treat with every meal; others can go weeks and weeks without indulging, and then . . . POW, a bad one. You know the drill. Some situation arises. You binge. You feel awful. So you binge again. What a waste. It's so sick and stupid and worthless, this kind of behavior. Compulsive behavior.

Back in the day, I figured out how to eat a pint of rock-hard frozen yogurt with a plastic spoon while driving 65 mph on a highway. I've gone to three different stores at midnight to fulfill a bizarre craving for Twizzlers Nibs—the red ones. I've driven thirty miles out of my way to get a Starbucks maple scone, hoping no one will recognize me. I've hidden candy wrappers in tin foil and disposed of garbage bags in shopping-mall parking lots. I've gone through weird phases where I've eaten big bags of Tootsie Rolls every night for two weeks. Then I'd switch to Mini Red Swedish Fish. (Sweet tooth, anyone? Couldn't give a crap about salty or fried stuff if you paid me.) I've stolen food out of friends' cupboards. I've eaten chocolate for breakfast and used mouthwash to cover up for myself. I felt like an alcoholic with a stash in the laundry basket. If I have something "good" in my house I can't stop thinking about it. If I don't, I'm thinking about getting it. I think and think and think and think (the kind of thinking that fen-phen put on pause). I can have the flu with a 103-degree temp in the middle of a blizzard, but if I want ice cream, goddammit, screw the bra, I'll put on boots and a down coat over my PJs and go down to the corner store to buy it. What the hell is that about?

It's about compulsion. But where did the compulsion come from in the first place?

Theory #1: It's an Addiction

Hi, my name is Wendy, and I'm a compulsive eater.

I'm using a little bit of addict talk here, but I don't consider myself "addicted" to food. I don't draw a clear analogy between eating and drinking and gambling. You can live without alcohol; you can live without blackjack; but you gotta eat. I tried Overeaters Anonymous. Works wonders for some people; it just didn't jive with me. There's a reason why I can smoke one cigarette and someone else needs to smoke the whole pack. Really, if I never had a cigarette again, it wouldn't make a difference to me. Is it because of nicotine? Is it because of genetics? Is it an emotional issue? Most likely it's a combo of all those things. Recent studies even suggest that high doses of fat and sugar found in fast and processed foods can become habit-forming in the same ways that nicotine or heroin can. Still, I wonder why I can eat one potato chip and lose complete interest, but if I know there are baked goods in my house, nothing can stop me.

Addiction itself may be genetic. Or maybe it's due to insulin reactions in my body. Maybe I'm self-medicating, trying to raise my own serotonin level using food—like my own personal Prozac. As I mentioned, fen-phen was a drug that helped me successfully manipulate my serotonin level, much like antide-pressants do. So maybe it's not about food, it's about mood.

Or maybe not.

Theory #2: It's an Eating Disorder

I don't think compulsive eating is an illness on a par with bulimia or anorexia. Go ahead and disagree, but if I really wanted to commit to a mental illness, I'd have learned to puke instead of sticking with the big nosh. I tried to go bulimic once in the dorm bathroom—it's practically a rite of passage for the modern-day gal on the go. But I couldn't make myself throw up. I've only thrown up a couple of times in my life, and it's a horrible feeling. No can do; I'm sticking with compulsive eating. When you're just packing on the pounds, then you've got some awareness and some control and just a little extra drama going on. What's the difference between a compulsive eater and a fat girl? Not much. To me, being fat is a dead giveaway for a compulsive eater. There are skinny people who are compulsive eaters—who are in a low-weight moment and will no doubt be porking up again soon. But truly skinny people are just skinny, not fat people on hiatus.

Bulimia and anorexia are devastating and lethal diseases and, like obesity, rise from a combination of physical and mental issues. As we do with obesity, we have to shake our heads and say, "Only in America." Only when we have it so good, when so much of the rest of the world goes without food, are we gorging and starving ourselves. We can't blame eating disorders on age or naiveté, as it's not only young girls who are getting sucked in: "Although medical literature in recent years has shown eating disorders spreading across class, race and gender lines and striking girls at ever younger ages, the next large group of sufferers, many experts predict, will be middle-aged women. The anxieties of midlife—divorce, marital strains, parental deaths, empty-nest syndrome and menopause—are powerful catalysts for older women's eating disorders, the experts say." Even African-American women, who traditionally have been resistant to body-image drama, are developing destructive eating behaviors in growing numbers. C'mon, girls, we are too smart to be doing this to ourselves. But I understand the lure. These are culturally specific diseases due to the way women see ourselves right now. To stop the proliferation of these diseases, we should start by relieving some of the pressure we put on ourselves.

Theory #3: I'm an "Emotional" Eater

Some experts, like Oprah's trainer, Bob Greene, refer to compulsive eaters as "emotional eaters." They say you eat because of some stimulus—like you're sad, or angry, or stressed, or bored, or in a place that reminds you of a specific food. Basically, any time you eat but you're not physically hungry, that's emotional eating. Every time you eat but you aren't using it as fuel, then you're an emotional eater. What a load! Okay, there are about seven people in the world who righteously use food as fuel. Six of them are professional marathon runners from Kenya, and the last one is Bob Greene. Everyone else eats birthday cake because it's a birthday party and eats hamburgers because they taste good. Sure, sometimes we eat for emotional reasons. But that doesn't entitle anyone to the label of "emotional eater."

Most diet books address emotional eating by trying to get you to break compulsive eating habits. They encourage you to find the root of your emotional problems, then teach you behavioral skills so you can "ride the anxiety" and "face the fear" and become a normal person who is not obsessed with food and weight and eating. These skills include making lists and talking to friends and working as a volunteer—all things that replace the emotional energy you supposedly give to food.

I don't know that any of us ever get to the root of our emotional problems. If you do, I'm not sure that taking a walk around the block or calling a friend or treating yourself to opera tickets really fixes anything. If anything is helping me address my own concerns and issues, it's not losing weight. It's staying where I am. I'm not surfing up and down on the scale anymore. I see the problems—emotional, physical, and other-wise—all laid out before me. I'm cognizant; I'm responsible—and I'm fat. And that's okay.

Theory #4: It's A Response to Cycles of Dieting and Deprivation

I love food. It can make me so happy. Food signifies family and celebrations and decadence and experimentation and dates and sleepovers and so many other special occasions. There are times when food is better than sex. A great dinner is a perfect night out on the town for me. I'd much rather dine out than go to a bar. Fat girls generally don't like to drink. Why have a cocktail when you can have dessert (unless it's a dessert cocktail, and in that case I'll take two!)? If you're a young American filly, you know how many calories are in a frozen margarita, so why not eat key lime pie instead? There's really no reason for a fat girl to go to a bar, because the chances of getting picked up are few and far between. Why not skip the bar and head over to that cute little café next door for a cappuccino and a sweet treat?

But food—and the way my body reacts to it—is also the bane of my existence.

We are so overprogrammed about health issues, so far from a natural state of listening and responding to our systems' needs. Eating is the same way. Like, something that comes naturally, that I've been doing since day one, has gotten so confusing that I'm supposed to relearn it somehow. But I can't. Too late. As the Scotland *Sunday Herald* reported in an article about Susie Orbach's class-action suit against Weight Watchers: "[Orbach] believes continuous dieting is partly to blame for the rise in obesity because it makes us lose touch with normal bodily mechanisms that regulate eating. 'Our girls are raised by a generation of mothers who've been so assaulted by this themselves that, from very early in their lives, their appetites might have been watched, curtailed and managed rather than simply developed,' she says. 'It's as though we've distorted the mechanism that would allow us to eat in a straightforward, engaged and enjoyable way. So food becomes an arena in which you're either depriving yourself or rebelling, and that really messes up your metabolism.'" My wires are crossed, baby. As a professional dieter, I learned that half of a banana is a single serving. Do you know anyone who eats half a banana and puts the other half away for later? A banana, dammit! A single serving of a banana is . . . a banana! Idiocy! No wonder I'm fat!

Even when I throw a harmless little apple in my mouth I suffer a mental meltdown: *Mmm, apple. I should eat more fruits and vegetables, this apple will give me gas, I couldn't even eat this if I was on Atkins, Atkins is dumb, Atkins works, tomorrow I swear five fruits and vegetables, but they are so expensive, and you have to keep buying them fresh all the time, what about grapefruit, grapefruit lasts for a while, I should have grapefruit for breakfast, grapefruit will never be filling enough, I need carbs at breakfast, why do I need carbs at breakfast, what I really want is a Danish, yeah I want a cheese Danish like they had at that bakery in Southfield where my grandparents used to go, the ones my grandpa liked, I'm gonna get one at Fairway market, they have some like that, my grandpa had diabetes, I'm gonna get diabetes, screw it, if I'm going to get diabetes. I'm going to eat that Danish* RIGHT NOW!

And I wonder why I'm stuffing a Danish in my face. Apple, Danish, drama.

When I eat, I'm still getting revenge for every half of a banana that got put away for later, every apple that I wished was a turnover, every little moment of deprivation I've had in my life. Other kids came home from high school and ate Doritos, took a swig of a Coke; there I'd be, sixteen years old, stirring up a delicious Quick Weight Loss Clinic butterscotch-flavored pudding! Mmm-hmm. My friends kicked off breakfast with a bowl of Froot Loops; I'd start with a piece of toasted Less bread (40 calories) topped with one-third cup nonfat cottage cheese that I'd sweeten up with cinnamon and Sweet'N low. If I'm not mistaken, I think that WW used to tout that as a "low-cal cheese Danish." Granted, the Froot Loops aren't exactly a healthy choice, but I think that all-or-nothing thinking, along with fussing around with my metabolism, is what got me screwed up in the first place. New research supports the idea that yo-yo dieting can alter the metabolism (which is the speed of the body's chemical processes), and the body's set point (which is the weight that your body tends to maintain over a long period of time). Paul Campos's research also concurred that those who lose weight by dieting or using a diet drug often wind up weighing more than people who start out at about the same weight, but never diet. Makes me wish I'd just sucked down the Froot Loops and called it a day.

I remember being in a hospital cafeteria with my stepmom, Myrna, one time, when my dad was having surgery. I was maybe twenty-five years old. We went down the line, and the thing I wanted was this really big, really good-looking muffin. With a pounding heart, I bought it. I was sure she was going to say something to me about it, ask me if there wasn't a healthier choice I could make, etc. With my heart racing, I ate it. Right in front of her. And I started to cry. She asked me why I was crying, but it wasn't about my dad. It was because for the first time I was eating a muffin in front of her. I realized how much of eating the food I really wanted to eat was done in secret— how many muffins I'd had in the secret space of my car or my bedroom.

I did that all the time. The by-the-book eating in front of the folks, then going home to fulfill my desires in secret. What a waste of time and calories. They could never figure out why I was so fat if I never ate anything bad. Duh. How stupid I was. Myrn's mind was on my dad and on our family. If I hadn't said something, she'd never even have noticed I was eating a muffin—a muffin that I cried over. Honestly, life is too short.

Theory #5: It Is What It Is

We're told that inside every fat person is a skinny person struggling to get out. I don't think that's true. I think that inside every fat person there is a skeleton and tissue and organs and just more fat than a thin person.

Fat can be a real stress on my life that holds me back from certain things. But I've realized that the emotional cost of the repair is much higher than the cost of the status quo. I can't afford to live through another renovation. Especially when I look back at all the stupid shit I've done to try to escape the body I'm still in. All the ass-backwards diets . . . I can't smell a beet without feeling faint because of the diet when I just ate beets, hot dogs, and vanilla ice cream for three days straight. Clipped it right from a women's magazine. I've eaten a gallon of ice cream every night for a month and nothing else after reading Geneen Roth's incredibly moving books about compulsive eating. I've tried to smoke cigarettes instead of putting food in my mouth—there's a genius idea. I've looked into joining the Army as some sort of weight-loss boot camp. I've spent hundreds of bucks on weird herbal supplements to curb appetite. I'm probably the only person who has been on chemotherapy drugs (methotrexate for the Wegener's granulomatosis) and not lost weight. The irony isn't lost on me either.

Truth is, I can eat and exercise "perfectly" for weeks in a row, or I can get lost in an occasional binge. In the big picture, it doesn't really matter. I go up a few pounds, I lose a few, but I always weigh about the same. With one steroid-induced exception, I've weighed between 215 and 225 for the past ten years. Time to put my self-improvement efforts elsewhere. Is that crazy? Defensive? Maybe. I reserve the right to change my mind. But my body ain't changing right now. I may not Break Free from Compulsive Eating. I may never Make the Connection. I can't always Stop the Insanity. Only recently did I begin to figure out that while I could lose a few pounds, or build some muscle tone, essentially I am always going to be fat. It was only when I finally understood it that something changed. I wasn't just fat, I was Fat—not just a physical state, but a state of mind.

So no more tapes, no more meetings, no more potions, no

more plans. No more hopes for a "lifestyle" change. I like my life. I like my lifestyle. I'm even starting—can it be possible?—to like my fat. Maybe someday I'll be able to define exactly what my fat is—-my fear and anxiety and sexuality and mother issues and father issues and bad behavior and guilt and feminism and laziness and chemistry and physicality and habits—and still NOT LOSE WEIGHT.

I'm fat. I assume I always will be. I spent my whole life waiting to get thin so my life could start. Now I realize that I can't wait for thinness to arrive in order for my life to begin. But I never would have known that if I hadn't finally gone to Duke.

Duke

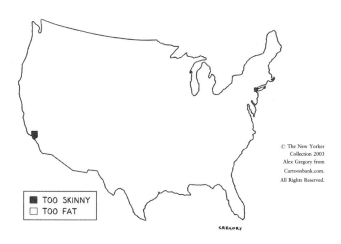

TOO SKINNY
TOO FAT

GREGORY

In case you've ever wondered, here's what rock bottom looks like: It's 11:59 on New Year's Eve and you're by yourself in a Walgreen's in god-knows-where Florida trying to figure out which kind of candy will best heal your pain (I went with Celebrations, by the way, so I could have, like, a little candy sampler). You're thirty years old, you just got canned from your dream job, the economy's dead, you don't have a boyfriend. You know you're going to become a complete shut-in, an agoraphobe with insomnia and an eating disorder. You're pretty sure they'll pull your bored, bloated, exhausted body out of your window with a cherry picker and profile you on *Jerry Springer*.

That's when you know for certain: It's time to go to Duke.

I'd always fantasized about Duke. It's the top of the line, the end of the road. Established in 1969 by Duke University in Durham, North Carolina, the Duke Diet & Fitness Center (DFC) is a renowned research center and weight-loss treatment clinic. Fat folks think about Duke like alcoholics think about Betty Ford: If they can't fix you, no one can. Every time I blew up after a successful diet I imagined the trip I'd eventually take down to Durham, North Carolina, to meet my skinny destiny.

I needed a boot camp, a hardcore new routine to start before I went down the wrong path again. I needed control of my body and my life. I wasn't looking for weight loss; I wanted A REGIMEN. I just wanted to have structure, one perfect month of eating and exercise and sleeping. That meant not getting caught up in a numbers game. Then my lifestyle would finally change, and my real life would begin.

Duke Diary

Sunday, January 13, 2002

This morning I pulled into the Duke Towers Residential Suites, the motel across from the Duke Diet & Fitness Center, where I'll make my home for the next month. A car pulled up next to me and a big, big guy lumbered out. I mean like four hundred pounds big. I thought, "What the hell am I doing here? I'm fat, but I'm not, like, FAT. What have I gotten myself into?" Am I being fattist? More like fear I'll be ostracized, the Britney Spears of the DFC.

The DFC building is your basic concrete, sixties-style educational facility. Met the other nine people who are starting in my week. A couple of moms with grown kids, a single guy, a married guy exec, a woman from England . . . a couple have been to the DFC before. One chick my age said she tried Slim-Fast, it didn't work, now she's here. Huh? There must be an in-between, sweetie! Then again, if I coulda nipped this in the bud . . . The staff put a fruit tray and a pitcher of water out on a table. I was hungry, but I was too terrified to take anything from it. Figured it was some sort of fruity trap.

The first thing the administrator offered us was a discount on a return trip to the DFC that we could use any time in the following year. But the payment is nonrefundable. So, if we didn't take the offer right there and then, we couldn't get the discount. It seemed strange to me that I'd be penalized finan-cially before I'd even officially started the program.

We spent a lot of time going over the menu plan and figuring out what we could order from the cafeteria. It's a very complex system, but it's all based on a basic food pyramid/exchange plan. They've recently moved away from calorie counting since it was confusing and made people get all crazy-compulsive about calories. We also get a stress test and a meeting with a personal trainer to figure out an exercise plan. I'm determined to maximize every opportunity. I want to do this TO THE LETTER. This DFC is my chance to do the ultimate body experiment, every variable calculated. Plus, it's expensive as hell, so I'm not about to let one penny go to waste.

Had our first meal in the cafeteria, a sort of tasty fish-and-vegetables thing. Not too diety at all. Lots of older folks here, maybe only three or four other people under forty in the room.

Tonight I stood in the hallway looking at the sign-up sheets for bowling nights and movie nights and Chinese-cooking classes.

This sweet and kind of sophisticated-looking older lady approached me in the hallway. She kind of reminded me of my grandma. "First time here?" she asked. I nodded. "Don't worry honey, you're gonna do great."

Monday, January 14, 2002

Day started early with a breakfast that we had to stuff down before the first class started. Our first session was DFC Obesity, with the guy who runs the program, Dr. Stuart Welling. Basic facts about obesity treatment, heart disease, etc. Welling looks like a guy who likes to go for a run in the morning. Not that you have to struggle with weight in order to understand what the fight is all about, but . . . it helps! Can you trust someone who has never had a weight problem to help you with yours?

The gym is hardly hoity-toity—looks like my high-school gym except that it has ten treadmills, a few elliptical machines, and a bunch of weight-training equipment. Most people were strolling on the treadmills; they pipe in disco music over the loudspeakers. On the far side of the gym, some clients were taking a lo-fi step aerobics class taught by one of the trainers. They offer aqua aerobics, but I ain't getting in no pool. Nothing grosser than a bunch of people sweating in a pool, I don't care how much chlorine they throw in there.

Back to our orientation room to discuss the "Hunger Scale." It's a line from 1 to 7, with 1 being absolute starvation and 7 being stuffed to the gills. It's posted in all the rooms. We're supposed to eat when we think we're at, like, a 2 and stop when we hit, like, a 5. I don't get why the damn thing goes from 1 to 7. Isn't the natural instinct to go from 1 to 10? People would say, "I'm at a 4," and the nutritionist would say, "Then you're probably done eating." Only we hadn't *started* eating yet. Or they'd eat and she'd say, "How do you feel?" "Oh, I'm at about an 8." "An 8! You must be sick to your stomach!"

At my medical assessment, the nurses weighed me in—224.2. I sat down for an intake with a physician's assistant named Neil Klein. Skinny and nervous and new. He looked at my extensive list of medications, most of them due to my Wegener's. One of the drugs is prednisone, which causes weight gain. I still take about 7 mg a day to help my joints; my body demands it. Neil and I decided to take me off Meridia, since that would sort of ruin the control of knowing how my appetite worked.

Later that day we took our stress tests to determine our maximum heart levels. I was so scared; what happened if I worked too hard and had a heart attack on the machine? Ah, no reason to worry. I'm pretty much the pinnacle of health compared to some of the other clients. I work out regularly; this kind of thing is new to people who consider frequent exercise to be getting in and out of the minivan or hitting the links twice a season. Passed my stress test with flying colors and they gave me the go-ahead to use the gym as much as I want.

Tuesday, January 15, 2002
Did a blood draw first thing, then went to Nutrition Fundamentals. I dutifully jotted down notes about vitamins and minerals. Four main risk factors for heart disease are: smoking, high cholesterol, inactivity, and high blood pressure (obesity ranks in at number 5). Happy to note that I was 0 for 4.

Duke's diet info is kind of like Dieting 101. Eat more veggies. Eat less fat. A deck of cards is a 3-ounce serving of meat. A tennis ball is a cup of veggies. A knuckle's width of a dessert is

100 calories. All the handouts have little cartoon guys on them, wearing terry-cloth sweatbands and running around.

There are four main areas of discussion here: nutrition, fitness, medical, and health psychology. Our first health-psych class was called Balancing Act—very "I saw this last week on *Oprah*." They asked us to write down answers to this question:

What am I hungry for?

Those chocolate-chip cookies they had at that place by my office.

This is so stupid.

C'mon, girl, give it a chance. You came all this way.

What I am hungry for?

Love/recognition.

I'm so stupid for getting myself into this situation.

I cannot live my life this way.

I do not have any goals.

If I make any goals, I'm setting myself up for failure.

Something bad happened to me to make me feel this way.

No one succeeds with this, so why do I have any reason to think that I'm the one who can do it?

This program is faulty.

Everyone thinks I'm a loser.

No one will ever recognize my genius.

I will never recognize my genius. I will never do anything great.

It's too late. My body is screwed up. My skin is screwed up.

I feel sorry for all of these people. They are pathetic. I hate them all. Why did they wait so long to lose weight?

I will always be alone. No one will ever love me.

Duke

I would never want anyone who could be interested in me—
there must be something wrong with them.
I'm going to be alone and die with cats.

Wednesday, January 16, 2002

Fast-ass breakfast again! So rushed, but line is too long to get in
any earlier—and I can't handle a wake-up call that begins with
a 6. So I was really late for a Meditation seminar. You're
supposed to relax and focus on your breath and dismiss
thoughts as they come into your head. I know a lot of people
dig it, but it just made me sleepy.

Took Boxing Aerobics at the gym, it's the highest-level aerobics
class they have. Still, I had to amp it up a little to keep my heart rate
in the zone. Haven't done a grapevine step in like nine years.
Seemed like a couple other ladies were annoyed with my hopping
around, but hey, I gotta do what I gotta do. Was feeling pretty bad-
ass till I nearly fainted. Dragged myself to the cafeteria to get some
salt just to stay conscious. But since a nutritionist hadn't approved
it . . . they told me no. Luckily another cafeteria guy took pity on
me gave me a teaspoon of salt. I dumped it into a mug, added an
ounce of hot water, and threw it back. Like a barfly.

Figuring out the menu here is like breaking DNA code. Once
the nutritionist signs off on your menu you aren't allowed to
deviate one bit. Say you sign up for the fish and get to the dining
room and the chicken looks more appealing. Well, screw you,
buddy, you're eating flounder tonight. Even if you want an
extra helping of steamed spinach—spinach!—no way, they say.
Good discipline, I guess, but hardly training for the real world.

*　　　*　　　*

87

People are nice but I don't really have, like, a best friend yet. One girl in her early twenties has been here for months, has lost a lot of weight. Some of the guys keep giving us the eye, it's very discomfiting. I mean, we're all fat girls in sweatpants—it's hardly a pickup joint.

Thursday, January 17, 2002

At each meal, I'm surprised to discover that almost every person around me has been to Duke many times. They all have success while they're here, but eventually fall off the wagon. Compared to other popular programs located nearby, like Structure House and the Rice Diet (where they test your pee!!!), they swear by this one. Then why are they unable to maintain their weight loss? Is it simply impossible? The few who do seem like heroes.

Signed up for a psychological session with Richard Reisman. He's a real New Yorky, Jewish guy with a beard, and I like that. He's also fat, and I like that. It takes a lot of chutzpah to work here and still be fat. Makes me think he's on my team, unlike the other skinny little psychologist they have on staff. Since Richard talks to fat folks all the time, maybe he's got some special insight.

The first thing he says when I sit down in his office is "Tell me the story of your body." I like that. Like, yes, my body has a story worth being told, and here it is. Then he starts in with "Fat is a layer of protection"—and I basically said, "Listen, Richard, you can skip to the back of the book. I know all the stuff about fat being a shield from intimacy and a sign of depression, and behavioral habits, and blah blah blah. Let's crack the code here, buddy." He seemed shocked. Like I said, I don't think they get a lot of kids like me down at the ol' DFC.

His advice? Lower my standards. Lower my expectations. Reneg on my "plus-size idealism." Stop being "such a feminist." He literally told me to read *Dating for Dummies* and to be nice to myself. Is that a real book?

Granted, I'm there in his office, and I'm in my sweaty sweatpants, and I'm vulnerable. But he seemed to make sense. He reinforced my suspicion that I've done something wrong . . . basically took the wrong exit at some point. Developed my mind too much and didn't think about my body enough. I'm going to take his words to heart. Shut up, basically. Be a good, quiet girl. Signed up for another session, $95 a pop.

Then I went to Making Peace with Exercise. It's an awkward truce. I'm trying to find other motivators besides weight loss. Also, I need to make it less of a pain in the ass if I'm going to do it more often. I get really unnerved about having to get showered and dressed twice in a day, and about schlepping my gym bag around. It's just a quality-of-life issue for me that I have to get over to make this work. C'mon, exercise, give peace a chance.

Good news, though! We got our labs back and I'm very happy with the results. My cholesterol is 191, triglycerides are 137. My HDL cholesterol (the "good" one) is 66, and my ratio is the incredibly low 2.8, prompting Neil to write "Excellent!" next to my numbers. I feel like a very successful second-grader.

But if my numbers are good, and my risk factors are low, then I'm here because . . . oh, because I'm a freak who can't trust myself. I need control.

Friday, January 18, 2002

I asked at the front desk where I can have my *New York Times* delivered. They were shocked; apparently no one has ever made that request. Need that paper; it's my thing to hide behind at breakfast if I get caught at a bad table or if I can't bear to start my day with idle chitchat. Love breakfast though, always a good carb and fruit and yogurt and coffee, almost too much to eat so I save my fruit for a mid-morning snack.

When you walk into the gym, people are sitting in the front lounge, READING. I swear, they're reading spy novels and romances and magazines. So I'm up on the treadmill, pumping away, headphones on to get some killer beats going, and when I finally get off to cool down someone approaches me and says, "Wow, you're really working up a sweat there, huh?" And it's not just once! Isn't that what we're here to do?

I work out in the morning and take yoga or tai chi in the afternoon. Occasionally some old dude joins the yoga class ("My kid told me I had ta,") and tries to do it from a seated position. As we're all oming ourselves into submission, he kvetches and asks questions and interrupts the teacher. Just tried to shine that benevolent love on him as Deepak would want me to do. Occasionally in the last part of the class—my favorite part, where you just lie there in "corpse" pose (genius, the guy who came up with that)—I just cry a little bit when I think about what the hell has gotten me to this crazy gym in the first place.

All of the classes are as beginner as they can be. I have to amp up my energy to the maximum levels to try and get anything out of a low-impact class. Lunging and squatting and V-stepping my way across the gym, the 1980s all over again.

On the machines, I put on my headphones and crank up the music as loud as I can take it, singing my head off to Madonna or Cher or Whitney or whoever can move my fat ass that day. My voice bounces of the walls of the empty gym, especially on the weekends, when I'm usually the only one there. Guess everyone else is taking the Sabbath day off. Or else they finished the latest Clive Cussler.

The other kooky thing? Everyone is constantly dressed in sweats and T-shirts, always on their way in or out of the gym (for library hour, I guess). Yesterday I went back to the motel in the middle of the day to change, to blow out my hair and put on some lipstick so I didn't feel like a total dirtbag. But I got HELL for it! "Where are you going all dressed up?" Somehow it's inappropriate for me to be clean or attractive, or to look young. I'm feeling disapproving stares from a few of the women and, worse, the oh-so-approving looks of the men. Ew, ew, ew. As if. Obviously, if I'm there, it's 'cause I'm at a low point. I'm fat, I'm sweaty, and I'm focused. I'm not here to flirt with middle-aged married/divorced men who are also fat and sweaty and apparently less focused than I am. I can't believe how many of them never got the message that we aren't at a spring semester at a dorm. And P.S.—Buddy, you'll definitely improve your shot with me if you COVER YOUR HAIRY-ASS SHOULDERS IN THE DINING ROOM and LOAD UP ON DEODORANT at some point during the day.

How can it be? In this alternate universe, I AM DFC BRITNEY. Oops, I did it again! I know what the Prom Queen feels like, I *almost* have sympathy for her. One girl said that a guy in our group followed her home to Duke Towers and tried to give her a "foot massage"! I don't think so.

Saturday, January 19, 2002

Did Cardio Circuit class, then more nutrition. Combination foods: what's in a burrito, how you tally up a chicken salad, etc. I can definitely recognize hunger now—it's a hot feeling in my belly, followed by a grumble that registers as a 3.5—damn it, I mean a 1.5—on the stupid Hunger Scale. Definitely have the sense of fueling my body for exercise instead of entertainment.

Sunday, January 20, 2002

Everyone loves Sunday here because they do brunch in the caf. A new group of victims started tonight. Ha ha, suckers!

Monday, January 21, 2002

Week 2 begins. Had a personal training session with Karen today. She's very pretty and kind. She teaches Pilates, which is the most contemporary class on the menu, focusing on upper-body strength and flexibility, free weights, etc. Then I did my regular exercise classes, so I'll probably be good and sore tomorrow. Also did yoga this afternoon. Two major sessions in one day. Who'd a thunk it?

Tuesday, January 22, 2002

Ate a silent lunch called Mentoring Mealtime that is offered weekly. We were supposed to sit and be mindful about eating while a staffer monitored us. I kept laughing and got in trouble.

Class o' the Day: The Pros and Cons of Weight Loss. We are asked to fill in a chart with four quarters: benefits of not losing weight, benefits of losing weight, drawbacks of not losing weight, and drawbacks of losing weight. While everyone else is really busy filling in the benefits of losing (better health, better clothes), I'm suddenly aware of the drawbacks: *Embar-rassing*, I write. *Hypocritical. Money. Relationships change when you lose weight. People change when you lose weight. Your clothes don't fit. You need to restructure your social life. You might gain it back. Then there's all the attention, attention I don't want: "Did you lose weight?" Reminder of what a loser you were when you couldn't lose.*

Went to the movies tonight and brought my after-dinner Jell-O as a snack. Oh God, I'm a dieter again.

Wednesday, January 23, 2002

I take back every snarky doubtful thing I've ever said. Today was Medical Check-in—i.e., weigh-in. 219.2! That's a loss of five pounds. Okay, maybe I was hoping for more, but that's a damn good start. Wow, maybe I can drop fifteen pounds this month . . . at this rate, I'll fit into my size 12 clothes a year from now . . .

Sunday, January 27, 2002

Slept over at my aunt Nancy's last night in Chapel Hill. I adore her and her husband, Andrew. Would be losing it if they weren't around. Got so tense this morning though, trying to make myself an egg-white omelet. I was measuring out vegetables in a cup when I freaked out with anger. Here I am, thirty years old. Am I going to have to spend my whole life learning how to eat, feeling like a three-year-old, measuring out things in spoons?

Tuesday, January 29, 2002

Bought an extra session with Karen ($65!) to discuss specific exercise goals. She introduced me to the concept of interval training. I'm so stagnant on my cardio . . . I can do an hour on the treadmill without really straining myself, or forty-five minutes on the elliptical trainer. She suggested that I stagger my workout. So I did a minute on the treadmill at 3.9 with 0 percent elevation, followed by a minute of 4.2 with 3 percent elevation. Did that five times. Then two minutes at 4.2 and 5 percent followed by 4.0 and 0 percent . . . We came up with an hour-long plan that kept me busy with an eye on the clock and my fingers jabbing at buttons. When it was over, the wind was truly knocked out of me. I felt it in my chest and throughout my body. Interval training. Rock on. Seems to be an appropriate metaphor for my entire dieting-and-exercise experience. I always thought it had to be all or nothing. An hour at 4.0 or forget it. Eleven hundred calories a day or else a food free-for-all. But I can go forward and back, hard and gentle, and then get back to it.

Wednesday, January 30, 2002

Weighed in again. Since I lost five pounds last week, was hoping for at least three or four this time . . . but the scale stayed exactly the same. Still 219.2. Neil and nurses went with the old "must be water weight/your period/don't worry about it," but I'm worried. Started weighing myself in the locker room every day. Bad habit.

Discussed situation with Diane, my nutritionist. She's skinny but she's very smart, very straightforward. Also works out here at the gym, which I think is very cool. We talked about trigger foods and how I could cure so many of my ills with a bowl of well-planned Jell-O! Ah, why didn't I think of that?

Had a "Polarity Massage" ($70) with the lady who teaches Meditation. You're supposed to lie there and focus and see if you can feel the energy streams moving around in your body. Couldn't be sure, although felt painful tingling in my left arm.

She says the left arm is like an antenna that takes on others' negative energy, and the right arm lets it go. Feel like I'm a negative-energy magnet.

Thursday, January 31, 2002
Proudly shared my interval-training metaphor in Processing the Program. It delighted the tiny behavioral therapist, but the eyes of the group members glazed right over. Same therapist teaches a class on Binge Eating that I hoped would be profound. Alas . . . 'twas not. Plus, therapist is about the size of my thumb and relentlessly cheerful. I'm guessing that her idea of a binge is eating BOTH Pop Tarts in the foil, instead of wrapping one up and saving it for later.

At least we had a cooking demo today. It's a super-popular class because you get to eat at the end.

Friday, February 1, 2002
Looking in the mirror every day for signs of muscle-tone change. All that Pilates! I stretch out my muscles hoping that I'm getting greater strength or flexibility. Pray every night that sometime in the not-too-distant future I'll take a crap. Trying to evaluate if exercise/sleep/food is helping my rheumatoid joint pain, or insomnia, or stress level, or constant constipation . . . but all hard to discern.

Took a class called Dining Out. Talked about the difference between restaurant portions and home portions, get rid of the bread basket, yada ya, I know this crap like the back of my fat hand. As a group, we got to choose from local Durham menus to go to a restaurant together, where our leader would join us with an assortment of measuring cups and spoons so we could have a real-life assessment of our restaurant tactics. (Do we get to take the "special" bus to the restaurant?) Naturally, the white male fiftysomething combover set chooses a steak joint. People are preordering the twenty-four ounce porterhouse and bacon skins and fried calamari. This is after the instructor has spent an hour explaining that one dinner-size protein portion is about the size of a deck of cards, and ixnay on the oo-blay eese-chay dressing, and watch the hidden salts. I'm wondering if it would be appropriate for me to smack my head into the concrete wall on the teacher's behalf.

Had another psych session with Richard. Now I have the sneaking suspicion that he really doesn't know what he's talking about. I mean, what is a fat guy doing working at the DFC? It's like having a guy sip a margarita while running an AA meeting. Getting seriously frustrated, on a slow deep burn, especially without seeing results on the scale.

Talked to my friend Emmy in California about my frustrations. I don't understand why the world is so small-minded about big people. My blood tests are stellar. My heart is a beautiful machine. I'm as healthy as anybody else, I just have more fat on my body. "Hmm," says smart Emmy. "It sounds like you're at a losing-weight place and you haven't decided if you want to lose weight." True, that. Emmy sighed. "I know that you want to change the system, Wendy. But I don't need to be a revolution, I just need to like how I look in the mirror."

Every night the same routine . . . evaluating my plan, double-checking my schedule. Control. Looking out the window as the

Pizza John's truck cruises purposefully by. Rumor has it that Pizza John's delivers to Duke Towers more than any other place in Durham.

Saturday, February 2, 2002

Today's special Saturday lifestyle workshop was called Cravings: The Magic of Chocolate. Skinny Minnie lecturer tried to gain our trust by saying her sister had a serious weight problem. She gave us each a baggie with a Dorito, a Hershey's Kiss, and a raisin in it. Inmates got all jumpy. She asked us to eat each one slowly. We sucked the flavoring off the Dorito first and noticed that what was left was a crappy tortilla chip. Then came the raisin. We smelled it, we rolled it around in our mouths. We bit into it and marveled at the multiple explosions of flavor on many different parts of our tongues! The raisin. Who knew? Had we ever really tasted a raisin before? The Hershey's Kiss was good, but it was hardly as complex as the little dried grape. Oh, tiny yet powerful raisin, we sing to thee!

Sunday, February 3, 2002

Worked out this morning. Power-walked the track outside on campus, then finished on an elliptical trainer. Again my blood pressure dropped to the point where I thought I was going to faint, but now I'm finally on the list for bouillon when I need it. Practically ate the damn cube straight. Got a massage tonight to help my aching muscles.

Monday, February 4, 2002

Bad omen this morning: no *New York Times*. I grin-'n'-beared it through half a bagel, one tablespoon cream cheese, a half-cup skim milk, and a cup of strawberries. Went to the locker room and peeled off my sweats. Against my better judgment, I stepped up on the scale. Same! 219.2. Damn it! Went to the gym and did forty minutes of interval training on the treadmill. Could feel evil no-goodnik voice nipping at the back of my mind as I hauled myself up onto the Precor. Hoped a little Madonna *Greatest Hits Vol. 2* would ease me out of my funk. Sure enough, it did. By track 2, I was singing and pumping on the damn machine as hard as I could.

One of the girl fitness interns sidled up to me and poked me in the up-and-down thigh. I peeled off my headphones and was greeted by the dusty sounds of Kool and the Gang on the loudspeakers. She gave me a little smile. "I can see you're having quite a time there today!" she said. "Oh—yeah," I huffed and puffed. "Well, um, do you think that you could, like, tone it down?" "Sorry?" "Do you think that you could just keep it down a little bit?" she repeated.

I looked around at the next-to-empty gym. I saw one Jackie Collins fan lounging near the door, and an old lady taking a leisurely stroll on a treadmill on the other side of the gym. "Am I bothering anyone? Did someone complain?" I ask.

"Oh, no." She smiled brightly. "I was just thinking that you *might* bother someone, and that wouldn't be good."

"Oh, okay, sure," I said as I put my headphones back on. The track switched over. "It's 'Don't Cry for Me, Argentina,'" I called out to the intern across the gym. "Guess I'd better skip that one!"

She gave me a thumbs-up and went back to playing computer chess.

I dialed down the volume but tried to keep my energy up. Too late—my buzz was officially killed. By then I was in a gray haze of low blood pressure and needed my bouillon fix anyway. I was seething by the time I made it to lunch (grilled cheese with pesto, one cup vanilla yogurt, one cup kiwi fruit, salad with dressing).

Okay, okay, I have to channel this negative energy. And my usual fallback—perhaps a nice cookie, or some other bakery treat?—is out of the question. Right, I have yoga at four. I'll put it all there.

Except yoga got canceled.

Dark cloud, dark cloud now hanging over the horizon. All day people keep saying, "Wow, you look so different. Wow, I can really see the change." I snarl back, "Oh yeah? I'm not a pound different."

"Well, we can see it in other ways," the nice fat ladies assure me.

But can *I* see it? Or any new muscle definition? A sense of strength that I didn't have before? An easing up of my arthritis? Am I sleeping better? Do I feel less stressed out? Can I even take a crap? NO. My left arm is KILLING ME!!!

I go back to my room at the inn to make a list of why I'm so angry about this gym sitchy. There, that's constructive. Changing Destructive Thinking.

Was the intern just annoyed or did someone say something about it to her?

Program doesn't give me what I need, music is what I give myself for motivation.

Been here three weeks. This is the first time anyone ever had a problem.

I'm paying for this.

Tell invisible complainers to come back a different time!

I work harder than anyone else in that gym, that's my reward!

I have to deal with everyone else's BS!!!

And so on.

Then, of course, the list devolves into complete self-deprecation.

The devil on my shoulder is laughing at me.

Why bother? No way I'm part of the "5 percent" that succeeds long-term.

My body is ruined already, and I ruined it. It's too late.

$ per pound not worth it.

I can do the Ben & Jerry diet and weigh the same.

I'm disgusted with myself.

I feel so defeated.

I feel lower than I did on January first. Feel like I could kill someone just by looking at them. And I might try.

Tuesday, February 5, 2002

Today in the gym I worked as hard as I could, as silently as I could, my eyes scanning over the ladies relaxing on the mats with their legs hanging over the big medicine balls. Am trying to root out any possible rat who said something to that intern. Apparently my seething is visible, since people stay away from me all day.

Roll out my yoga mat and start to stretch out a bit. Notice that the guy next to me has some open sores on his legs, but he's rolling all over his mat. Oh my, disgusting! Any common decency here? No! I look down at my mat and see a spider crawling across it.

That's it. I can't take it. I'm gonna blow it. Fuck this diet, fuck this whole thing. I drive out to the grocery store. Stalk the aisles with revenge on my mind. And I buy . . . a Kashi bar! That's right, 290 calories and 4 grams of saturated fat. Take *that*, I think, chowing on it in my car. Can't sing on the damn machine? Hah! Monitor *this*, you bastards! And I drive back, in time for dinner (6 ounces sea bass, one-half cup potatoes, salad with dressing, and one-half cup pineapple).

I can't handle this for ten more days. I can't.

Wednesday, February 6, 2002

The day starts with lab tests and weigh-in.

220.2 pounds.

Oh my god. I'm up one pound. Murder. Murder someone. Murder the intern. Murder gangly Neil Klein.

In Bringing the DFC Home, they give us a weekly meal plan sheet for home use, so we don't have to make our own or go out and buy expensive monitoring software programs. Monday is already filled in to show us what an example day looks like. But if we want to record our Monday, there's no room to do it on the sheet. I mention it to Diane, and she is surprised. "Huh, you're right. How do you like that? No one has ever brought it up before." Aaarrrgh! Diane is kind enough to make me another sheet that has Monday left empty, all ready for me to monitor myself.

Unhappily, I start making plans during my weekly evaluations with fitness and nutrition about what I'm going to do when I get home. I'm going to make an exercise schedule at the beginning of each week. I'm going to invest in more workout wear and have a bag ready to go at any time. I'm going to get over the hump of hating to shower twice a day. I remind myself that it's better to get twenty minutes in than none at all. Someone mentions the goal of being on target 80 percent of the time, as long you don't front-load your other 20 percent.

Murder, murder . . .

I'm trying to remember that I didn't come here with the intention of losing weight. I just wanted to reprogram my system so that I was used to working out every day. So that when I went home and didn't have work I wouldn't sit around in my apartment all day in pajamas eating ice cream and sobbing. That's all. But have I accomplished that? Is it even possible?

The title of the handout in Perfectionism reads "Dare to Be Average." The DFC connects perfectionism to moderation, because they feel so many of us are "all or nothing" thinkers who just need to set our expectations lower.

But what if I don't want to be average? I'm not a shrink-to-fit person. I don't have a shrink-to-fit body, so why would I want a shrink-to-fit life?

Still, when I go home, I'm gonna plan out my meals, sticking to 1,500 or 1,600 calories a day. I'm going to buy a colander and shop with a list. I'm gonna monitor with the best of 'em; I'll be beautifully, perfectly average.

Thursday, February 7, 2002
Took the grocery-store tour this morning. Like putting a diabetic kid in a candy store. Torturous. Saw about a thousand things that made me think, "Note to self: Eat that later."

Tonight me and two of my pals got dressed up in pretty clothes, did our hair, and snuck out before any of the creeps could give us the twice-over. It was a pleasure to read off a menu and to hear specials, to drink from a real glass. We ogled cute busboys and gossiped about the other weight-loss contenders and, yes, even ordered dessert, which we ate as mindfully as could be.

This sweet lady, Lorraine, said that one time she was here

with an Arab sheik who went out to dinner all the time and got people drunk and had sex with all the women at Duke Towers.

Murder, murder.

Friday, February 8, 2002

Only two other people in Welling's Obesity Medications seminar this morning. I think that the chemical stuff is the future of obesity treatment, but apparently I'm in the minority. Of course, Popular Fad Diets was packed yesterday.

This afternoon was Eating for Exercise, then Preventing Stress, and then my final Medical Check-in.

Breath held. Too scared to hope. But how could this not work in my favor? I've done everything right.

I step up to the scale.

222.2. Up another two pounds.

I break down in tears, terrifying unprepared, unequipped Neil Klein. He says, "Well, maybe it was the medications. Maybe you exercised too much. Maybe we gave you too little food." Good work, Sherlock. Did you want to think about this before Day 26? Maybe the red flag should have gone up in Week 2? I am trusting you, I am putting myself in your expert care. This is so WRONG. "We should have put you on more calories, maybe. Maybe it was the prednisone. Maybe it was the Meridia. Maybe we should have done a caliper test." Enough maybes. You're the experts!

As I lose it, they hustle me into a quick session with Janice, the head of the behavioral psych department. (Bless her soul, she does the session off the books, as she well should have.) She tells me to look at the big picture, to acknowledge that at least I'm being healthy. She tells me to look at this as an experiment, an experiment that continues.

Lorraine sees me in tears and tries to comfort me, but it's no use. I have a total breakdown in a Kinko's when I stop there on my way over to Nancy's house. The world's nicest Kinko's man not only lets me e-mail for free but writes me a note telling me to hang in there.

I can't believe that I'm caught up in this numbers game again. I can't do anything right. I lost my job, but I can't lose weight. How unfair is that?

Saturday, February 9, 2002

The last Saturday. I go to my final lifestyle workshop, Anger: What to Do with It. In that seminar I see the flash—a cognizance that comes alive in all the DFCers as they give words to their anger. Especially the older guys. We fat people aren't sad sacks, or losers, or depressos, or weaklings. We're pissed. It's just under the surface, under the fat . . . anger at parents, and wives, and kids, and bosses. Even if they weren't aware of the connection, I saw it there.

Of course, in true DFC style, they advise us not to express our anger. Leader suggests that venting anger just leads to venting more anger. Don't vent it, but don't eat it, either. Make some lists, break it down, take a bath (geez, fat people must be soooo clean). Yeah, that's just not going to work for me.

As far as I am concerned, Duke just doesn't get it. The whole thing is one step off. It's a hunger scale that goes from 1 to 7 instead of 1 to 10. It's a complete lack of offerings that have to do with body image or self-esteem, except for the behavioral-health seminars. (Feeling hungry? Try knitting instead! There ya go.) It's a sales pitch that makes you buy before you've even seen the product. Get a discount on your return—before you've

even started the program! Get a break on maintenance—before
you even lose a pound!

I can't believe the DFC is so . . . elementary. And so relentlessly positive, with the worksheets and the cartoon characters
and movie night. And so black-and-white! There's no room for
the gray area of weight loss. It's all math and time-outs. We all
know full well that it's not. But they don't want to touch that
ball of wax. They're nickel-and-diming you when you're paying thousands to be here.

Oh, right. The money. The cost for four weeks of the DFC
program?

Program fee	6,594.00
Chinese-cooking class	15.00
Therapy	110.00
Polarity massage	70.00
30-minute massage	40.00
$\frac{1}{2}$ personal trainer	35.00
Car rental	598.00
Airfare (one roundtrip)	168.00
Room and board at Duke Towers	1,800.00
TOTAL (not including expenses)	**$9,430.00**

With a total loss of 2 pounds, that works out to $4,715.00 a
pound.

Maybe my expectations are too high. Maybe they can't
deliver what I need. But at the very least, I should have lost
more weight here.

And the bottom line is, a Hershey's Kiss will always taste
better than a raisin. Hands down. Who are they trying to kid?

Epilogue

I called Dr. Welling to discuss my time at the DFC and my feelings about the program. Looking over my papers, he said, "According to our expectations, you did great." I was dumbfounded. Great? Great? He explained that they can't expect anyone to lose more than 1 percent of their body weight in a month, and at 224.2 with a two-pound loss, that counts as pretty much a 1 percent loss!!! Does this make me part of the 5 percent that succeeds over time? I told him (in slightly more professional words) that I thought the program was really dusty. He told me to stay in touch and that he was open to speaking more if I had more questions.

Over a year later, I'm still keeping a food journal, exercising, and my weight is still the same. I eat whatever I want to eat. I am a Duke dieting success story. Is that a load of crap or what?

Of course, Duke, so sold in its low-fat lifestyle, is now starting to eat its words and hedge its bets by offering a "low carbohydrate diet option." Hmm, all that fruit and veggies and rice for nothing, huh?

When I look back at the money, and the stress, and the time, and the effort, I realize that I did learn one major thing at the DFC, where I went to find the diet that would end all diets. I did finally make that one major lifestyle change: No more diets. Ever. Again.

CHAPTER 7

The Science of Fat

Our belief that fatness and fitness are in fundamental tension is based on myth, not science . . . There is no reason why there shouldn't be millions of healthy, happy fat people in the United States, as there no doubt would be in a culture that maintained a rational attitude toward the fact that people will always come in all shapes and sizes, whether they live healthy lives or not.

　　—Paul Campos, "The Weighting Game: What the Diet Industry Won't Tell You," *The New Republic*

I can decide what course is best for my body, but it's hard to defend my choices against a medical industry and a media drive that have us convinced that being fat will kill us. Being fat might be healthy for my mind, but is it good for my body?

The Blame Game

Every day you open up the paper and read another article about why Americans are so fat. There are a million reasons why, most of them having to do with technological advances that have made us much more sedentary people. There's blame on the fast-food industry for introducing us to huge portions of high-calorie, delicious faux foods for a low, low price. We blame schools for serving the aforementioned fast food in cafeterias and for cutting physical education programs. We blame the weight-loss industry and a government-sanctioned low-fat movement that created lots of low-fat, high-calorie snacks that we big dumb Americans eat right up. We blame the media for presenting unattainable body images that we nonetheless strive to imitate. We place puritanical blame on our cultural excess: We crave too much, we want things that are too big, we're gluttons, we're sinners! Remember, we live in a Christian country. We're not fat-'n'-happy Buddha people, celebrating our Buddha bellies; we're represented by a slender and suffering Jesus.

One failed Atkinator said the following about sinning and dieting: "I consoled myself with the thought that gluttony is a crime only against oneself, not against one's neighbor, much less humanity, while Atkinsim, with its promise of a long, sleek, healthy life, is idolatry, so to speak, of the self . . . But like all innate puritans, Atkins never grasped the incurable waywardness of human beings: the desire to have both this and that, rather than choose one and renounce the other, especially when the popular culture celebrates polymorhpous excess."

My favorite kind of ironic blame goes to those who blame fat on the feminist movement. See, with women in the workforce, we're not around to make good, healthy foods for our families or supervise what our kids are stuffing in their mouths. Let's not look for compromises, like Dad learning how to make a meal or kids learning how to cook. C'mon, America, get those women back in the kitchen where they belong! In a recent study, some economists suggested that work in general makes us fat: "As women devoted more time to paid work, the theory goes, they had less time for cooking, a burden that the men in their lives (who typically spend more time at their jobs) presumably had little time or interest in assuming. Fast-food restaurants—offering cheap, convenient meals dense with fat and calories—rushed in to fill the vacuum." In actuality, moms are doing a better job of mothering than ever before, according to the *New York Times*. "Mothers today spend as much if not more time with their children than they did in 1965, even though the percentage of mothers who work rose from 35 percent to 71 percent (How do they do it? Answer: less sleep, less housework, more time together when they're home)."

We blame our mothers or fathers or a life event that caused us some emotional damage. We blame stress and jobs and money and TV and the guy who was mean to us in eleventh grade and the girl who was rude to us at summer camp and the boss who just won't give us any respect. We blame the delicious taste of chocolate. Some of us stick with addiction models, or blame sugar, or carbs, or potatoes, blood types, or God knows what else.

And, of course, we blame our awful, rotten, no-good, very bad selves most of all.

There are a million reasons to be fat. To tell you the truth, I'm surprised that anyone is thin. But blame is just blame. It's finger pointing. It doesn't accomplish much; blame just sells magazines and starts lawsuits.

Here's the problem, all you America-is-too-fat boo-hooers. The planet is not going to start turning backwards. We aren't going back to working in fields instead of driving to the office. We aren't going to ride letters over to the next town on horseback instead of sending e-mail. (As the *Times* pointed out, "People used to be paid to exercise, since most work involved heavy physical labor. Now we have to pay to exercise, by taking time away from sitting in front of computers and TVs.") You can't stop the advances of technology and science. You can't stop cloning, you can't stop stem cell research, and you can't stop Americans from eating crap and getting fat.

What we can do is use science and technology to our advantage, to find new avenues for better health. I'm not talking about a "magic bullet." I get pissed every time someone mentions a "magic bullet" solution for weight loss. No one talks about a magic bullet for cancer, or a magic bullet for homelessness. I'm not looking for magic, which implies that you don't have to work for something. I'm not indulging in a fantasy, where a magical fairy will float down and grant me a weight-loss wish. I'm not expecting a miracle from God. I'm not waiting for a "bullet," which is the creepiest metaphor of all in terms of weight loss. A bullet is a violent weapon that injures, hurts, kills, and destroys. A bullet punctures things—like big, doughy fat people, I guess. It's an insult. So I don't use that phrase, and I wish other people wouldn't, either.

Our current-day fattitude is a sign o' the times, baby. Industrialization, fast and processed food, computers, easier travel. We know a lot more about how our bodies work, and we diagnose problems faster (often without the help of a doctor). Victorian bodies vs. contemporary bodies, blah blah blah. Our bodies were designed to survive the elements, and now we're busy playing Sims on our planes, trains, and automobiles. We were bound to puff up sooner or later.

Big News

Someday soon we'll be doing leptin shots and popping gherlin supplements and fat won't really be an issue. We'll probably have pills instead of food, like something out of *Willy Wonka and the Chocolate Factory*. We'll find something else to freak out and discriminate about, like longevity or Botox intolerance or peanut allergies. Until that day, I am waiting for more research. Every time I think fat is a hopeless cause, or I'm a hopeless person, I learn something new about obesity. Here are some of the latest developments in obesity studies:

- "Researchers have identified a gene that directly causes obesity."
- "Scientists have identified a hormone that caused the sensation every dieter craves: the feeling of fullness."
- "A recent study reported in the *New England Journal of Medicine* 'makes the strongest case yet that a genetic mutation can cause an eating disorder.' The study suggested that a gene may cause binge eating."
- "Researchers who have been testing the biological effects of fast food are discovering that they can trigger hormonal changes in the body that could make it difficult to control eating."
- "A new study suggests that eating disorders may stem from some type of immune system abnormality that causes other difficult-to-treat diseases like rheumatoid arthritis, multiple sclerosis, and lupus."

Genes? Hormones? Immune disorders? The very idea of mitigating factors seems to frustrate the Indignant Thin. "People lose weight if they stop eating bread," they claim. What about this whole no-carbohydrate business? I know people do it and lose a lot of weight. I know fewer people who do it and actually keep the weight off. The "prep" diet I did at Quick Weight Loss Center was three days of red meat and green roughage, and I dropped a ton of weight (at least the first time). Medical professionals still aren't sure about the biochemistry behind low-carb and low-sugar diets. They figure that these diets contain fewer calories overall and cause a state of ketosis, where the body burns stored fat for fuel rather than carbohydrates. For me, it's not worth it; a bagel-free life is not worth living. A brunch is not a brunch without French toast. How much are fat people supposed to give up to fit in?

Is Fat Fatal?

"Americans are being threatened with something far more dangerous than weapons of mass destruction," a journalist wrote recently. "Call it the weapon of mass. 'Obesity represents a much greater risk to Americans than any chemical or biological weapon that Saddam Hussein might be hiding underneath one of his sprawling compounds,' U.S. Surgeon General Dr. Richard Carmona said . . . '[Obesity is] almost entirely preventable through proper diet and exercise,' said Carmona, who added that he was at the gym working out at 5 a.m. Wednesday."

You're telling me that my fat ass presents a bigger threat to mankind than SADDAM HUSSEIN? You must be joking. FYI, folks, our Surgeon General is a laugh a minute: " 'And eating healthy doesn't mean substituting Krispy Kreme donuts instead of Dunkin' Donuts,' he jokingly told the audience comprised mostly of police and fire officials." Hardee-har. Get it? Police-men eat donuts! That's a new one. Oh, somebody stop this guy.

Push the discrimination, bad jokes, and emotional drama to the side, and a question remains: Can you be fit if you're fat? Can you be healthy if you're heavyset? Fat is still fat! Fat will kill you! Right?

Mmm . . . probably not.

Plenty of research suggests that obesity—at least as it's clinically defined—is not nearly the death sentence that most media outlets and weight-loss companies would have you believe. Half of the obesity battle is won when you start reading between the lines. You have to look for alternative opinions, because they don't get a lot of publicity. No one makes money from telling you you're fine just the way you are. Writer Paul Campos re-evaluated the weight-loss-industry standards in a shocking essay in the *New Republic* called "The Weighting Game: What the Diet Industry Won't Tell You." This essay is the Pentagon Papers of fat. Campos reveals the following mind-blowing facts:

- "A moderately active fat person is likely to be far healthier than someone who is svelte but sedentary. What's worse, Americans' (largely unsuccessful) efforts to make themselves thin through dieting and supplements are themselves a major cause of the ill health associated with being overweight—meaning that America's war on fat is actually helping cause the very disease it's supposed to cure."

- "There is in fact no medical basis for the government's BMI recommendations or the public health policies based on them . . . The BMI range correlating with the lowest mortality rate is extremely broad, from about 18 to 32, meaning that a woman of average height can weigh anywhere within an 80-pound range without seeing any statistically meaningful change in her risk of premature death."

- "In a decided majority of studies, groups of people labeled 'overweight' by current standards are found to have equal or lower mortality rates than groups of supposedly ideal-weight individuals."

- "Large-scale mortality studies indicate that women who are 50 or even 75 pounds 'overweight' will on average still have longer life expectancies than those who are 10 to 15 pounds 'underweight,' a.k.a. fashionably thin."

- "Numerous studies have shown that weight loss of [20 to 30 pounds] (and indeed as little as ten pounds) leads to an increased risk of premature death, sometimes by an order of several hundred percent."

Campos summarizes: "In the end, nothing could be easier than to win the war on fat: All we need to do is stop fighting it." Not a popular or widely publicized opinion, I assure you, because information learned is minds relieved and money lost.

Campos is not the only one reassessing traditional weight-loss beliefs. In his book *Big Fat Lies,* Dr. Glenn Gaesser states, "The idea that a given body weight, or percentage of body fat, is a meaningful indicator of health, fitness, or prospects for longevity is one of our most firmly-held beliefs, and one of our most dubious propositions . . . [When] you scrutinize all the relevant data it becomes apparent that the health risks of obesity, as well as the purported benefits of weight loss, have been greatly exaggerated."

Similar conclusions are being drawn in the Ivy League. "Some people are quite heavy, yet are fit," proclaimed Dr. Kelly Brownell, a professor of psychology at Yale University and director of the Yale Center for Eating and Weight Disorders. "Maybe to the outside world, you don't look healthy, but you still can be. It's relatively new thinking, that you can be fit and fat at the same time." Keep in mind the most important part of the equation is the "fit" part—regular activity as part of one's life.

The exercise industry is being forced to examine this revised point of view. Aerobics instructor Jennifer Portnick filed a case against Jazzercise Inc. in San Francisco, saying she was fired because of her size. At 5'8" and 230 pounds, she didn't fit the profile of the standard Jazzercise instructor. While her skill as an aerobics instructor was never questioned, the size of her body was. She went to court, and she won. In a statement released by Jazzercise, the company said, "Recent studies document that it may be possible for people of varying weights to be fit. Jazzercise has determined that the value of 'fit appearance' as a standard is debatable."

Here are more new and interesting statistics about weight from reputable sources that you haven't seen on the nightly news:

- "About two dozen studies support the notion that the standard treatment for excessive weight—dieting—is insufficient and perhaps even misguided, at least for any individual who isn't working out."
- "The Federal Trade Commission also released a study last week proving that quick-weight-loss products don't work—despite the fact that Americans spend $40 billion on dieting every year."

- "A study of 692 teenage girls in Northern California found that those who exercised and dieted with the express purpose of losing weight were more likely to end up obese. 'This was a bizarre finding,' said one of the investigators. 'Dieters were two to three times more likely to show onset of obesity than nondieters.' Similar results were found among adults who diet."

Sure, you can find just as many studies that contradict these. The goal is to be able to read between the lines and advocate for yourself. For example, "A recent study of more than 5,000 men and women found that being overweight does indeed affect your health, regardless of how much time you clock at the gym." That's from MSNBC.com. On the same Web page, running next to the article, you'll find ads for a pedometer from drugstore.com, GNC, E-Diets, E-Fitness, Danskin Plus-Size Exercise Bras, and MSNBC's very own BMI calculator. Is the information correct? It certainly could be. But is the motivation for putting it on the page to sell you something? Definitely.

You also have to be discerning when it comes to medical studies. Say you read an article that says more people die of cancer in New York than in Boston. Does that mean that there's something wrong in New York? Is it the water? The air? The medical facilities? No. There are simply more people in New York than in Boston. Larger population. Read between the lines.

For example, women taking birth-control pills have been told that they increase their risk for cervical cancer by 50 percent. What's in that pill? I gotta get off of it! Hold on a second, cowgirl. Read between the lines. "Experts believe this is because Pill users may be more sexually active and thus more likely to be infected with human papillomavirus (HPV), the STD that causes cervical cancer." See, it's not the Pill itself; it's just your potential behavior that puts you at risk.

I've mentioned that the basis for the current two-thirds-of-Americans-are-fat! statistic comes from a sample of only 1,446 people. In a much wider study of over thirty-five thousand people, Dr. Steven Blair, director of research at the Cooper Institute in Dallas, studied how body size and fitness connected in terms of lifespan. He discovered that "overweight" people who exercise regularly often have a longer lifespan than "normal weight" people who do not. Blair's best advice? "I'm not saying eat, drink, be merry, and get as fat as you want. But at some point we have to say, 'Get a life,' instead of obsessing over every ounce."

In his book *Eating Well for Optimum Health,* alternative health expert Dr. Andrew Weil concurs: "The fact is that Western medicine, being part of Western culture, has taken on its prejudice against body fat. That attitude, I believe, has warped medical research and practice, compromising objectivity in assessing the actual health hazards of obesity. For example, most doctors assume that being fat decreases longevity, and that losing weight will increase it, but recent studies by exercise physiologists cast doubt on that assumption. If fat people remain active and head off further weight gains, there is no association between being fat and dying early."

Sick of Fat

Fat has long been linked to a litany of illnesses, including heart disease, hypertension, arthritis, and diabetes. But does fat lead to an increased risk of cancer? Recent studies conclude it does, saying more fat in a woman's body can lead her to produce more estrogen. High estrogen is considered a risk factor for breast cancer. "Losing weight could prevent one of every six cancer deaths in the United States, more than 90,000 each year, according to a sweeping study that experts say links fat and cancer more convincingly than ever before," The Associated Press reported recently. "Researchers for the American Cancer Society spent 16 years evaluating 900,000 people who were cancer-free when the study began in 1982. The researchers concluded that excess weight might account for 14 percent of cancer deaths in men and 20 percent of those in women."

In 2003, the American Cancer Society launched a campaign to link excess fat with cancer. "The society said that being overweight or obese is associated with a higher risk of several forms of cancer, including colon and breast cancer. It also says there is strong evidence that being physically active can reduce cancer risks, especially for colon and breast cancer. So the society is starting by trying to link fat and cancer in the public mind. And it is focusing most strongly on women, because they not only feed the family, they are more likely than men to make changes in their lives."

What the American Cancer Society is not so clear about is this: "The society's effort is being funded by the Weight Watchers diet program, which will promote the cancer group's program at its centers. Other business sponsors may be added for future Weigh Ins." There may be a connection between fat and cancer. But there's definitely a connection between the American Cancer Soceity and Weight Watchers. The American Cancer Society needs money. Weight Watchers has money. I suspect that Weight Watchers' funding is not entirely altruistic.

Still, you have to give credence to the fat-related cancer theory when health writer Jane Brody supports it. She writes:

> As the authors point out, "potential biologic mechanisms include increased levels of endogenous hormones—sex steroids, insulin and insulin-like Growth Factor I—associated with overweight and obesity." These substances, produced in excess in overweight people, can stimulate the growth of nascent cancer cells in various organs. For example, the sex steroid estrogen is firmly established as a growth stimulant for most cancers of the breast, as well as cancer of the uterine lining, or endometrium. Excess fat around the abdomen increases the risk of heartburn, or chronic reflux disease, which causes chronic acid irritation of the esophagus that can lead to the development of esophageal cancer. Obesity also increases the risk of developing gallstones, which, in turn, increase the risk of gallbladder cancer. Excessive production of insulin by the pancreas in people with a high B.M.I. may explain their increased risk of pancreatic cancer. And so on.

But is it the fat itself that's the problem, or sedentary activity that raises the risk? Brody writes, "Physical activity 'may decrease exposure of breast tissue to estrogen' and 'may also affect cancers of the colon, breast and other sites by improving energy metabolism,' or the burning of calories. It also may reduce 'circulating concentrations of insulin and related growth factors,' the guidelines state." Sounds again like the emphasis belongs on fit rather than fat.

Luckily, Paul Campos again countered the above study:

Now consider the study's actual data. Among supposedly "ideal weight" individuals (Body Mass Index 18.5 to 24.9) the study observed a mortality rate from cancer of 4.5 deaths per 1,000 subjects over its 16-year course. Among "overweight" individuals (BMI 25 to 29.9—a category that currently includes about twice as many adult Americans as the "ideal weight" cohort) the mortality rate was 4.4 deaths per 1,000 subjects. In other words, "overweight" people actually had a lower overall cancer mortality rate than "ideal weight" individuals! . . . In short, what this study actually found was a negative correlation between increasing weight and cancer mortality for the majority of the 135 million Americans who are currently categorized as overweight or obese, and only a small increase in risk for all but the very fattest people.

Looking closely at this information, I draw the conclusion that it's not the FAT that causes disease (except perhaps in the case of estrogen-related breast cancer), but a SEDENTARY LIFE-STYLE that causes fat, that causes disease. That's why we need to make weight less of an aesthetic issue and more of a medical issue for women. What could we learn about hormones, sexual dysfunction, and other female medical issues if we weren't being distracted by weight loss? Or issues that are directly related to estrogen production caused by excess fat, like poly-cystic ovary syndrome and infertility? Could we spend more of our time exploring preventive measures for heart disease and lung cancer, far greater killers of women than breast cancer or overweight? Surely there's a different responsibility we could shoulder once we give up diet shakes and get serious about health.

Drastic Measures

Most everything we hear goes against that grain. That's why so many of us are willing to risk life and limb for vanity and/or health. For example, we take dangerous drugs and untested "supplements," like chromium picolinate, bitter orange, pyruvate, mahuang, and ephedra. Ephedra is the dietary supplement that killed Baltimore Oriole Steve Bechler on February 17, 2003. New York Yankees pitcher David Wells said he still took ephedra for weight loss even though he flatlined on it in 1996. Federal officials have proposed warning labels of heart attack, stroke, and death for products containing ephedra, and the FDA finally announced an outright ban on it in January 2004: "No other dietary supplement on the market has stirred as many warnings and frightening medical histories as ephedra. It has been linked to deaths, to strokes, to heart arrhythmias and even to psychotic episodes." Be careful if you're taking a supplement with ephedrine alkaloids (the active ingredient in ephedra) or mahuang (the Chinese name for ephedra), you're taking ephedra.

Surgery is another drastic antiobesity option exploding in popularity. "This year, 60,000 Americans who are morbidly obese, meaning 100 pounds or more overweight, will have major surgery to seal off most of their stomachs and shorten intestines to lose weight," the *New York Times* reported in 2002. You want to scream, "Stop eating! Forget the stomach surgery, just wire your freaking jaw shut!" But this is not a matter of willpower. Especially when you consider the side effects of gastric bypass surgery: waves of nausea, pain, and bloating—the so-called "dumping" syndrome—if you eat more than a few ounces of food at a time, especially foods high in sugar or fat; an inability for the body to absorb vitamins and minerals; a total change in your social psychology; and the risks (5 to 20 percent of patients—the published reports conflict on the exact number—regain weight despite the surgery). "As many as one in five will endure side effects ranging from unpleasant (vomiting, dehydration) to serious (ulcers, hernias) to potentially fatal (intestinal leakage, blood clots in the lungs)," reported the *New Yorker*. "The death rate is about one in 300 but may be as high as seven percent for those with complications from their weight." If the risks of living with obesity outweigh those, then surgery might be an option. But if you're doing it for cosmetic reasons, you'd better think twice.

Gastric bypass surgery is a legitimate option for people who are morbidly obese. (Sadly, one overachieving doctor offered it to me even though I didn't medically qualify for it. Thank goodness I have a strong sense of self.) When you're talking about something this extreme—both the surgery and the situation that got you there in the first place—it's more than a lack of common sense or a lack of willpower to blame. This is about how your body and brain are wired, not about your attitude. The *New Yorker* report, profiling a man who had undergone gastric bypass surgery, found: "A 1993 National Institutes of Health expert panel reviewed decades of diet studies and found that between ninety and ninety-five per cent of people regained one-third to two-thirds of any weight lost within a year—and all of it within five years. Doctors have wired patients' jaws closed, inflated plastic balloons inside their stomachs, performed massive excisions of body fat, prescribed amphetamines and large amounts of thyroid hormone, even performed neurosurgery to destroy the hunger centers in the brain's hypothalamus—and still people do not keep the weight off

. . . We are a species that has evolved to survive starvation, not to resist abundance." Guess there's something to that Caveman Famine Theory after all.

As Dr. Stephen R. Bloom, an obesity researcher at Hammersmith Hospital at the Imperial College School of Medicine in London, explained to the *New York Times*, "People can't stop eating any more than they're going able to stop having sex or grabbing money or anything else . . . When you crash in a plane in the Andes and there's no food, you eat your neighbor. Here we have the action of a very important, basic human drive." Do you understand? Humans are so nuts about hunger that when push comes to shove WE WILL EAT EACH OTHER. Now, I've had a mad binge or two, but at least I've never chewed off the leg of my next-door neighbor.

Dr. Bloom expects that appetite will eventually be controlled the same way high cholesterol or high blood pressure is—with a pill. That doesn't mean you take the pill and the problems go away; obviously we can complement drug treatment and/or lower cholesterol and high blood pressure through healthy diet and exercise. But it certainly takes a load off my mind, if not my body, to know that biochemistry can safely shoulder some of the weight.

I've personally had a lot of success with weight loss drugs like fen-phen and Meridia. But drugs aren't a one-hit wonder. Obesity, like diabetes, is a disease that can be treated with medication but that can be helped by lifestyle. Obesity, like depression, is a disease that is chemical in nature but can be triggered by emotional events. Obesity, like alcoholism, is a disease that seems to be transferred genetically but that some people can carry and not suffer from while others are destroyed by it. It's not that there's one perfect weight-loss solution; it's a matter of finding the combination of tools that helps each individual reach an individual goal.

Fit and Fat

As lawsuits begin and labels shift, there is one big conclusion that researchers can make about the causes and effects of obesity: a big old "I dunno." They inch their way down the list—fast foods, giant portions, sedentary lifestyles, round-the-clock noshing—and still are unable to understand exactly why some of us are fat and some aren't, and whether losing weight definitively benefits our health.

And just as cause is unclear, effect is hardly a lock as described by health writer Gina Kolata in the *New York Times*.

"Here is what we know," said Dr. Gary Foster, an obesity researcher at the University of Pennsylvania. "If you have diabetes and you lose weight, it is likely to get better and you will go on less medication." That's important, he stressed, because in addition to causing immense suffering, diabetes is expensive to treat and has extensive complications—amputations, kidney failure, blindness. But he added, it is not yet known whether losing weight will help with other medical conditions: "Will it prevent or decrease the risk of heart attack or stroke or will you be less likely to be hospitalized? We don't know that yet."

It is true that blood pressure may go down slightly or that cholesterol levels may improve. But does that translate into fewer heart attacks and strokes, the so-called hard outcomes? After all, hormone therapy for menopause improved cholesterol levels, but studies showed that women who took it ended up with more heart attacks and strokes. With weight loss, Dr. Foster said, "we don't know what happens to hard outcomes."

Let's take the focus off "fat" and put it on health. Let's take the focus off "skinny" and put it on good common sense. Let's take the focus off body image and put it on education, women's rights, human rights, the economy, baseball cards, anything. And while we're at it, let's stop showing that same shot of some random flabby midsection jiggling around city streets every time the nightly news does a story on obesity. That same midsection is the "before" in every newspaper and magazine photo. I live in horror at the thought that I'm going to see my big wide ass swinging by as some cheesy newscaster intones, "America's obesity epidemic is out of control!" If you want to show anonymous fat people a fat person on TV, have some guts, show their faces, and ask them to sign releases and give their permission. Or show us exercising, or working, or hanging with friends—not just slowly lumbering through a park, eating a hot dog, without a friend in the world.

If weight were really just the math problem most experts would have you believe, then we would be able to make a nice little loss formula for ourselves based on calories (caloric intake minus caloric output equals weight loss). However, just about anyone who has ever dieted or worked out has discovered that the formula isn't quite so clean-cut.

CHAPTER 8

Listen to Your Gut

How dare anybody try to tell me what I should look like,
or what I should be, when there's so much more to me
than just my weight!
— from the film *Real Women Have Curves*

I always believed that one day I would find the one perfect
weight-loss plan that worked for me, or the guru who would
inspire me—I just hadn't found that plan or person yet. Even
plans that had multiple elements to them—food and exercise
and monitoring, for example—would always suggest that the
real shift would be a "lifestyle change." Oh, all I have to do to
be thin and happy is CHANGE MY LIFE. And then stay
changed, forever.

I didn't get fat just one way. I don't stay at my current weight
just one way. I won't stay healthy just one way. Taking care of
my body and mind is a complex system, so I don't look for
simple answers.

One single plan doesn't work, and it certainly doesn't work
every day of my life. There are times when I'm working at a job
that takes me away from my exercise routine. Okay, so when
the job's over, I go back to the gym. There are nights when I

can't eat the healthy dinner I want, so my food choices get compromised. So what? I improvise. Life throws curves. I know that I can't plan everything, can't control everything. That's okay too.

Eat Me

I'm not going to tell you what to eat. If you're reading this book, my hunch is you know plenty about nutrition and diets already. I can tell you what I do, and if you want to borrow elements of it, knock yourself out.

I try to eat a balanced diet. That means lean protein (chicken, turkey, fish, tofu, etc.), carbs (whole wheat flour instead of white flour, brown rice instead of white rice), fruit (a real piece of fruit for the fiber, instead of a sugary juice), veggies (never enough), dairy (women NEED dairy), a little sweet, a little fat. I try to eat lots of little meals instead of three big meals; I tend to feel fuller and digest food better that way. I eat breakfast every day. I take vitamins. I drink lots of water. I enjoy an alcoholic bevvie now and then. I try to avoid soda. I try to avoid sodium. I rarely eat fast food. I read food labels. I try not to eat a lot of processed or prepackaged foods, especially foods with trans fats or hydrogenated oil in them. I don't like a lot of sauces or dressings or butter, so they're easy for me to avoid. I try not to eat late at night. I try not to starve myself till I'm famished; I try to stop when I'm full.

I try not to deprive myself; I've found that it's better for me to eat one piece of bread out of the bread basket at the restaurant than a whole loaf later. I'm a lot less worried about eating what I want than eating what I don't want.

How many calories do I consume in a day? I guess around

two thousand. Do I ever eat more than that? Sure. Do I ever eat less than that? Sure. Do I eat popcorn at the movies? If I want to. Do I eat a hot dog on a whim on a hot summer day? Every once in a while. Do I order dessert in a fancy restaurant? Let's hope so; I never understand the people who order the twenty-dollar fruit plate. Do I eat dessert every night? No. Do I eat too much? From time to time. Do I eat too little? From time to time. Do I push back from the table and say loudly, "Oh, I ate so much, I'm really going to pay for this at the gym tomorrow!" Never. No one wants to hear it, least of all me.

Do I feel crazy about food? Much less than I ever have before.

Work It Out

Fat girls don't want to go to the gym. Very few of us say things such as, "Well, I just *like* working out, it's sort of part of my routine, I feel bad when I don't exercise." That's a Skinny Chick thing to say. I hate exercising. I hate sweating. It takes me nine thousand years to cool down. I hate getting dressed for it, I hate going to it, I hate doing it, I hate taking a shower afterward. It never feels natural. It never feels fun. It never feels like part of my routine. It's always hard. It can be expensive (you can walk for free, yeah yeah, but not in the freezing cold or the rain or the disgusting heat, and you still need shoes and at a least a bra, so shut yer trap). I don't get a thrill from the progress I make. I don't comprehend what people are talking about when they discuss endorphin rushes. My body is covered with too much fat for me to notice much muscle definition. Exercise doesn't relieve stress, it doesn't help me sleep better. It's literally a pain in my ass.

But I do it. Because I have to do it. Because it's good for my heart and my health and my cholesterol and my blood pressure. Because I take responsibility for my body. Because it enables me to eat without guilt. Because I want to prove something to my parents. Because I want to show the weight-loss industry that I can be fit and fat. Maybe if I do it, some other fat girl will see me and decide that she can do it, too. I exercise because I want to live a long and healthy life. As the *Wall Street Journal* recently stated: "The unfit lean—as measured by performance on a treadmill—were twice as likely to die earlier as the fit, including the obese fit." I believe that exercise is a major component in long-term weight loss or maintenance of current weight.

Everyone I've known who lost or maintained weight for the long term has done it on their own. Not with Zone Delivery, not with Pilates—at least not completely. The long-term weight-loss winner generally makes her own pupu platter of what works. It's usually some cardio plus some stretch and a hike once a week, along with a low-carb diet and a daily treat. Or else it's dance aerobics twice a week and yoga twice a week and a walk with the kids plus a vegetarian diet and a lot of Popsicles. Whatever it is, it's about assessing all the information and making the plan that works for you.

That's what I'm doing now: some of this and some of that. I've been going to the gym forever and I've been fat forever, so I modify my routine when I learn something new. When I switched gyms and got a complimentary session with a new personal trainer, I started up a small-weight regimen and I liked that. Even though I couldn't see any real definition, I could poke around under my flab and tell that something was firming up under there. I make myself go even if I don't have a full hour (ten minutes is better than no minutes). "All or nothing" will destroy. I invest in good shoes and good music. I make myself put on my gym clothes first thing in the morning as a sort of insurance policy. I figure if I'm already strapped into the outfit, I might as well go. I try to focus on strength and keeping my heart rate in a certain range instead of on calories burned.

Everything used to be cardio, cardio, cardio. Lately, it's all about weights, since the news came out that muscle burns more calories than fat (a pound of muscle burns roughly thirty-five calories a day; a pound of fat burns about six). Hate to burst the bubble, but . . . Dr. Claude Bouchard, the director of the Pennington Biomedical Research Center at Louisiana State University, now says that weightlifting has virtually no effect on resting metabolism. As Bouchard explained in the *New York Times*:

> The reason is that any added muscle is minuscule compared with the total amount of skeletal muscle in the body. And muscle actually has a very low metabolic rate when it is at rest, which is most of the time . . . A corollary to the hypothesis that you burn more calories simply by adding muscle is the belief that muscle can noticeably change your body weight. The idea is that when you do resistance training you may actually be thinner yet weigh the same or a little more, because muscle is heavier than fat. That holds a grain of truth, because muscle is more dense than fat. But, Bouchard said, the problem is that few people put on enough muscle in proportion to their total body mass to make a noticeable difference in their weight. The idea that you will weigh the same or more but you really are thinner may be true if you work hard at

weight lifting for many months, but otherwise it is another myth.

Oh, crap, there goes that idea. Should I just go back to hula-
hooping? High-impact aerobics? Again, you have to be your
own advocate. Be moderate, and consistent, and hope that you
can find a teacher or trainer to trust for a while.

The gym is repetitive and a schlep and I get sore sometimes.
So I tried the hot new old thing: yoga. One zillion Indian people
can't be wrong. When you take Gucci mats and Christy
Turlington out of the equation, there is something to it.
Body-mind connection and all. Aside from the spiritual thing
(which I admit still gives me the heebie-jeebies), it feels really
good to stretch out my muscles and use my body strength and
concentrate when I exercise, instead of trying to distract myself
with hard-core Mary J. Blige beats just to get through it. I really
feel yoga in my muscles the next day. Plus, you have to love any
kind of exercise that ends with a ten-minute nap.

The other great thing about yoga is that it's very democratic.
Anyone can do it anywhere. They have Kid yoga and Elderly
yoga and Pregnant Lady yoga and Hot yoga and Madonna
yoga. Unfortunately, they don't seem to have Overweight
Jewish Girls with Big Boobs and Good Intentions yoga. See,
yoga was invented many moons ago by slender people who
spoke Sanskrit and survived monsoons. Which is great and
everything, but I don't think the yogis counted on a big tube of
boob suffocating you when you do a shoulder stand. Some of
the poses that are meant to relax you and give your body a
break are actually a lot harder for Fat Girls because we've got
gobs of flesh where the ancients had a breeze of sandalwood.
The teachers don't get that quite yet. As much as they help you

fine-tune positions and adjust to compensate for injuries, they still don't seem to understand why I can't hunker down on my haunches for any great length of time, or why it's no fun for me to rest the entire weight of my body on my head.

Most fat people are afraid to go to yoga or dance class or the swim club or the gym because they think the skinny people will be mean to them, or at least think mean thoughts about them. Well, okay, that's legit. But you know what? It's a gym, not a playground. You're a grown-up, not a kindergartner. You are a strong enough person to get over it and do what you have to do for yourself. Screw everyone else. Besides, when you're actually there to work out, you sort of give a cursory glance to everyone around you and then you do your thing. No one is giving you nearly the amount of attention you think you deserve. So invest in a good pair of supportive shoes, a supportive bra, and a T-shirt that's not full of holes and get your big fat ass to the gym or yoga studio or dance class or basketball court. As Natalie Angier reminds us in *Woman: An Intimate Geography,* "Over-weight people not only have more fat than the slender, they often have comparatively more muscle. When you gain weight because you're overeating, you put on three-quarters of that weight as fat but one quarter of that weight as muscle. Fat people are so cowed into self-loathing that they don't realize the potential they carry. If they choose to exercise their submerged muscle on a regular basis, they'll be able to beat the sprat out of any thin ones who call them pigs."

No one deserves to be at the gym more than you do. When I look at those skinny people lugging their big weights around and thrusting their bumpy biceps all over the machines, I think, "What a shame. You don't have something better to do with your life than spend two hours a day at the gym?" I've never understood women who spend hours building muscle mass just to look at it. Never for strength, just for vanity. It's definitely not a life I can live. It's not a life I could keep up with for long. So I do my cardio, a little bit of weight conditioning, hit the locker room, and I'm outta there.

What's Up, Doc—Besides My Weight?

I know eating Twinkies makes me gain weight. I know that exercise is good for my heart. I get enough uninvited flak about my body from well-meaning friends, family members, and coworkers—not to mention my own endless inner monologue. It's no wonder I'd rather not pay for one more round of scolding from a medical professional. But I won't avoid the doctor when I have health concerns. I have to take care of my body. Bottom line. No excuses. Weight is just one part of having respect for your fabulous, unique, holy body. And respect for your body includes regular medical checkups, no matter how much you weigh.

I can't think of one woman who looks forward to her annual visit with her gynecologist. Who wants to hunch down on a table with your legs pointing out like a protractor while some lady in a lab coat pokes inside your various orifices? But one time, in my mid-twenties, I was looking forward to my annual visit. When I'd seen my gyno the year before, she had asked me to address the idea of losing some weight. She was concerned that my weight was going to affect my overall health and raise risk factors that could adversely affect my reproductive system. Her words came at a time when I was mentally ready to make some changes in my body. I increased my exercise level and put a stronger focus on a balanced diet. When that didn't work, I did Optifast for three or four months (round two of three). Sure enough, I'd lost enough weight to want to show off to her.

When she came in the room, I was already down on the table with my legs splayed open. But she noticed the change! "You look great," she said, warming up the speculum (gulp). "Thanks," I said. "I worked really hard." She smiled and fished around in my nether regions while I counted holes in the ceiling. She pressed inside my uterus with one hand and squeezed my abdomen with the other. She shifted her hand and squeezed some more. "You know," she said, "if you did some crunches, you could really tone this up!"

Snap. Horror. I burned with shame. As if it wasn't humiliating enough to have someone prodding me like a brisket in the meat market, she had to goosh around in the softest part of my whole body and tell me that I was still too fat. All that hard work, all that sweating, all that starvation! All out the window. At my most vulnerable moment—literally, with my gut in her hand—I was still a fat chick.

It was three years before I went back to a gyno again. A different gyno.

I've heard a ton of stories like this. One friend went to the doctor for antibiotics to heal strep throat and got a lecture about dieting instead. Another wondered why she needed to be put on a scale when she had just come to the doctor to have stitches removed. A pregnant friend was told she'd better "lay off the fruit" before her doctor even bothered to open her chart and review her medical history.

Most doctors treat us with something between ambivalence and fear when it comes to the subject of weight. Although I did once meet a white coat who tried to "tough love" me. Keep in mind, I'd gone to see him about a sinus infection. But he made me get completely undressed so he could give me hell about my weight. Wanted to scare me thin, I guess. Diet or die, you know the drill. At first I was impressed with his bluntness; someone was going to give me a long-overdue confrontation. He fed my secret self-loathing; he confirmed what I'd always expected: that I was a bad, weak person. Then I realized we weren't having a dialogue; he was delivering a monologue. He was humiliating me. I felt too ashamed to do anything about it.

We know how complicated fat is. So is it any wonder that weight is a mysterious thing that doctors don't completely understand? This is frustrating and confusing to medically trained professionals who are trained never to say, "I don't know."

Doctors live in a black-and-white world. You're fat or you're thin. You smoke or you don't. You're sick or you're healthy. Most of them don't have the time or training (or patience) to sit with a patient and help her figure out the reasonable choices and options around weight loss. Of course, you're generally half-naked when the discussion comes up. You're wearing a tiny little paper dress that never seems to wrap all the way around. The nurse has got you locked in a blood-pressure cuff that's so tight it cuts off your circulation. Still, you'll take a little upper-arm pain over a harried nurse screaming "She needs the big cuff!" down the hallway. You've just had to weigh yourself, and now someone else knows the number and is making one of those little comments you can read into ("Oh, we're up a bit this time, huh?"). You're a physical and emotional mess, and then the doctor enters the room to talk about how fat you are? Forget about it.

When I was diagnosed with Wegener's granulomatosis, I wondered if my weight had anything to do with it. Did my fat make me sick? Did I only have myself to blame? One of the first doctors I went to see told me just that. He said that I wouldn't be sick if I wasn't so heavy. Turns out that he was just a fat Nazi in a lab coat. More experienced, better-informed doctors (with much better bedside manners) assured me that while a healthy lifestyle can ease the symptoms of almost any autoimmune disease, my weight was not to blame. Any doctor who blames you for your disease—be it cancer for a smoker or heart disease for an overweight person—has his or her priorities screwed up. Over the past four years I have conducted my own experiments to see if fluctuating diet and exercise changed any of my autoimmune symptoms, like rheumatoid arthritis, sinusitis, and fatigue. In my case, it doesn't. But fending off one life-threatening disease doesn't mean I'm willing to set myself up for another one by avoiding proper medical care.

Some patients turn to alternative health solutions as a way to avoid seeing Western doctors. But in my experience, it's not just Western medicine that has an institutional lack of sensitivity. I recently accompanied a nervous friend on his first visit to an acupuncturist. While sitting in the waiting room, the doctor came out and handed me a flyer about how acupuncture could help me lose weight. Why, fuck you very much!

Seeking a new form of therapy, I did body work with a Japanese doctor who practiced moving *qi,* or energy, from different sources in the body. With the help of two female assistants, he silently rolled me around on a bed for an hour. When we finished, he asked in halting English, "You Jewish?" I said yes, hoping that he would have some insight into how my heritage influenced my current health. "Ah," he nodded. "One question. Why all Jewish women so fat?" "Because of the

Holocaust," I replied tartly before writing him a check and never seeing him again.

Can Shrinks Help You Shrink?

You may pursue psychological medical help with your weight issues. After all, not only can a psychiatrist prescribe certain medications (like antidepressants) that may help you control your appetite, but therapists can also deal with the emotional connections we have with food and eating. Your mom rewarded you with food when you were a kid. Or your brother teased you about your weight. Or your ex-boyfriend objectified your body. A therapist can help you work through it. As previously mentioned, some fat people consider eating an addiction, which can be treated in therapy like an alcohol or drug addiction. Sometimes it works, sometimes it doesn't.

Though it's failed for me before, I go through phases where I'm convinced some Freudaholic will have the key to unlock my drama. I used to think that female therapists were too nice to me, so I should just go to a guy and get it over with. (See? I'm always looking for some mean man to confirm my inner, most self-hating fear: that I'm a horrible, horrible person.) I told this shrink from the get-go that my weight was my weight, and I'd rather address emotional issues. We worked for months before I finally opened up and trusted him with my deepest and darkest drama—no "Boo-hoo, I'm so fat," mostly family stuff. I was a crying wreck walking out the door, but proud that I'd opened up to him. That's when he turned to me and said offhandedly, "You seem very concerned about your weight. Some people have told me about a thing called the Atkins Diet . . . maybe you'd want to look into it?"

I'm sorry—have I heard of a "thing" called "Atkins"? Let's see. I'm a lifelong dieter. I'm currently fat. I see a newspaper every day. Yeah, I think that's come into my realm of awareness. Are you really going to ask me that question—when I'm halfway out the door—and when I've just laid my guts out to you? When I told you that I didn't want to talk about weight? You're gonna suggest that I go on a DIET?

I debated long and hard before I broke off our therapy the following week. At first he didn't understand why. He assured me that he was only trying to be helpful, that he didn't judge me based on what I weighed, that he was just looking out for me . . . but in my heart of hearts I knew that HE JUST DIDN'T GET IT. Another doctor with good intentions and faulty execution. Another "A few crunches will tighten this right up." Another "It's all your fault." Another "I'm only telling you this for your health."

What I told him, and what I would tell anyone in a white coat, or anyone holding out his or her arms to me, is that IT'S NOT THE FAT. You can't be overweight in the twenty-first century and not have a clue. You can't carry extra pounds and not know every diet in the book. If you're fat, it's not because you want to be. It's a pain in the ass to be fat. It adds stress to your musculoskeletal system. You sweat a lot. You have to deal with comments from the peanut gallery all day and night. It's hard to find clothes that look good on you. It's literally more challenging to pack a suitcase, because your clothes are bigger and can't be wadded up into little balls and thrown in an overnight bag. Fat Girls have bigger baggage, in every way. If we had it in our power to wish it away, we probably would. I would. I'll say it again: No one wants to be fat.

Even though I often forget, I know in my gut that no one

knows me better than I know myself. Not a therapist, not a dietician, not a friend. It's time to stop thinking that someone knows something that you don't, that someone has an answer that is being withheld from you.

I can't sanction an unhealthy lifestyle—at any weight. I wouldn't want a doctor to ignore an obvious risk factor like weight, which can lead to diabetes and hypertension and other diseases if it goes unchecked. But we know that exercise and diet don't always do the job.

My gynecologist didn't realize how much she hurt me. She thought she was being encouraging. I ended up writing her a letter some time later, discussing my feelings and concerns with her. Luckily, she was very receptive. I'm sure she has more sensitivity now in dealing with other fat patients. I discussed my concerns with the well-intentioned therapist instead of cutting off our therapy with a message on his machine. I hope he'll think again before tossing out diet tips to overweight patients as they walk out the door. If I didn't speak up, how could these doctors have known that I even had an issue with their assumptions?

The medical establishment has always been nervous about women, always hoping to "tame" women surgically. In the late 1800s, our ovaries were removed. As the nineteenth century turned into the twentieth, we were diagnosed as "hysterics" and given drugs to calm us down, or else the doctor would invite us into his office to fondle our genitals in order to check for "rampant sexuality." In the middle of the twentieth century, we were given hormone-replacement drugs that turn out to put us at a much greater health risk than our natural estrogen. Now, in the twenty-first century, fat is the new hysteria. When a woman looks just "too womanly," when there is literally too much woman to go around—many doctors want to cut her, drug her, or at least try to make her feel like shit.

I'm angry at myself for letting all that time go by without a checkup of my reproductive system. I'm angry I let a hateful ENT run a trip on me; I'm angry a weird Japanese guy made an anti-Semitic, antifat remark to me, and I paid him for it. I let it go then, but I won't do it again. I hope you won't, either. If you go to a doctor who makes you feel compromised, or a doctor who humiliates you, switch immediately. You don't deserve that. But don't avoid medical care because you're embarrassed about your weight. Talk to friends, find someone sensitive. Before you set up an appointment, get a consultation to address your concerns with a potential health-care professional. Take responsibility, take the lead. Educate doctors, because they need it the most.

CHAPTER 9

Such a Pretty Face

Feminists may frown (and frankly, Botox could work wonders on those frown lines), but the desire to feel special and pretty is a primal urge. Dress it up in psychojargon—call it self-fulfillment or empowerment—but it boils down to wanting to feel special and pretty. Whole industries orbit this need. It speaks to the girl with her nose pressed up against the lunchroom window, the society wife, the Ophelias, the Marilyns, the Monicas. It can inspire, it can defeat, it can tempt and it can elude. And it can build a hell of a dermatology practice.
—Ellen Tien, "The Doctor Is In," *Harper's Bazaar*

All my life I've been told I have "such a pretty face," but what I really wanted was a beautiful body. I don't know who made up the beauty rules, but they're recited to me on a daily basis in every ad that I see, and visible in every magazine that I read. Most of these images are manipulated or airbrushed, if not completely unreal. Drug companies put different people—two different human beings!—in the before and after photos for weight-loss treatments that you see in magazines. They quote doctors that never practiced medicine; they make up their own studies. Celebrities endorse products they don't use. For example, *Days of Our Lives* star Alison Sweeney lost thirty pounds and is a spokesperson for the diet supplement Xenadrine, but she did not use it to lose weight. Beyoncé Knowles does an ad for Feria hair color IN WHICH SHE IS WEARING A WIG. But we're such dummies, or such naïfs, or such wishful thinkers, that we run out and buy the dye and have the nerve to be surprised when it looks different on us. It's you, only . . . exactly the same.

A Model Life

"These days there's just no excuse for not being beautiful like a supermodel. If you're not drop-dead gorgeous and toned and skinny with dewy, kissable lips, I'm sorry, but you must be doing something wrong. If you've got blemished skin, if your lipstick is smudged, if you're more than 110 pounds and look older than a 15-year-old girl, if you haven't fixed that bump in your nose yet—well, all I can say is, I hope you're not expecting any kind of favorable treatment from anybody or that any sort of good thing is going to happen to you."

That's taken from a tongue-in-cheek *Allure* article called "Get With the Program," but it hits uncomfortably close to home. You know full well what you are supposed to look like: a model. Like a model home, or a model car, you are supposed to be a model woman. That's where the word comes from, because models represent an ideal, the example to which we futilely aspire.

Now, everyone knows that models are very, very skinny, and that they are very, very tall, and that they come from a special gene pool. The rest of us poor suckers can diet every day for the rest of our lives and never look like models do. There are only eight women in the world who look like Barbie, and eight zillion who don't, and blah blah blah.

We know it intellectually, and yet WE DON'T BELIEVE IT. We tell ourselves that if we just tried a little harder, or we hadn't eaten that tiramisu last night, or we had gone to spinning class instead of sleeping in on Saturday . . . if we really, really wanted it badly enough, we could look like Gisele or Naomi or Cindy or whoever the girl of the month might be.

We can't process this logically, because we never see models in the context of reality. Models are always standing (or slouching) in the Louvre, or bending over a car, or stalking down a runway next to other models. We see them splayed out on marble floors of Italian mansions wearing thongs and demicups and high heels. But you never see models in Laundromats. You never see them catching the bus, or shopping at Macy's, or dropping in on parent/teacher conferences. Until you see these women in reality—YOUR reality—you will not understand that they are anatomically structured in a completely different way from the rest of us human beings. The structural difference between you and a supermodel is the structural difference between you and a dwarf (unless, of course, you're a dwarf). Compare a Yugo to a limousine. Yes, they are both cars. Yes, they both drive on wheels and have engines. But that's all they have in common. They are built with all different parts. Their dimensions are completely different. The Yugo can wish and try as hard as it wants to. It can drive for miles and miles at its fastest speed, or starve itself from gasoline, and yet it will never be a limo. Models are limos, my friend, and you and I are just European trash boxes driving on a completely different highway.

Think of models the way you think of basketball players. On the court, they all look the same. But if a basketball player walks into your living room, he's going to smack his head on the door frame. Michael Jordan looks like an average guy on TV, shooting at the foul line or showing off his cute little boxer briefs. But stand next to him in the locker room, and you'll think again. Michael Jordan is Gisele; you are just the ball boy. In the context of other players, Mike is normal. You could be just like him. On the subway platform? He looks like a completely different species.

It wasn't until I started working at fashion events that I understood how different my body was from a model's body. First of all, most professional models are incredibly young. I mean, sixteen, seventeen, eighteen. They're often fresh from Algeria or the Czech Republic or wherever they got scouted. I remember meeting two models at a TV shoot for a makeup demonstration. I was determined to be nice, so I'd be able to bust down the snobby-model stereotype. When I said hi to these two girls, they were so rude. They sort of smiled blankly, but mostly looked right through me and started whispering to each other. So obnoxious! Screw 'em, I thought, models *ARE* rude. It wasn't until after the shoot that I found out that neither one knew a word of English.

Second, models have incredible height. 5'10" is about as low as you can go unless you've got some sort of unique star quality; believe me, they can always find another striking Romanian who is at least six feet tall. Models tend to have really long legs, shorter torsos, surprisingly large breasts, and smaller width across the shoulders. Their heads generally look too tiny for their bodies. They have straight hair and unmarked skin (they're teenagers, remember! wearing a ton of makeup, sure, but they are still high-school age!), big eyes, and white, even teeth. Their features have incredible symmetry, which we unconsciously acknowledge as something beautiful. It's not their skinniness that's so shocking and threatening about models; it's their homogeneity. Each one looks almost exactly the same as the next. Remember, these are models—ideals. They represent a beauty standard which we support. We pick the best of the litter, the juiciest apple on the tree. We are looking for a few dozen women out of five billion here, so we can be really picky. This girl's got the height and the eyes and the tits, but weird teeth? Forget her, there's another Polish chick coming up right behind her in the mall.

Former *Bazaar* editor-in-chief Kate Betts said, "The average model in 1985 was a size 8, while today the average model is a size 0 or 2 . . . These days, fashion's anti-fat bias and obsession with thinness, so ingrained among those who make careers in the business, is looking increasingly like a blind spot, one that could ultimately shortchange designers, retailers, and even magazine publishers. While sales of sizes 0 to 12 have been flat or have grown modestly in the last two years, what is called the 'plus size' market has surged as much as 18 percent." Even Twiggy, the legendary model of the 1960s, who weighed ninety-six pounds during her reign, is stumped. "Next to these girls, I'm very fat and pretty tiny," she told a reporter after the Milan shows in fall 2002. Of course, today we don't just have models; we have supermodels. That's right, we actually super-sized the anorexic modeling industry.

The average American woman is 5′4″ tall and 152 pounds; the average American model is 5′11″ tall and 117 pounds. Do you understand that no matter what the Average Woman does, she can never change herself into the Average Model? Sure, she could work out and have plastic surgery and starve, but she'll never approximate those dimensions. She'll never be as tall; her bones will never be that tiny. It's not an issue of intent or willpower or work; it's a physical impossibility. An academic paper that studied popular contemporary television shows discovered that the ideal 36–24–36 body on TV

> represents a woman who, by garment industry standards, simultaneously wears a size 4 (hips), a size 2 (waist), and a size 10 (bust) . . . What is curious about this ideal figure is its unusual fat distribution. Breasts are composed mainly of fat, not glandular tissue. Because breast fat is positively correlated with total body fat, it is impossible to lose body fat without reducing breast size. Thus, women who wish to meet the skinny-yet-busty body ideal generally cannot do so through diet and exercise alone. The demands of meeting this ideal put women at risk for doing "double damage" to their bodies, through extreme dieting or disordered eating to reduce the lower half and surgery or the use of potentially dangerous drugs or herbal treatments to increase the upper half.

Chant it with me, ladies: We mustn't, we mustn't, we mustn't increase out busts.

Becoming a supermodel is a lot like becoming a world-famous concert pianist. One requires an aesthetic talent; the other is based on skill. You either got it or you don't. Your parents can make you take piano lessons all your life, but it's going to be clear from day one whether or not you're a virtuoso. You can learn and practice and study and play, but a gift is a gift, and if you don't have it, you never will.

That's not to say you can't be in a band, and play at parties, but there's a big difference between Patty Schmeltzer's sixth-grade recital and Rachmaninoff's debut at Carnegie Hall.

Same with beauty. It's a gift. It's hitting the genetic jackpot. Sadly, even if you are a natural beauty or a natural piano player—have all the "skill" to make it—you still need the God-given luck of being in the right place at the right time to meet the right person in order to turn your gift into a career.

If you can believe it, even models are persecuted for invisible excess fat. An unintentionally hilarious article called "Model Boot Camp" talks about models who are put to the test right before shows. "During the two weeks before the collections, Miami trainer Ruddy Esther sends girls from Next and Elite on 45-minute runs every morning with nothing but sugar sweetened coffee and an over-the-counter Xenadrine fat-burning pill in their stomachs. 'You burn an incredible amount of fat if you have no food in your system.'" Wouldn't know, myself.

It continues: "New York nutritionist Michelle Luhan, who helped Claudia Schiffer drop five pounds several years ago (Schiffer, who is six feet tall, panicked when her scale hit 130) . . . estimates that her model clients are 20 to 25 percent below ideal body weight on average . . . 'Claudia had never been to a supermarket when I met her,' says the nutritionist. 'She had no idea that there was such a thing as fat-free. Neither did [Heidi] Klum.'"

Rinse and repeat: Claudia had never been to a supermarket. I can't relate personally. Thank goodness she and Heidi were able to work it all out. When the article was reprinted as "The Bod Squad" in *Vogue Australia*, a group of nutritionists and eating-disorder counselors spoke out, saying it "conveyed dietary information that was confusing, wrong, obnoxious, irresponsible and potentially dangerous." How right they are. You know we girls learn all of our bad habits from those magazines. For every tip on how to rewrite a résumé or "make him want you so so bad," that's where we pick up tips on how to make ourselves barf or snort cocaine for the first time. For example, in one of the most self-deprecating profiles I've read about attempted postpartum weight loss in a long time, actress Tisha Campbell says, "I went on a fast for 10 days, only drinking a formula of water, lemon juice, cayenne pepper, and maple syrup. I lost ten pounds from that alone." Oh, Tisha. Don't you think some foolish girl might try that because of you?

The Idea and Ideal of Beauty

We all want to be beautiful. We all have the fantasy of eating ice cream at the mall and having some guy stop us and say, "You really are gorgeous! Come to New York City and let me take photos of you that we can put in *Vogue* magazine! Here's my card!" Wouldn't that be great? To be thought of as special and adored without having to do anything but stand there and look hot? To not have to cultivate a personality or an opinion or an attitude or a skill? To just be, and be paid for it, and be loved for it?

I get that, truly I do. It's my fantasy, too. I want to feel special and pretty. Fat girls fantasize about "discovery" even more than regular girls, because we hope that someone will see past our fat and notice not only our physical beauty, but our inherent beauty. All fat girls want to be models in magazines like *Mode* or *Grace*. When I did actually get tapped to be a plus-size model (you know, that pretty face is such a calling card!), I couldn't believe it was true. I went to the agency and got my measurements taken and everything. I stopped when I discovered that I had to put up the money to get a photography book together (a common requirement). To tell you the truth, I would not have made it as a plus-size model. They too are built differently from the rest of us fat girls. They are taller, more symmetrical. Plus-size models represent a greater variety of features than straight models do (e.g., different-size busts, some have waists, some don't). Still, they are models, not regular people.

When I say I'm fat, more often than not someone says to me, "You're not fat, you're really beautiful." Or the classic "such a pretty face" comment rears its ugly head. Not that I don't appreciate it. I know that I'm beautiful, and striking, and attractive, and that I have a great haircut and clean skin and great style. Fat and beautiful are not opposites. They do not cancel each other out. I am fat and beautiful. I know lots of people who are skinny and ugly. I can look in the mirror and see lots of things I think are beautiful about me, my face, my body. I can see the elements come together and get a feeling of "Ooh, I like that." Occasionally, *verrrrrry* occasionally, I look at my body and think, "Okay, there's some fat. What's so bad? What's everyone so scared of, freaked out about? What the hell am *I* so freaked out about?"

But usually I look at my body in the mirror and I go, "AAAAAEEEEWWWWWW!" Especially when I look at my stomach. My weight is pretty evenly distributed, but all the extra goes straight to my abdomen. My belly sometimes looks so big that I debate going to prenatal yoga classes. I swear sometimes that I must have stretch marks on my eyeballs. I wish I could just give myself the 100-percent stamp of approval, but I'm not there yet. Don't even get me started on the pouch. You know, that slab of flab below your belly button but above your vagina? Women hate that little pouch, don't we? But what's so wrong with that pouch? We're supposed to have that. It's good, it's supposed to be there. That's where we grow babies. Somehow we came up with the idea that our bellies are supposed to be ironing-board flat and perfectly pouch-free. Sure, Goldie Hawn is like sixty years old and you could bounce quarters off her belly. Good for Goldie. But you aren't her. (Plus, Goldie keeps her Oscar in her meditation room—does that make any sense at all?) Who knows for sure, anyway—did you ever see Goldie's belly up close? Smoke and mirrors, my friends. There are rare birds with completely flat bellies, but it's like someone who has eleven toes: genetic mutation!

And thighs. It turns out that thighs are supposed to touch! That's our storage space for the energy our bodies need to sustain pregnancies. "During puberty—a typical girl gains nearly 35 pounds of so-called reproductive fat around the hips and thighs. Those pounds contain the roughly 80,000 calories needed to sustain a pregnancy, and the curves they create provide a gauge of reproductive potential." Ah, those thighs that *Allure* magazine couldn't nuke, though they tried EIGHT different ways in an article called "A Leg Up": "Seven candidates followed seven different regimens designed to tone, shape, and dejiggle their thighs, undaunted by the fact that there is a biological (read: maternal) reason women tend to accumulate fat on the hips and thighs." Again, what's that reason? " 'There is evidence that estrogen is stored in fat on the outer thighs,' says Rhoda S. Narins, clinical professor of dermatology at New York University." Hmm. Thighs equal estrogen. Estrogen equals female. So if you get rid of your thighs, are you getting rid of your femininity? Your womanhood?

The Eye of the Beholder

I can't argue with the sex appeal of skinny chicks with flat bellies and thin thighs and big tits. Sexually and aesthetically, Victoria's Secret models have it all over the fat girls and always will—if you think of sex and beauty as something cold and hard and cruel. In that case, sex *is* stomping women in high heels and snapped-up thigh-highs whipping long hair over glass desks and fast cars (i.e., male). But if you think of sex as something wet and hot and dirty and crazy and funny and intimate (i.e., female), and we can project sex as something hot and wet and dirty and crazy and funny and intimate, then a different picture comes to mind: a picture of you or me.

Maybe it's just the difference between the way men and women see our world, and ne'er the two visions shall meet. This is how a female critic at the *New York Times* reviewed the Victoria's Secret lingerie fashion show that aired on CBS in 2002: "Portrayed with a cheerless mock innocence as angels, or as Christmas packages waiting to be unwrapped, the models stalked the runway looking like skeletons with strategically placed pads of fat, hitting their paces hard so breasts bobbled atop demibrassieres in time to the music, which included lyrics like 'took her to the bedroom/she was stripped down' to a driving beat." Definitely not a fan of the show or the models in it.

On the other hand, a male writer covering the Victoria's Secret show wrote this story in the *Pioneer Press,* under the headline "Lingerie Models Look Like Real Women Should":

So, along comes a special in the middle of prime-time television that featured runway models who have obviously watched their figures. In other words, if we have an obesity problem in America, doesn't it stand to reason that you might show by example what a gal is supposed to look like? Of course it does. Put another way, a young gal might take Tyra Banks as a role model over some tub of lard who finds a lawyer desperate enough to sue McDonald's. When it comes to style, aerobic fitness and skin care, I would imagine that a gal will go with this Banks or Bundchen any day of the week. Gee, the way these experts babble on, you would think that these models were dropped out of some spaceship or something. No, these are hard-working gals who watch what they eat and make sure they get their jog in every day and otherwise lead the kinds of lives that they need to lead in order not to have an obesity problem.

First of all, now we understand why the first reviewer works for the *New York Times* and this guy writes for the *Pioneer Press*. Second, what's with all the "gals" and "gals" and "gals"? Even this guy doesn't see the models as "women." Third, we see Thin Logic in action, where Tyra Banks is a "hard-working gal" and a fat chick like me is a "tub of lard." Maybe men and women see things differently. Or maybe we should just hunt down this specific man and set him straight.

I thought regular women made big strides when the Lane Bryant lingerie fashion show began to get a lot of press coverage. Big, beautiful, curvy women strut their stuff during that show in a truly inspirational way. What kind of comments did some men make about the women in the show?

- "Are these really women?"
- "[My wife's] a size 3, and that's how I like it. Those girls are too tender and plump for me."
- "They look like guys to me . . . after six or seven beers, I might be happy."
- "I like thick girls, but these girls need to work out."

This is what are we up against in terms of defining contemporary beauty. In our defense, fat chicks always like to point out that Marilyn Monroe was a size 14. Turns out that "Ms. Monroe, who was 5 feet 5 1/2 inches and weighed between 118 and 135 pounds, may have been just busty enough to fill out a size 14, but partly because sizes were smaller in the 1950's." Marilyn struggled with her weight and her body image just like we do now. In a book called *Lift,* former *New York Times* medical writer Joan Kron revealed that Marilyn had a chin implant, and a crude breast-enlargement surgery that left her with an infection near the end of her life. If she was alive today, I have a feeling Marilyn would be doing Atkins and Yogilates and have more surgery than Joan Rivers.

Evil-utionary Psychology

Scientists say that our attraction to beauty is explained by a theory called evolutionary psychology. JD Heyman writes, "The evolutionary argument about beauty starts from this assumption: Human beings, like all other animals, seek out certain traits in prospective partners when it comes to reproduction—among them, resistance to genetic and infectious diseases, physical fitness, and of course, the ability to produce healthy offspring. And, the theory goes, certain external signs—facial symmetry, full breasts and hips on women, specific waist-to-hip ratios—are indicators of these traits." When a man is evaluating you, he's really not looking at *you*—he's looking at your facial symmetry. He's checking to see if you have features like a high forehead, fuller lips, prominent eyes and cheekbones, and a small chin that indicate you'd be good at reproductivity. (No coincidence that these are features on little girls, huh?) He doesn't need a hot chick, just one that can reproduce. So those reproductive traits became what we consider to be "hot."

There's this little problem, however. We *need* fat. We need it to be high-quality mates. We need it to sustain pregnancies. But not too much of it—just that perfect "hip-to-waist ratio" that indicates how well we'd reproduce. "A low waist-hip ratio"—the ideal is that a woman's waist is 60 to 80 percent the size of their hips—"is one of the few features that a long, lean Barbie doll shares with a plump, primitive fertility icon," sums up Heyman. Say what you want about the Venus of Willendorf and Empire waists—if they can't have girls that look like boys, men generally prefer an hourglass figure. Usually our fashion choices throughout the ages—whether it's a big belt or a girdle—are designed to show off our hip-to-waist ratio.

Between those hips you'll find a vast new land of unexploited terrain: the abs! Now that everyone can buy a great rack if they weren't born with one, we needed to move on to a tougher piece of female-body real estate. By baring our abs to the world in the twenty-first century, we're finally like "Screw the camouflage—I'll let it all hang out!" Just be careful with your fashion choices—they could be lethal. According to the ever-alarming *New York Post*, "Those tight and trendy low-cut hip-huggers you're wearing could be dangerous. A Canadian doctor has warned that the popular women's jeans can squeeze a sensory nerve under the hipbone and cause a tingling or burning sensation in the thigh called 'paresthesia.' "

To me, the belly-baring look is an advertisement to men showing that we're not pregnant. Come on, baby, come fill up this empty womb! Then I'll be fat (i.e., pregnant) and off the market again. "The symbolic nature of the region beneath a woman's rib cage [represents] her potential for procreation. 'A flat belly is a modern-day virginity symbol,' said Stephen Beckerman, an associate professor of anthropology at Pennsylvania State University, who has studied marriage and mating rituals. 'What it suggests is a woman who has never borne children and thus has all of her years of fertility in front of her' . . . A darker view suggests that one's stomach, especially if it is as taut as a trampoline, presents an all-too-literal billboard for the triumph of denial over appetite, the struggle between the two in some part characterizing the plight of the modern affluent woman."

What's even stranger about all this flat-mound madness is that from the neck down, you can't tell if you're looking at a girl or a guy. So the most desirable woman—with a blowout bust, cut abs, and a flat, hairless stomach—is really just a dude with implants. Girl, you'll be a . . . man, soon?

There's a reason that Natalie Angier dismisses evolutionary psychology in this way: "In sum: higgamus, hoggamus, Pygmalionus, *Playboy* magazine, eternitas. Amen." Debunking these theories, she calls for "revolutionary psychology" instead.

Maybe She's Born with It (Psst—She's Not)

If you're not born with beauty, at least you can buy it. In a recent poll of 1,500 patients done by a Beverly Hills plastic surgeon, patients revealed that they wanted Heather Graham's eyes, Heather Locklear's nose, Halle Berry's cheeks, Denise Richards's lips, and Britney Spears's body. (Brits would build Ms. Frankenstein with Jennifer Aniston's hair, Catherine Zeta-Jones's face, Elizabeth Hurley's bust, Elle Macpherson's legs, and J-Lo's butt, according to a survey of 3,000 British women.) If you don't want a cut-and-paste job, pick just one icon: It would cost you $100,000 to buy all of Britney. That includes a nose job for $6,500, an eye job for $4,000, lip augmentation for $5,000, breast implants for $10,000 (then again, you could get just one boob done to cut costs), cheek and chin implants for $7,500, white porcelain veneers for your teeth at $25,000, a laser facial and Botox injections for $3,200, lipo for $20,000, human hair extensions for $5,000, your own home-tanning machine for that year-round precancerous glow at a bargain rate of $6,480, a year's worth of manicures for $6,000, and an annual full-body-wax tab of $3,600 (but does that include a tip?). Here's the problem: Now you look like Britney, but you're still you. And you're out a hundred grand.

When diet and exercise fail, we turn to more foolish and/or drastic means to get beautiful. I'm horrified by what we do to ourselves in the name of beauty. I understand why we do it; I feel the temptation myself. But it doesn't matter how you fix the outside if the inside is all messed up. Still, we cut, we suck, we burn. You can try hypnosis to drop weight; you can "sniff yourself thin" by inhaling special lotions. Why not get electrocuted for $150 a pop? That new method promises weight loss from an old machine: "Called Visadera, it uses Electronic Muscle Stimulation (EMS) machines, used by doctors and physical therapists for more than two decades to help heal and strengthen muscles." We smoke to suppress appetite and speed up our metabolism. We get fake bake suntans, breast implants, body piercings. We wear "Wonder Pants," a WonderBra for the butt—just to give your booty a boost. Are you ready to purchase a "breast-building Biometric bra" for $2,000–$2,500? It will suck your boobs for ten hours a day to make them bigger, like Austin Powers's Swedish-Made Penis Enlarger Pump, but for girls. We can get toe surgery for prettier feet, or have the nerves on the soles of our feet desensitized so our high heels won't hurt so much. We can buy cadaver-cell lip injections, get makeup tattooed on our faces, inject drugs to prevent our sweat glands from . . . sweating. There's a whole litany of freaky stuff you can play with at personalsurgeon.com (did you ever think you'd see the day?), leading to plastic-surgery addicts and body dysmorphic disorders for everyone!

So, many of us go under the knife. In 2002, nearly 6.6 million people had plastic surgery, 85 percent of them women. Liposuction (the only way to physically rid your body of fat cells, since losing weight makes fat cells smaller but cannot rid the body of them) is positively old-hat at this point. Why stick with fuddy-duddy liposuction when you can get Lipo-Dissolve or microliposuction? C'mon, how risky can it be? To quote Dr. Robert Del Junco, former president of the California State Medical Board: "To put it in perspective, the incidence of death from liposuction is two to three times higher than that of dying from a normal pregnancy." Instead of a time-consuming face lift, how about a new process called "feathering," where a dermatologist weaves a thread under your skin and pulls your face tighter by hand? Or she can shoot you up with some "Radiance" to tighten that saggy face—unlike Botox, this fake fountain of youth will last for two whole years.

You may be relieved to know about "the new bottom line: after years of shrunken status, bountiful butts are on the rise again." How can you get that Kylie/Tara/Thalia/Gisele/J-Lo/Beyoncé/Shakira look? For $9,000, a butt implant oughta cover it. Apparently they're becoming quite common. There are butt-lifting exercises you can do to put more junk in your trunk; but when those fail, buy the Tone-A-Matic. Simply attach conductive pads to your butt and shock it into shape!

And why stop with your external body when you can change your very female self? That's right, there's female genital reconstruction for those of you who have saggy labia that need some snipping, or loose vaginas that need to be tightened up. " 'Whatever needs to be fixed, I fix it,' says Dr. Jane Norton of her patients, who are often embarrassed to be nude in front of their partners." Oh, maybe that's why your partner doesn't love you—it's because your labia is just so unattractive! Dr. Norton is one of the few female plastic surgeons in the game: Only about 4 percent of all the board-certified surgeons in the United States are women. "It is men who are lifting the eyebrows, enlarging the breasts, and suctioning away the fat to remake women's faces and bodies," observed the *New York Times*.

Women's Magazines

It's mostly female editors and publishers who create the false idols we see in magazines. We tend to think of magazines as entertainment, like a TV show or a movie. But magazines are really just big books of advertisements, interrupted by articles and a couple of photos of models lying around gondolas in Venice. Sure, they reflect our own interests, but they primarily sell us an idealized image. There's also a huge crossover now between magazines and Hollywood; it's much more common to see a celebrity on a magazine cover than a model. You could get mental whiplash just perusing the newsstands each week. If you were to just use *People* as your body barometer, you'd have an immediate insecurity complex. The gamut runs back and forth from LUV YOUR BODY THE WAY IT IS to FAT BUSTING SECRETS OF THE SUPERSTARS, usually within the same issue.

We could give *Vogue's* editor-in-chief, Anna Wintour, some props for finally including plus-size model Kate Dillon in its first "body" issue in 2002. Granted, they posed Kate next to a diminutive man in order to emphasize what *Vogue* called her "Amazon stature," but progress is progress. Catherine Zeta-Jones, Minnie Driver, Rita Wilson, Kate Winslet, Sophie Dahl, Jewel, and Jennifer Lopez were featured in the "curvy" section of the magazine. As Anna sniffed in her editor's letter in that issue: "I fully take on board the complex issues of body dysmorphia, isolation, and manipulation that presenting images of idealized women may give rise to. That said, some-times people overlook a simple truth: To be slim and fit is healthier than to be seriously overweight and 'out of shape,' whatever one's natural body type."

In 2003, plus-size rock royalty Mia Tyler earned the curvy spread. In that issue Wintour explains, "This issue celebrates our physical diversity and our ability to look fabulous given what we were born with." Of course, their "short" model was 5'6", but we won't sweat the details. Still, you can tell Anna is on the defensive from that issue's letter from the editor: "I couldn't help but thinking, as we prepared this issue, how confused we all are about matters of size, weight, and speech. If it's politically incorrect to call someone fat—in a country where one in three people suffers from (medical) obesity—why is there no similar prohibition against labeling a skinny person 'skeletal' or 'anorexic'? The *Wall Street Journal* feels within its rights to call me 'entirely too thin,' when the truth of the matter is that I don't gain weight, never have, no matter what I eat . . . It's tiresome. Why can't we just accept that people come in different sizes?" Hey, Anna, you tell me! This is of course the same magazine where in a story about day-spa relaxation, a model lounges in a pool, a giant hot fudge sundae waiting to greet her when she steps out.

Vogue may set the pace, but many follow. Liz Tilberis was the legendary editor of *Harper's Bazaar* who died from ovarian cancer. As she was memorialized in *New York* magazine, "She shared her delight in the fact that her weight loss [from chemotherapy] finally allowed her to wear the clothes she championed." She found an upside to chemo? My god, wouldn't you trade snappy suits for LIFE?

It was Tilberis's successor, Kate Betts, who finally came around, saying she owed Renée Zellweger an apology for bumping her from *Bazaar's* cover during Renee's bodacious Bridget Jones phase. "Over a year ago, as the editor of a fashion magazine, I pulled her picture off the cover of an issue at the last minute, swapping it for a photo of a lanky swan in a whiff of Dior chiffon. The problem wasn't the usual one that kills covers. The lighting was impeccable. Her dress was a glamorous Galliano, and there was a lot of talk about her new movie, *Bridget Jones's Diary,* and a starring performance that would be hailed with an Oscar nomination. No, the problem was much more primal, born of one of the not-so-secret obsessions of the fashion world: she was too fat."

As you can see, she certainly gave poor Renée a complex. As Lisa Schwarzbaum so aptly wrote in her review of *Bridget Jones's Diary* in *Entertainment Weekly,* "This is not what 'fat' looks like; this is what ripe, sexy health looks like, and she needn't have dropped the weight afterwards—except, perhaps, to eat lunch again in the demented, scale-obsessed town of Hollywood."

Sadly, in *Chicago* Zellweger seemed determined to prove that she had nothing in common with her onscreen alter-ego Bridget Jones. Her skimpy costumes revealed skin stretched too tautly over her chest, ribcage, and nonexistent rack. It only served to make Catherine Zeta-Jones look that much sexier, her sexuality smoldering with every luscious curve. She's the one who took home the Oscar. Cheers to Kate Winslet, the perfect example of a Hollywood star who is not fat but keeps getting lumped in there anyway. Instead of getting angry, she just wonders why? As she told the *Daily Mail* after the February 2003 issue of British *GQ* retouched her already slender legs, "I do not look like that. And more importantly, I don't desire to look like that."

There is a shift opening up in the media, a trend of body acceptance floating around. There are so many big people making such a big noise, something has to give. Part of the shift has to do with teenagers who understand that they don't have to take it anymore. "The evidence that an evolution is taking place in young women's attitudes is preliminary—eating disorders do, after all, remain a serious health hazard—but glimmers of a new mind-set are emerging from teenagers, from professionals who deal closely with them, and even from images purveyed by the mass media," opines culture critic Ginia Bellafante.

Magazine editors say, "We put pictures of big women in our pages and we got a lot of hate mail." Well, keep doing it. Once upon a time, people resisted seeing photos of black or Asian women, or women with curly hair, or women with big noses in those shiny, glossy layouts . . . Granted, there are those who break the mold. Barbra Streisand came along in the sixties and redefined American beauty. Isabella Rossellini has challenged the age/beauty barrier in modeling. Halle Berry has broken a racial barrier for beauty in the twenty-first century. As Steve Martin said at the 2003 Oscars, her Oscar win "broke down barriers for unbelievably hot women . . . now, at last, they have hope."

I don't hate Halle Berry or Hollywood. I love beauty, I love glamour. I love movies and movie stars. I know that skinny girls like Tyra Banks and Cameron Diaz kvetch about how they were mocked in high school, called Skeletor and Pelican Head, just like us Butterball Babes. When models talk about zits and ugly-duckling childhoods, *Allure*'s editor-in-chief, Linda Wells, says they do it compensate for their beauty. "Beauty makes us all uncomfortable, confused, unnerved. People laughed at the ad that went 'don't hate me because I'm beautiful,' but hate is exactly what many of us feel. Hate and envy and profound unease—as well as, of course, attraction, awe, and wonder." At least Tyra and Cameron had the satisfaction of knowing that they were gonna make good when they filled out. When we grow up (and fill in), we Hefties are still . . . garbage.

It's a Small World

We big fat Americans are doing our best to mess up the world's metabolism with our Big Macs, and so far, we're doing a great job! "A wave of obesity is sweeping through Asia as its population shifts into vast new cities where the food is faster and the lifestyle more sedentary," said the *New York Times*. Reuters found: "It is not only fast food chains that have changed the Asian diet. Milk, ice cream, cookies, soft drinks, and potato chips—these once alien foods are as common in many parts of Asia now as in the West. Meat and eggs are making inroads on rice and vegetables." The thinking used to be that we were giving Western kids a sweet tooth by feeding them sweet things when they were babies, like milk and then sweet cereals, applesauce, etc. Nutritionists wondered if we ate more of a traditional Asian breakfast (miso soup, white rice, a poached egg), we'd be less fat. Now it's too late.

As much as we borrow elements of Indian and Asian style in our home design and in our fashion influences, Western beauty ideals still set the pace around the world. In the hope that they'll look more Western, Korean women "get their cheekbones chiseled narrower, their eyelids sliced open, and their legs broken and stretched." In China, "hundreds of young Chinese, more women than men, obsessed with stature in this increasingly crowded and competitive society, are stretching themselves to new heights on a latter-day rack developed by a Russian doctor 40 years ago to treat dwarfism and deformed limbs. The often painful procedure . . . adds lengths by allowing new bone to grow in the gap left by the gradually separating ends of broken bone." How is it done on one patient? "A doctor cut her shin bones in two, applied a medieval-looking brace to her legs, and taught her how to turn its screws so that metal pins would pull her bones apart nearly a millimeter a day, or around four-hundredths of an inch." It takes six months for each leg to heal in the device, then three more months before the victim—I mean patient—can walk again. The price for this high-risk procedure? Just $6,000 to $7,000 per leg. Why do they do it? For the same reasons we starve and slice and dye: to attract potential employers and husbands.

The downside of our American cultural influence is spreading to even the most remote locations. "Just a few years after the introduction of television to a province of Fiji's main island, Viti Levu, eating disorders—once virtually unheard of there— are on the rise among girls . . . Girls who said they watched television three or more nights a week in the 1998 survey were 50 percent more likely to describe themselves as 'too big or fat' and 30 percent were more likely to diet than girls who watched less frequently, the researchers found." The shows they were watching, by the way, were *Beverly Hills 90210* and *Melrose Place*. Boy, if you didn't have a reason to hate Brenda before . . .

Western beauty is planting its tentacles all over the world. In Iran, where religious law forces women to cover their bodies and hair, women are manipulating the only visible part of themselves by getting Western-looking nose jobs. And in Africa, the woman who won the annual Face of Africa pageant in 2001 was said to look the least typically Ugandan—i.e., the most Western. As for the Nigerian winner of the 2001 Miss World Pageant: "In a culture where Coca-Cola bottle voluptuousness is celebrated and ample backsides and bosoms are considered ideals of female beauty, the new Miss World (18-year-old Agbani Darego of Nigeria) shared none of those attributes. She was 6 feet tall, stately, and so, so skinny. She was, some said uncharitably, a white woman in black skin," reported a local journalist.

At the 2002 Miss World Pageant held in Nigeria in Darego's honor, 105 people were killed in clashes between Christians and Muslims after a local reporter implied that the prophet Muhammad might find the contestants attractive enough to be wife-worthy. The pageant itself had already inflamed Nigerians who found the concept of a beauty pageant promiscuous and offensive to female morality. We're dying for beauty, in so many ways.

At least, we sigh with relief, there are places in the world untouched by butt implants and Lean Cuisine. At first I was relieved to read a story in *Marie Claire* called "Where Men Love Big Women." It explained: "In southern Niger, West African nation, Maradi women will go so far as to eat themselves sick and take weight gain supplements to fatten up for their weddings." Well, I don't want to eat myself sick, but at least the tyranny of the tricep isn't in play here, right? Maybe I'll just move to West Africa! The *New York Times* covered the same story: "In Niger, as in many other places in Africa, fat is the beauty ideal for women." Love it! "At one festival, called Hangandi, women of the Djerma ethnic group compete to become the heaviest . . ." This keeps getting better! "Among the Calabari people in southeastern Nigeria, brides are sent to so-called fattening rooms or fattening farms before their weddings . . ." Wait, did they just use the phrase "fat farm"? "So popular is fat that here in Maradi, a sleepy town just north of the border with Nigeria, women take steroids to gain bulk, or pills to sharpen their appetites. To gain weight, some women even ingest feed or vitamins for animals—though few will admit it." Wait a second, that's disgusting. I hate to say it, but this sounds like the same thing we do in America, just opposite, right? "And so, if the beauty concept here is the reverse of the West's, its motivation appears the same: seeking men's approval." Give me back my passport!

Look Out

It's not that beauty is bad or inherently evil. Beauty is good. I want to look beautiful, and feel beautiful. I admire it when I see it, whether it be in a face or a body or a work of art. There's a reason that a group of American businesswomen approached several beauty companies (including *Vogue,* props to Anna) to open a beauty school and wellness center in Kabul. Under Taliban rule in Afghanistan, the right to be beautiful was taken away from women—just like every other right.

It's just that the beauty image we've developed is so convoluted. The goal is to have a body with the breasts of a woman, but the face and hairlessness of a little girl. A body with the curves of a woman but the muscles of a man. A body that's part flesh and part plastic. No wonder we fail; we're not Barbies. We're not Terminators. We're people.

You have to read Emme's book, *True Beauty.* You'll understand that she's more than just a model; she's a mogul. She was the first plus-size model to appear in *People*'s "50 Most Beautiful People" issue, shot in a full-on nude. Her clothing line is gorgeous, and she absolutely shines kindness onto others. She also offers the world's best beauty advice: "I've changed my psyche, my self-esteem, the 'good girl, bad girl' thing. If you cheat on your husband or commit murder, that's bad. A cookie is just a cookie. I got tired of fighting myself every step of the way. I live my life now, I don't get crazy. Each person has to ask, 'What's not making me happy?' My story is a story of hope, and maybe it can re-educate people. Everyone should start to become their own role model in their own image."

Do yourself a favor. Take the magnets off the fridge and the stickies off the computer screen. Stop taking cues from others—whether they are fashion editors or people you know—and let yourself set your standards. Don't renew your commitment to losing ten pounds, or getting into last decade's sun dress. Don't vow to transform yourself into someone else. Don't renew at all; take on a new idea instead. Try this: "Well, here I am. Maybe I'd like to be in the process of change, but today I'm in this body. So why not work with myself instead of against myself?" Right now, try to honor the skin you're in.

CHAPTER 10

Hollywood

It's not my job to be thin.
—Julie Burchill, "I'm Fat, So What?" *The Guardian*

In 1991, *The Silence of the Lambs* made a gazillion dollars and swept the Academy Awards. In the movie Jodie Foster plays an FBI agent tracking a serial killer who kidnaps big fat women, starves them so their skin gets loose, then skins them to make himself some sort of . . . skin suit. When Jodie comes to the killer's door and asks him about one of the victims, he says, "Oh, wait, was she a great big fat person?"

Jodie replies, "Yes, sir, she was a big girl," like she's sort of embarrassed. Meanwhile, when they cut the victim's tag out of her sweater, it's a size 14. Here they've been talking about how gigunda these women have to be so their skin is all loose, and she's just a size 14. Just my size, at the time. "Okay," I thought. "At least fat chicks are good for something in the movies—like making skin suits for serial killers."

It's Not the Suit, It's How You Wear It

These days fat suits—which are really just updated versions of the skin suit—have become even more common in Hollywood. Here's a list of just some of the recent celebs who've gotten suited up: Julia Roberts, *America's Sweethearts*; Eddie Murphy, *The Nutty Professor*; Martin Lawrence, *Big Momma's House*; Mike Myers, the *Austin Powers* sequels; Goldie Hawn, *Death Becomes Her*; Courteney Cox Arquette, *Friends*; Jane Leeves, *Frasier*; Robin Williams, *Mrs. Doubtfire*; Cynthia Nixon, *Sex and the City*.

Allison Anders, writer and director of *Gas Food Lodging* and *Mi Vida Loca*, said it best:

> This practice of skinny actresses donning fat suits is essentially the new and acceptable blackface in Hollywood . . . At the end of the day, after she sheds her blubber in the makeup trailer, she still gets to be Gwyneth Paltrow; slim, famous, clad in designer clothes, and much richer because of this project, while the girls and women she's supposed to embody in this film (including her body double) have to live with the painful stereotypes she has helped perpetuate. I hope the next actress offered millions to play "the fat girl for the day" stops to think about this before she signs the contract—even just to ask, like any other professional actress would in any other situation, "Why does she weigh 350 pounds? And why me for the part?" If the director can't answer these questions, don't do the movie.

Ah, yes. Gwynnie. When ex-boyfriend Ben Affleck said that Gwyneth Paltrow is "actually the funny, down-to-earth fat girl in the beautiful girl's body," I nearly stabbed myself. Gwyneth thought she was doing fat girls some kind of favor by donning a fat suit in *Shallow Hal*. Frankly, I've been wearing a fat suit for fifteen years, and trust me, it's hardly Oscar-worthy.

In multiple interviews, Gwyneth said that when she wore her fat suit around a hip hotel lobby bar, no one even wanted to look at her! As a fat girl, she felt virtually ignored—for the first time ever. That's weird. I get lots of positive feedback when I'm out and about. Maybe it's because I wear bright red lipstick and sexy, low-cut clothes. Or because I like to dance and sing and laugh. When I say something funny or smart, which I frequently do, men often turn to listen. Sometimes I get so much support that I forget I'm even wearing the suit!

Isn't it weird that I've had such positive experiences in my fat suit, but Gwyneth felt insulted or ignored? I'm not saying that my life is perfect, but it just doesn't occur to me to blame all my problems on the suit. It seems to me that it's not the suit you wear but how you wear it that determines whether or not you're dressed for success.

Celebrating Celebrities

Everyone wants to be famous, because celebrities—at least, the ones we admire—are thin and rich and beautiful. We assume that if we were famous, we'd be thin and rich and beautiful and universally beloved. Since just one person—be it a mother, best friend, boyfriend, or sibling—can't love us enough, then maybe the whole wide world could fall in love with us and our lives would be just perfect.

Jennifer Aniston is thin and rich and beautiful, but she doesn't speak to her mother and can't go shopping without a police escort. Few actresses have let their personal body traumas play out in public like Jennifer has. Here's a woman who clearly longs to put on five pounds, Zone diet be damned. She lost weight because her agent told her to, and says, "I curse that day, because from then on, I became body conscious." As she told *Rolling Stone,* "I'm 110, I've been 130, and I'm five feet five . . . I was just as happy before I was thinner, by the way. My life wasn't different, except people, mostly men, changed." Would we stop watching *Friends* if she gained weight? I don't think so. Would Brad Pitt stop loving her? He'd better not. Just because you're thin and ripped and famous, doesn't mean you're happy. As the cover of *People* magazine described the then-single Nicole Kidman, Meg Ryan, and Julia Roberts, "Sure they're rich and gorgeous. But that doesn't make it any easier to find a love that lasts." No matter how hot you are. And how hot you are now isn't necessarily an indicator of what's coming down the pike; Julia Roberts, Angelina Jolie, and even Lara Flynn Boyle have been photographed with their lovely, fat moms.

It's not just movies; music is obsessed with bodies, too. Did Mariah Carey sell more albums after she got a boob job? Nope, but she did earn herself a mental breakdown. Janet Jackson is the only person I've ever seen with, like, a nine-pack. I fear that her belly button is going to open up and start having a dialogue with me. It scares me half to death. And it's not like she's psyched about *all* of her body, so she wants to show it off—she only allows us to ogle her cleavage and her stomach. Think about it: Have you ever seen Janet's knees? It's so sad. I can tell you a lot about Janet's body and her personal life, but you tell me: What was the name of her last great song? Has a new body made her more money? I find it ironic that in the hip-hop world, men's clothes keep getting bigger and bulkier, but women's keep getting more and more fitted. Men are taking up more space, while women are forced to take up less and less. Men's bodies become more and more protected, while women's are more and more exposed. Guys could get lost in the clothes that Sean "P. Diddy" Combs designs for his line Sean John, but women are supposed to slink around contentedly in Diddy's leather panties, with a fur collar snug around their necks.

As celebrity bodies have gotten smaller and smaller, we the audience have become even more obsessed with them—and even more rigid in our opinion of what an attractive woman is supposed to look like. Hollywood personal trainer Valerie Walters said, "Size 4 is fat. Everyone wants to be a size zero . . . I've had clients say their managers flat out refuse to send them on auditions until they lose 10 pounds. I'm talking about very thin, very beautiful girls here." We can't give managers and casting agents that kind of choice. If we stop offering men idealized images of women, idealized images of ourselves . . . if we stop offering options, they will have to make do and mate with us ugly chicks—or else let our race die out.

It took major guts to do what Jamie Lee Curtis did—pose for *More* in September 2002 without any makeup, clothing, lighting, or retouching. "There's a reality to the way I look without my clothes on. I don't have great thighs. I have very big breasts and a soft, fatty little tummy. And I've got back fat. People assume that I'm walking around in little spaghetti strap dresses. It's insidious—Glam Jamie, the Perfect Jamie, the great figure, blah blah blah. And I don't want the unsuspecting 40-year-old women of the world to think that I've got it going on. It's such a fraud. And I'm the one perpetrating it."

Puffed-up Pamela Anderson, Curvy Carmen Electra—they might be nice people, or smart people, but let's face it, it's all about their bodies. And we think that we are supposed to look just like them. Why do we scrutinize movie stars and assume we're supposed to look that way? Why do we adopt our standards from film and TV, but not from other places? We watch the Olympics on TV, but we don't berate our inability to make a record-breaking luge time. We do come home from *Tomb Raider* mad that we're not as thin as Angelina Jolie; we don't come home from the World Series mad that we can't hit a baseball as far as Derek Jeter. No one comes home from the Cirque du Soleil cursing themself out for not being double-jointed. But we clip photos of celebrities in bikinis and tape them up on the fridge so we glance at them every time we open and close the fridge, snacking on last night's chicken cacciatore. Apparently we think Rebecca Romijn-Stamos's belly button is some sort of evil eye that will ward us away from temptation.

The Trouble with Oprah

And then there's Oprah. She's our national stand-in for the craziness we feel about weight; she's the Jesus of dieting, taking on all our sins. We're ashamed of our bodies and appetites, we feel like failures, and she does too. It doesn't matter how rich or successful she is; her body is the one battle she can't completely win. We do what she does. We do Optifast, we hire trainers. Every time she starts a diet she says, "This time it's for real!" and within four months she's back to eating macaroni and wearing stretchy clothes. She's the most famous woman in the world, and yet she's one of us.

Oprah wields so much influence over us. We relate to her; we follow her advice. We long to be as well-read as she is, as spiritual as she is, as connected to people we love as she is. I felt so proud when she took a recent stand about diet and exercise based on health instead of vanity. Still, Oprah's resistance to body-image satisfaction is evident when you read between the lines.

In a recent issue of *O: The Oprah Magazine* themed "Confessions," I found this article: "Behind Every Great Woman Is a Butt She Can Learn to Love." In it, author Veronica Chambers confesses to liking her big butt. She pooh-poohs media messages that tell us "there's an ideal butt and it's our responsibility to get it." She says, "It's ridiculous to think that we can achieve one so-called 'perfect' size. Wouldn't we all be happier if we idealized a shape that hewed more closely to our own?" As Oprah herself might say, "You go, girl."

But opposite this derriere diatribe is photo spread of a muscled athlete working out under this heading: EQUINOX'S KACY DUKE SHOWS YOU HOW TO GET FIRMED TONED AND PROFOUNDLY UPLIFTED. Wait—one page ago, didn't you say that my big old butt is just fine the way it is?

That tonal seesaw is evident in almost every issue. The "Learning to Love Your Body" issue included articles like "A Guide to Getting Happy in Your Own Skin" and "Life Isn't a Beauty Contest: How to Stop Competing." Inside, Oprah tells us she has made peace with her body. And yet there she is on the cover, smiling and hiding her body under a big, baggy shirt.

I know what Oprah is doing wearing that big, baggy shirt: She's hiding her body. We all have photos like that. I know that when you tie a sweater around your whatever-size-your-ass-is-is-fine-but-here-are-some-squats-you-can-try ass, it's not because you were too warm and you had no place to drop your sweater so you casually wrapped it around your waist. I don't care. I like Oprah this way. I think she's beautiful. I long to hear her say, "I don't know what is true. I know what is difficult. I know body issues are hard. I know they are not black-and-white. Maybe I'll just be a little fatter than I always hoped . . . and maybe that's okay."

If anyone can alter our self-image and our beauty standard, Oprah can. She's brought literacy, spirituality, and entrepreneurship to the masses; why not a new attitude about weight? The women in her studio audience look like me: big—in other words, perfectly average. But I never see plus-size models in her magazine. They put "regular" women in there, but no one who looks like any of the thousands of size 12's and 14's and 20's and 22's who go to Harpo Studios for some wise words and maybe a free book. I'm delighted that Oprah tells her audience to honor the spirit. I just wish that she, like each of us, wasn't so conflicted about the body that houses it.

Hooray for Hollywood?

Who knows if it's just a Freaky Friday situation, or if in light of 9/11 we're trying to get a grip on what's actually relevant to our lives. But size options are opening up all over the media. For example, *Hairspray* is the hit of Broadway, and its Tony-winning star Marissa Jaret Winokur was signed to a production deal at ABC. ABC also produced *Less Than Perfect,* a sitcom featuring plus-size lead actress Sara Rue (well, whatever they consider plus-size in TV-land. Still, it's a start!). The *New York Times* noted:

On a new ABC sitcom, *Less Than Perfect,* it is the heroine who looks more like Anna Nicole Smith than Ally McBeal—breaking what is perhaps one of television's last taboos . . . As the ideal feminine form keeps getting thinner, real Americans keep growing larger . . . The sudden embrace of the Rubenesque seems to span all across popular culture . . . movies, mass market fiction, romance novels, television soap operas, the fashion industry, advertising, and now prime time television seem to be accommodating that reality.

"Going into a crowded field, we thought it would be a plus to have a heroine who looked more like America," [said Susan Lyne, president of ABC Entertainment]. She noted that the hardest part was finding an actress larger than a size 4. "Casting was tough," Ms. Lyne said. "We auditioned a lot of people who were too close to the typical TV ideal."

Thankfully, Diane Bliss, an L.A.-based actress, has initiated the Screen Actors Guild Plus-Size Task Force, hoping to call attention to size discrimination in Hollywood writing and casting.

At the movies, *Real Women Have Curves* won multiple awards, and sleeper success *My Big Fat Greek Wedding* became one of the most profitable films of all time—even though there was nothing fat about it but the title. (You tell me, would it have made the same impact if it was called *My Big Greek Wedding*?) Kathy Bates bared her way to an Oscar nomination in *About Schmidt,* stealing the movie with her bravery and her brilliant performance. I just wish the filmmakers could have made her a sympathetic character instead of a caricature. (In the same movie, the audience sucked in its collective breath in horror when it saw a shot of an old woman's doughy armpit. Hello, what do you really think is going to happen to your body? Don't we know that's what bodies look like?)

Author Jennifer Weiner sold TV and film rights for her first best-selling book, *Good in Bed,* to HBO, and just did the same with her second, *In Her Shoes*. Both feature blessedly big heroines. In the music world, best-selling American Idol Kelly Clarkson dismissed the usual music-industry makeover with an *Us Weekly* cover story reading I WON'T STARVE TO BE A STAR: Curvy, confident, and with the No. 1 album, the singer, 21, tells *Us*: "You don't have to be 100 pounds to be beautiful." Inside the magazine Kelly says, " 'Who wants to die on a diet?,' she said. 'I eat like I've always eaten. If I want a frozen Ding-Dong, I'm damn sure going to have one.' "

Just so you know, Hollywood executives and production staff and publicists don't look like Hollywood stars (writers definitely don't). They look like all of us normal folks: fat, skinny, ugly, pretty, curly-haired. Some do look ultra-glam; and of course women working in Hollywood are also held up to a double standard that the men don't have to achieve. However, as plenty of execs still look like real people, they should feel ashamed and guilty of the product they promote. Columnist Liz Smith, who has always been an advocate of body acceptance, defended movie mogul Harvey Weinstein after a blistering media attack: "If Harvey Weinstein resembled someone like the slim, trim and handsome Bob Iger of ABC, nobody would be running around feeling perfectly free to blast him . . . Harvey is sometimes loud, aggressive and just plain plump. In a society overwhelmed with anorexic longings, Harvey's size alone makes it easy to give him a hard time."

Who knows if Harvey is or isn't a good guy; what we do know is that he's an easy target. Still, I'd like to see this "easy target" hire someone besides Gwyneth or Renée to star in his movies. Maybe providing us with semi-realistic stars will make his own vindication a whole lot easier.

The Hollywood defense, like the magazine defense, is always that the audience doesn't want to see reality; we want to see fantasy. Hmm, must be why all those REALITY shows are such a hit. My sense is that we want to see stuff that's good, not stuff that's crap. Good stuff is always worth seeing and spending money on. There must be an image between fantasy and reality that's less physically damaging for actors and less emotionally damaging for the audience. If we can't change the celebrity standard, then we need to create a second, more realistic reality standard. Or else let's adjust the aspect ratio of height to width on TV and movie screens, so everyone can look tall and thin but still eat lunch.

We think life would be a dream if we had tight abs and cut arms, like the stars on the cover of *Vanity Fair*. But all they do is complain about what a drag celebrity life is in the first place. Unrealistic beauty standards. No privacy. Fake friends. All drama all the time. If it's a trade-off between flashing cameras and the ability to go to the grocery store without causing a fuss, I'll take stretch marks over celebrity any day.

CHAPTER 11

The Fat Girl's Dance Card

Above all, in our culture being fat means you get no love, because you deserve no love. Being fat, and therefore failing to be the person you ought to be, probably could be, certainly will be one day (dammit), you have no right to receive any love—if you love yourself so little as to be fat.

—Richard Klein, *Eat Fat*

The feeling starts when you're a little kid. You know that you are . . . different, somehow, even if you can't put a finger on it. Your parents keep pushing you away from your natural inclinations, even though you can't figure out what's wrong with them.

By the time you get to high school, you know that you're cut from a different cloth. You have a hopeless crush on the cutest guy in school, but he won't give you the time of day. You hide from the other kids in the locker room, but they don't want to have much to do with you, anyway. You find solace in the arts. You become friendly with a couple of other misfits who seem to be in the same boat you are, but you shy away from them publicly because you're embarrassed by their company.

When you're alone, you indulge in your secret pastime, hoping no one will discover the truth. You pray to God that you will change, that this is a phase, that surely one day you can be like everyone else. You believe that if you really wanted to badly enough you would change, but you don't, so you're a sinner. Obviously there's something wrong with you, but deep down inside you know there's no "cure." You are doomed to suffer, doomed to be an outsider, doomed to be the subject of secret whispers and occasional obvious mockery. You try to wear regular kids' clothes, listen to their music, talk the way they talk, do the same things they do . . . but it's too late, because you are . . .

FAT.

That's right, Fat Girl, it's time to come out of the closet.

Stop hiding. Stop sucking it in. Stop dieting at work and gorging at home. Stop covering up. Stop staying out of swimming pools. Stop pining for cute guys who won't give you the time of day unless they need you to write a paper for them. Stop wishing for change. You're here, you're fat, get used to that! And develop your social life accordingly.

Fat Girls and Gay Guys

Growing up fat and growing up gay have pretty clear parallels. Fatness and gayness both seem to be a combination of nature and nurture, attitude and destiny. Some of us can fake it, some of us can try to avoid it, but when push comes to shove, fat girls and gay men are both rejected by the norm. We have to take ownership of our outsider status in order to succeed in a straight, skinny world.

Many of my gay male friends knew from the time they were

kids that they were gay. I've heard every stereotype in the book—they were fascinated with their mommies (Daddy was often distant or demeaning), they wanted to play Barbie instead of sports, they were more comfortable with girls than with boys. While many of them could "pass" for straight (or had to at least try to pass to avoid a world of trouble) into their adolescence, most had a hard time covering up their sexuality. Their sexual preference became obvious in the way they walked and talked, the clothes they wore, the kind of books they read. I know how hard it is to be a fat teenager; I can only imagine how tough it would be to be a gay teenager. I don't blame anyone for trying to conceal it. Somehow, our little gay/fat bat signals are tuned into each other. Luckily, the gay boy and the fat girl seek each other out to find comfort, acceptance, and the best glitter eyeliner on the market.

Our physical attributes give both of us away—I weigh too much, his walk is too swingy. We have the same taste in clothes (funky, adventurous), and the same taste in men (not a chance in hell). We both turn to pop culture for artistic outlets to help us make it through the tough times. We both audition for the high-school plays. As John Waters said, "The real reason I'm praying that *Hairspray,* the Broadway musical based on my 1988 movie, succeeds is that if it is a hit, there will be high-school productions, and finally the fat girl and the drag queen will get the starring parts."

We're both ostracized by the "in" crowd. That's not to say that the fat and the gay aren't popular or accepted or smart or outgoing or gregarious. In fact, we often are. But we aren't prom queen material (though we'd certainly be each other's toughest competition). We aren't winning varsity letters (except in debate, maybe). In high school, you know damn well that a huge part of your social status is based on your physical attraction as evaluated by the opposite sex. It's like one big round of Are You Hot or Not? Well, chances are if you're fat or gay, you can check the "not" column. So we take each other to the prom. Your high-school prom date evolves into your standard "and guest" invite at weddings.

We're both drawn to larger than life characters—divas and drama queens and superstars. Madonna, Barbra, Cher, J-Lo, Liza, Beyoncé. They are wildly sexy, they have great clothes and dramatic love affairs. They lead the lives we secretly want to live.

We also get portrayed in the media in a stereotypical way that's not really that close to our reality. Sure, there are flaming gay men just like there are raging fat women. But for the most part we're just doing our thing, making our choices, and wishing that life were just a little bit easier.

This is why fat girls and gay men seem to have a special bond. If *Will and Grace* were really true to life, then Grace would weigh about two hundred pounds. And you know that *Pretty in Pink* should have starred a size-16 chick. C'mon, Duckie is so gay! We both admire Wonder Woman, but for different reasons. We both wanted to be Olivia Newton-John in *Grease*. Princess Leia was our favorite character in *Star Wars*. We're both big *Buffy* fans. (Many people think that Samantha on *Sex and the City* is modeled on a gay man; I think Carrie is modeled on a fat girl.)

Fat Girls could really stand to take notes from gay men who have come out of the closet. They've found strength in numbers. They've created their own entertainment culture and businesses when the mainstream wouldn't have them. They've advocated for health, social, and discrimination reform. They build small communities where they can celebrate and play together. They often have to sit down and tell their families, "I'm gay, there's nothing you can do to change me, so you'll just have to learn to love me." Can you imagine saying that to your folks? "Mom and Dad, I'm fat. There's nothing you can do to change me. I know what's important and what's healthy, so please stop sending me stories cut out of newspapers with before-and-after photos. Please stop mentioning how much weight your neighbor's daughter lost on Jenny Craig. I'm not going to change. This is me. You're going to have to learn to love me the way I am."

Gay men and fat chicks can be as close as a romantic couple without any of the scary pressure of unknown sexual stuff. Hopefully, we are able to love each other without judging each other. That kind of acceptance continues throughout life if we make choices that are outside of the mainstream, like unusual living situations, marriages, adoptions, and lifestyles.

While many gay men can be very sensitive about a woman's extra flesh, they're not about to have sex with you. So they don't have to be scared or threatened or curious. They can hug and touch without fear on either end. Sadly, in some parts of the gay community, men can be very self-hating about their own bodies. They hold themselves up to an unattainable standard, just like we fat girls do. They have a fascination with achieving a certain body type, and a sense of failure when they can't or don't. Many look down on men who are fat, or old, or bald . . . all things that can't be helped.

I'd like to see fat girls embrace the word "fat" as the gay community has embraced the word "queer." I'd like to see us advocate for ourselves. We need to take legal action against discrimination and hate crimes. We need to hold the media accountable for our portrayal on TV. As gay men have done before us, we need to show that stereotypes of fat girls aren't true—we aren't all jolly, we aren't asexual, we aren't lazy, and we aren't all depressos zoning out in front of TV sets with ice cream melting down our chins.

Take a risk. Be defiant, be Fat, and be proud.

High-School Crushed

I was oblivious at the time, but now I remember how hard it was to get through high school as a fat chick. Back then I thought my body was just a stylish sack that carried my personality around. That was before I'd internalized everything that was wrong with my body, and therefore wrong with me. Of course, if I was in high school now, I'd use *Teen Vogue* as a cheat sheet to prove that I was a full-time resident in Fault City. But back in the eighties, hot chicks wore big hair and big sweatshirts, none of my friends saw modeling as a logical career choice, and getting a good score on your SATs was a much bigger accomplishment than developing flat abs to showcase your belly ring.

My high-school girlfriends were funny and skinny and stylish, but luckily not Heathers (phew). Every day in the cafeteria we'd slurp down soft-serve vanilla ice cream and chocolate-chip cookies. That was lunch. (And the government wonders why teenagers are getting fat.) Lunch didn't seem to linger on my friends' bodies the way it stuck on mine, but we never really compared ourselves to each other. We were smart and outgoing, and popular enough. We had lots of Boy Friends, but no real Boyfriends. It never occurred to me that the opposite sex would have more interest in my body than in my mind.

Whether it was stupidity or naiveté, it's what happens when your teenage daughter does not read nearly enough Harlequin romances.

We are so extraordinarily concerned about what everyone else thinks about our bodies that we make decisions based on not what we want, or what we think is right, but what someone else will think of us. So we often make the wrong decisions. Whew.

That's why Jordan, Captain of the High-School Football Team, can't love you, the fat girl, back. See, you're smart and beautiful and funny, but he's Jordan, Captain of the High-School Football Team. He's too worried about what everyone else thinks. He has standards to uphold.

I believe that when Jordan listens to you make that comment about William Faulkner in English class, or congratulates you on the banner that you made for the school dance, or laughs at the joke you made during lunch, some part of him thinks, "Ah, there's an attractive human female that I would like to mate with." Maybe he notices your curly hair, or your pretty smile, or your sparkly eyes. Maybe he notices that you're wearing sexy knee-high boots (with a spandex insert in them so that they can stretch over your calves). Maybe he notices your cleavage. Or your laugh.

But, like you, Jordan has a fragile ego. While he may think, "Hey, I'd rather roll around in the back of my dad's truck with Wendy, that plump human female, than with Christy, that skinny, snotty head cheerleader," he'd need maturity beyond his years to choose you over her. He has to consider The Contract. He has to think about what his asshole buddies may say in the locker room. He has to think about offensive strategy for Saturday's game. That's a lot for one seventeen-year-old

American boy to have on his plate. What Football Captain Jordan really wishes is for you to be skinny, so that he can date you and not Christy the Head Cheerleader, impress his friends, have fun, and win the game. Go, Team, Go!

Chances are he'll decide that it's just not worth the energy, and Christy is nice enough anyway, and it's what he's expected to do, it's what his dad wants him to do, and he's gonna just do it. I'm stereotyping all three players here (if you as a Fat Girl really want to be a cheerleader, I insist that you try out and use it all for fodder in your own book twenty years from now), but stereotypes do start somewhere.

Dating Drama

I have found that there are an inordinate number of Fat Girls who have mad crushes on Football Captains. Just like there are an inordinate number of Fat Executives who have mad crushes on Rick, the Head of Finance. And Fat Makeup Artists who have crushes on Zeke, the Movie Star. And Fat Interns who have crushes on Bill, the President of the United States. (Did I mention that the guys who break The Contract by going for a fat girl wind up getting a lot of shit for it? Like, their political leader gets impeached for having semi-sex with a fat chick?)

Unfortunately, high-school guys are just big ol' wusses, and it really doesn't get too much better as they grow up. Men get scared about taking risks. Which is such a shame, because Fat Girls are perfect candidates for loving, sexy, interesting, supportive relationships. We spend a lot of time watching friends from the sidelines. When you spend a whole life observing, you get really good at relationships from all that objectivity. Since you're rarely in the center of the love action, you listen to friends complain about how they haven't gone out on a date in three weeks while you chuckle to yourself. You see which ploys of attraction work and which don't. You watch everyone else make mistakes and do the dirty work for you. Men tend to tell you a lot of honest things about themselves because they take out the sexual component of talking to you. After all, you're fat . . . so you're asexual to them. Until they get really, really drunk. I'm not talking about all boys, I'm talking about a majority. And I'm not talking about all fat girls, either. Just the ones I know.

As a fat girl, you learn to live without the little touches of civility usually accorded to the fairer sex—sure, you're female, it's just that you're not fair. I'm talking about gentlemanly things like opening doors and lighting cigarettes. No one is flirting with you, so you do without. It hurts. You try to compensate by proving that you're strong—your girth is good for something. You can schlep your own bags, thank you very much. You don't mind reaching for the toilet paper on the high shelf, no problem. You're just as tough as any man. You can run, you can climb, you can carry it just fine. Which is the problem in the first place.

I used to have enormous crushes on pains-in-the-ass that never went anywhere. Pathetic. "Stop going for assholes!" I'd tell my friends, as I'd swoon over some arrogant dork. "Don't play games," I'd remind them, as I set up the game board for myself. "Don't let a guy treat you That Way," as I went ahead and let a guy treat me That Way. I have journals full of hopeless crushes, unrequited loves who would plot with me to get my best friend's attention while telling me what an awesome person I was. I've dated guys who loved me up in private but refused to introduce me to their friends—ashamed to be seen with me in public. Men who were too scared to be honest about their own weaknesses and would tell me that I was too "intimidating" to date. What a copout. Is it my size or my personality that's too intimidating for you? Would you like me to have *LESS* of a personality? Would you like me to be less of a person?

I have a litany of fabulous qualities—just like you, I'm smart and inquisitive and beautiful and funny. Too bad funny can't buy you love. A profile of cool fat-chick playwright Wendy Wasserstein in the *New Yorker* said it best: "While a sense of humor in a man is universally regarded as a good thing, a sense of humor in a woman is often thought of as a handicap—an unnatural growth that obscures rather than reveals her femininity. It often leads to popularity, but only rarely does it lead to intimacy. Wasserstein says, 'It's always "You'll love her, she's really funny," not "I'm *in* love with her, she's really funny."'"

I check out other superstar girls—fat and skinny and in-between—all the time, so I know what I look like when I have my shine on. Like Queen Latifah glowing at the Oscars. Or my friend Sam shaking her world-famous booty so hard on the dance floor that I have to step away and laugh. Or Deb washing raspberries for her kids. Or Kim opening gifts at her twenty-nineth-birthday party. I think of this gorgeous full-figured woman I saw recently swing into a dinner party. I looked at her and thought, "Wow, she is so beautiful . . ." And it occurred to me that I look a lot like her. People get confused when they hear me talking about this stuff, as if I think I'm not beautiful or attractive to men. I'm trying to tell you folks, it ain't me who has got the goggles on.

Maybe it's just that white guys have different standards of

attraction than other races. God forbid a white man be attracted to a woman as big as or bigger than he is—what an affront to his Neanderthal masculinity! But if I had a dime for every black guy who hit on me . . . I get lots of attention from guys who are nonwhite—or at least non-white-collar. I can't get in a cab without being hit on. I wonder, are white guys just snobs? Have men of color in America learned to expect sloppy seconds? Or do men from other cultures genuinely feel attracted to bigger girls?

Farewell to Fairy Tales

These days I'm much more interested in pursuing guys I find attractive than waiting around for them to hit on me. Ideally I like a tall, broad, Semitic-looking guy . . . big noses turn me on. But fat, skinny, bald, hairy, short, I'll take ya. I've gone out with men who have weird hair patches and breakouts and wrinkles and funky soft spots, too. I have yet to meet a six-pack live and up close. But that's us girls, right? We can be physically attracted to just about anyone. Can you imagine what would happen to the human race if we gave up on runty guys and only went for hotties? No way. Boy beauties freak me out. Double the narcissism, half the fun.

When it comes to personality, I insist on a kind man. A funny man. An educated guy who has enough cynicism to be smart, but not enough to throw off his value system. A guy with manners. A guy who turns on my mind before he turns on my body. I have a million qualified good-guy friends, but rarely has one ever wanted to date me. Why date me when there's a slightly less interesting (aka less intimidating) teeny little Jewess just off to my side? ("If only I could meet someone like you," they'll often sigh. Whatever!) Many people see that I'm over thirty and single and suggest that I drop any standards I may have, and simply find a mate IMMEDIATELY. Oh yeah, that always works out great.

If we expect men to establish new beauty boundaries, then I say we girls have to shake things up first. Please, I beg of you, reconsider the crushes on men who won't go for you. I say it to Fat Girls, I say it to Skinny Girls. There are exceptions to all kinds, of course; but generally, the more beautiful the man, the more fragile the ego, and the less of a chance that he's going to take a risk at loving a beauty who is outside the standards of the system. If you want to go for it, great, but you may end up doing a lot of work with a lot less to show for it. And if he is foolish enough not to see the glory of you in front of his big, brown eyes with the thick lashes that make you just melt, remember that it's truly *his* loss.

We're bred on fairy-tale visions of romance and true love. Cinderella starts us off and rules throughout our lives. The Prince can't see through her dusty outfit (i.e., her fat? her zits? her flat chest? her cheap shoes?) to know who she really is: his true love. She needs a "makeover" (i.e., bariatric surgery? Accutane? a boob job? Manolos?) to qualify. Even if he digs her makeover and declares true love, he still needs PROOF (that glass slipper) to stay in love with her. If she "changes" (i.e., gets old? wrinkled? fat?), he doesn't recognize her or love her anymore.

This is what we are taught to believe in. It's the same theme replayed in all of our favorite romance novels and blockbuster films (*Pretty Woman, Maid in Manhattan, My Fair Lady, Clueless,* any John Hughes movie ever . . .). You can't be acknowledged for who you really are. You have to go through a visible and major transformation to be desired, accepted, and loved. Then the spell can only last so long, so you'd better keep up those impossibly high standards, or plan to do it all over again. Hey, Prince Charming, don't you know it's still me? It was always me?

Some nights I'll go into a bar with friends of mine and look for straight guys (I know there are a few left). It takes just as much courage for me to hit on a guy as it does for him to hit on me; I'm constantly bracing myself for rejection. Every once in a while I'll score, but more often than not I don't. In a bar, looks are your calling card, and I understand that not every man is big enough to be attracted to a big girl like Yours Truly. When I end up going home in a cab solo, I feel bad for the boys in the bar instead of myself, because they aren't going to have the pleasure of spending time with me!

Now I look for my equivalent in the social hierarchy and get to work. That's the smart, funny short guy. Or the dry, witty guy with the receding hairline. Or the shy brainiac who could use a wardrobe makeover. These are our men. We don't see them as Prince Charmings because they don't see themselves as Prince Charmings. We know that we see ourselves as Sleeping Beauties, so imagine how they feel. They have the same insecurities that we Fat Girls have. So we both have to put in the extra work to get over the insecurity hurdles, build the friendships, and not be scared when love comes to town. Even a Fat Girl is entitled to live happily ever after.

CHAPTER 12

The Fat Girl in Bed

*Our generation certainly has been encouraged to grab life
by the balls, be super-independent, get a great education,
follow our dreams, kick ass, all that stuff, and I feel like I
woke up one day holding the golden ring and realized that
smart, sassy girls who accomplish a lot and have their
own cash and are independent are frightening to men. I
felt like, "Why didn't somebody tell me? Why didn't
somebody warn me?"*

—Madonna, "What It Feels Like for a Girl," *Interview*

Back a zillion years ago, before the sexual revolution, women
were repressed and life was easy. I'm sure there was a lot more
play going on than *Happy Days* would have you believe, but the
tables sure have turned. Now that we've won our sexual freedom, we've also run into some pretty big problems. The biggest,
of course, is that sex can kill us; our parents never grew up
fearing AIDS. Then there's all the fun of STDs and unplanned
pregnancies. It seems like unwanted advances and sexual molestation and rapes have also become all too common.

Society is now wildly vagina-centric—in all the wrong ways.
Instead of the Era of Repressed Virgins, women have entered

the Age of the Super Slut. It's not enough to be sexually active at an early age; you also have to experiment with multiple partners and be well versed in multiple orgasms, sadomasochism, voyeurism, stripping, blow jobs, erotic lingerie, public displays of affection, and barely there bikini waxes. Naturally, we do it all with a wink and a smile, and keep reading *Cosmo* to continually up the ante. I'm thrilled that women have the leeway for exploration and adventure. I think it's great that we can have all the fun that men have supposedly been enjoying for years. But this Madonna/whore switcheroo puts a whole lot of pressure on women in general, and on Fat Girls in particular.

Fat Fear

In my limited and nonscientific survey, fat girls get a lot less play than the average chick. Why is this? Well, first of all, if you're fat in adolescence, then you're hardly the pick of the litter. (Although there is a corollary to this—the Fat Slut—which I will address later.) Not your fault, it's just the way the cookie crumbles (often directly into your mouth). There's our anxiety about our bodies: We don't look like the idealized images we see of women in sexual situations, so we're afraid to put ourselves out there to put out.

Then there's the fear of mockery. I swear, if I hear "It's like fucking a fat girl" used as a punchline one more time . . . Working in comedy clubs, I'd hear it all the time. My face would burn. I was pretty sure that the whole room was looking at me. I used to just chuckle wryly along with everyone else, while inside I'd curl up in shame. I'd try to make my face look like, "See? I'm cool, I can laugh at myself." It's like going to the movies on a date and trying to figure out what facial expression to wear during an intimate sex scene. Look, I understand that standup involves equal-opportunity humiliation—the same guy would probably substitute "old" or "gay" or "Polish" for "fat" if it suited his needs.

Now that I'm a Fat Girl, though, I don't laugh. I don't pretend to look comfortable. Now I make my discomfort known. I'll go up to the comic after the show—especially if I know him (it's always a him). Of course, he's probably short or bald or alcoholic or pockmarked, 'cause if you're a hottie, you don't go into comedy. Hotties become movie stars, not standups. Hotties get series on The WB; standups get a special weekend slot at the Shits & Giggles Comedy Factory off I-95. Beautiful people don't need to hone their comedy skills to succeed in life.

Now I'll go up to this comic and say, "I didn't like your joke about fucking fat girls." He'll always stammer and get embarrassed, which is just fine with me. Then I'll say to him, "You just have to try harder. It's an easy joke. You're a talented guy. So why don't you think of something more clever next time?" Who knows if he'll actually change his act? But I bet he won't make a fat-girl joke without thinking about it first.

Here we are, getting the message from standups and magazines and movie stars and little brothers and friends that you are only sexually desirable if you look a certain way. It's taken me a long time to figure out that while almost every guy prefers to be seen with a supermodel, they're pretty much happy to get play with anyone. I've rarely met a man who feels like he has TOO MUCH vagina access. Once a man is in the moment, it really doesn't matter if you look like me or Mini-Me. The dude's more like, "Psych! I get to put my penis in a vagina! Hooray for me!"

Trying to Be a Fat Slut

The Fat Slut isn't all that different from the Skinny Slut. Both push themselves into sexual situations for compromised reasons, usually to compensate for poor self-esteem or body image. Seventeen-year-old Hannah Leach explored these reasons in a video-taped diary on a recent edition of ABC's *Primetime* about teen obesity:

Looking back at the tape, Leach—who is now a much happier 21-year-old, and 75 pounds lighter—was overwhelmed at the memories it brought back. She said she made the tape at a time when she felt "insignificant" and "not important"—and was using sex as a way to make her feel better about herself. She said her display on the tape was more about "self-hatred" and loneliness than sexuality—something that was reflected in a more recent edition of her video diary. "I want so badly to be loved by somebody," she said into the camera. "I just go through these things to make somebody love me, and I end up feeling like a f—ing whore afterwards." [Pediatrician Michael Rich of Children's Hospital, Boston] says weight problems often make teenage girls vulnerable to sexual exploitation. "They are perceived as being older and more mature than they truly are. That they are easy. That they are more willing to trade sex for affection than somebody who everybody wants because she looks like the front cover of a magazine," he said. Leach said she had no problem finding boyfriends: "I had something that pretty much every guy wanted. Whether I was 300 pounds or not, it didn't make a difference . . . Somebody wanted me. Somebody finally wanted me."

Do you recognize that pathetic feeling? I sure do. Back in high school and college, when it seemed like everyone else was sleeping around, I felt nervous and insecure. For me it wasn't concern about body-image issues as much as a general sense of fear of the unknown. To make matters worse, when I actually got up enough courage to have sex, I didn't feel the bells and whistles everybody talked about. My first few forays were hardly the blooming effervescence described in Judy Blume books and portrayed in Julia Roberts movies. Even my friends who were the high-school and college equivalents of Happy Hookers didn't seem all that thrilled with the sex they were getting. Sure, they'd have fun stories to tell during "I Never," but there was always a catch: She'd have to do it in a room with some other guy "sleeping" in the bed across from them. Or her date would get all huffy when she asked him to use a condom. Or he'd get his rocks off while she was left humiliation-heavy and orgasm free. Didn't really seem like a fair trade to me.

By the time I got out of school, I decided to ignore my qualms and force myself out there more frequently (note to self: "force" is not a great concept when thinking about sex). I'd bring condoms on first dates; I'd do my best at the end of an evening to score a one-night stand. I wanted to stack up those "I Never" tales, too. While this was supposed to be cool—I assumed it was what all my peers were doing—I secretly felt ashamed of myself. I never talked about it with my friends. It was all just too embarrassing.

Plus, I was fat. I'd live in fear that the guy lurking down below would suddenly lift up his head and scream, "*Ewww!*

You're fat and disgusting! What the hell did I just touch? Is that even a body part that other people have?" Worse, maybe he would keep his disgust to himself, and then share it with all his buddies the next day. I could picture the conversation: "And then I reached down, and it was like feeling a bowl of . . . I don't know, dough or something. I nearly puked!" And so on, and so on.

Now, I've been through some awkward moments. Everyone has weird concerns about their bodies. However, to allay your fears, I have yet to hear of anyone running a Fat Girl out of bed with the words, "Ew, get out of here, you disgusting fat fat fattywad." If you step past your own insecurity and see this scenario as at all likely to happen, here is my advice: DO NOT GET IN BED WITH THIS MAN. If you can't trust him to treat you with respect, then why on earth would you sleep with him? If you can picture him running to his buddies the next day to say how gross it was, then why are you putting his penis in your mouth?

In those years, I rarely came close to experiencing the kind of pleasure that I thought was my inherent right. Maybe I was doing something wrong. Maybe I was with the wrong kind of men. Maybe I was having sex instead of making love. I hoped if I was in a committed relationship, it would be different. It's not like the average hookup fulfilled my sexual needs—a quick order from Good Vibrations and two AA batteries could take better care of that in no time. It wasn't like it was bringing me closer emotionally to anyone. If anything, it was distancing. The element of trust shut down right when the lights went out. I was trying to be a Fat Slut, but I was really, really bad at it. I'm just lucky that I came out of it safe and alive.

Clean Sheets

At some point in my mid-twenties, it occurred to me that my sexcapades weren't working for me. According to magazines and movies and drunk friends, they were supposed to be wild and carefree and ooh-la-la. But I sure didn't feel that way. I always thought sex was supposed to be special and intimate. The first people I saw having sex were in the book *Where Did I Come From?* given to me by my mom. They were puffy cartoon people who didn't specifically look like my parents but were close enough for me to understand that they were representations of them. Nowhere in that book did it say that only skinny people were allowed to copulate. No chapter said that only those on the Zone diet were allowed to procreate or have a funky good time. I never associated sex with hard bodies or fake boobs. Just with parents. Just with people.

So I began to think about my body a different way. Maybe I wasn't just a disposable, disenfranchised penis holder. My body was special. I should treat it with more honor. I shouldn't just let any old dick dock there. So I stopped—not having sex, but trying to prove a point to anyone but myself.

I began to see how many of us were offering up our bodies publicly but paying a price for it privately. I was talking to a friend of mine who had been recently diagnosed with an STD. Even though she was using protection, she wondered how she'd tell the guy she was dating about it. I asked her, "Well, isn't that usually a part of the conversation you have with someone before you sleep with him?"

"What do you mean?"

"Like, don't you ask if he's been tested for AIDS?"

"Oh, sure, but it's not like I'll actually believe his answer. I mean, he could totally be lying—I don't know him well enough to know for sure."

But she sleeps with him anyway! Because it's what we do. We're independent, sexual, twenty-first-century women, and we deserve to get off! I think: If you don't know a man well enough to trust him when he says he's been AIDS tested, why are you sleeping with him? If you think some guy is going to mock your body when he's going down on you, why are you sleeping with him? Not worth it, ever. I know how much we long for affection; I know it's difficult to find the right partner; I know we deserve wonderful, uncompromised sex—which is next to impossible to find. Something's got to change—and I say we start with our attitudes.

I've stopped talking about how many men I've been with, or how long its been or hasn't been, or what went down (or didn't). I love to flirt, but it's just too compromising for me to be cavalier in bed. The sexual shift isn't ideal, but it beats the feeling of lying next to some man I barely know in the middle of the night, waiting for four more hours to pass by so I can wake him up and get him the hell out of my house.

I keep hearing this rumor that loving someone actually makes a difference, and I guess I'd rather hold out for that instead. Confront that fear instead. It's hard to tell if I'm saying this because I'm thirty-one or because I'm just me and that's the way it is right now. Maybe it's just a good old-fashioned defensive move, because I'm insecure about my body. I wish I could tell you I was madly in love with my kickin' bod, but that ain't 100 percent true.

I go through phases of incredible panic when a relationship falls apart. I'm sure that my Dream Date isn't going to come find me while I'm watching TV in my apartment. Half the time I feel like a Mengele baby, caught in some terrible lack-of-love experiment that's going to cause me permanent mental damage. But all I have to do is look at one of the girls who caved in to her panic—who married a guy as a defensive play, who is caught in a loveless relationship she is too afraid to break off, who had a baby to "fix things"—to know that I just have to hold my course and do the best I can do.

For the longest time I was convinced that no man could be attracted to me because of my big ass; now I've finally realized that my big mouth is a much bigger obstacle for any man to overcome. But baby, you gotta take all of me. I know a lot of gorgeous thin women who can't find a date, so there goes the full-on fat defense.

It's not just fat girls who feel insecure. All women feel it; men, too. Straight, gay, you name it. Married couples tell me that they aren't having sex because one or the other is embarrassed, or thinks that the other is embarrassed. Even Skinny Chicks feel insecure about their bodies, which is even more of a reason to get over it. If they're feeling shaky, what do you have to worry about?

Fat Versus Skinny in the Sack

There's no reason to assume that a Skinny Chick is better in bed than a fat girl. As a matter of fact, a recent study revealed that fat women have better sex than thin women. In an article headlined POUND FOR POUND, PLUMP WOMEN HAVE MORE FUN IN BED, researchers said that fat women had a better-quality sex life than thin women, asserting that "thinness is never associated with sexuality." This is shocking. Fat girls got it goin' on? It runs totally contrary to our vision of sex. In mainstream movies, in soap operas and on TV shows, we're used to seeing shadowed fingers running down a chest cut into muscled segments. We're used to seeing breasts that stand up like big cupcakes, perfectly formed and always the same size. I've never seen a stretch mark in a love scene, I've never seen a vein or a weird patch of hair on a big-screen body—but I see them all the time in real life.

We can throw these hypotheses around: Maybe a thin woman gets more play on average than a fat girl, and therefore has more experience, and therefore is better in bed. Or we can assume (not necessarily correctly) that a fat girl is more nervous, and more anxious to please, and therefore better in bed. Why not just go with the theory that everyone works at his or her own pace?

As I mentioned, men (and women) are socialized to think that one kind of body is sexually attractive and another kind is not. The ideal hot bod is tan and slender, with big boobs and long, tousled hair. She has a small forehead, big juicy lips, bright white teeth, and long dark lashes. Her body is hairless, like a little girl's. A foreign accent or a complete lack of English vocabulary is wholeheartedly welcome. So many men are getting their sexual education from pornography—even the light, "harmless" stuff that you see on late-night cable or on a magazine stand—that they have no visual vocabulary for the real, funky thing. It's a sexual fantasy built and sustained on repeated viewings of $9\frac{1}{2}$ Weeks. (By the way, if you do a search for "fat girls" on the Internet, you come up with tons of porn. Methinks the boys doth protest too much.)

We need to move away from the visual aesthetics of sex—which disappear the second the lights go off—and focus on the tactile sensation of it all. Smooth is all well and good. Muscles feel nice to the touch. But fat feels nice, too. It moves around, you can squeeze it in your hands. You can press your fingers into it and feel it shift. You can move your fingers along the tiny valley that your stretch marks form, one next to the other, all in a row.

When you lay your head down on a skinny or muscular stomach, it will feel hard, like wood. But when you lay your head on a nice, fleshy tummy, it cuddles your head like a pillow. I hate to inform men that natural big boobs—the ones that so many dudes long to touch—are big because they are full of fatty tissue. That's what makes 'em full. Not air, or silicone, or wishes from genies. Real breasts shift and puddle. The fat we hate so much is what actually feels so good.

Standup comedian and Ultra Fat Girl Mo'Nique, author of *Skinny Women Are Evil,* is super-sexy and not afraid to talk about it. She definitely supports the theory that black women are way more comfortable with their bodies than white women. She does a hilarious routine in which she says two fat people can't have sex with each other—there's just too much "shit" in the way. But I think there's all sorts of things to do, no matter what size combo platter you're dealing with.

There are men who fetishize fat women, especially supersized women. There are gatherings where obese women go to meet these men. I don't think this has as much to do with body image as it has to do with psychological drama. I don't want a man who just focuses on one part of me to get sexual satisfaction. It's sort of like a man who says he can only get turned on by a skinny girl. Hon, there's more to me than my body. At this point it's sort of an all-or-nothing deal.

Confront your fear of fat on your own body. Feel it, get comfortable with it. When you're with someone else, move him (or her) towards it. Ask him questions about it. Ask him to describe how it feels when he touches it. Have him compare it to different textures on your body—the fat parts, the lean parts, the muscled parts. Areas with hair and areas without. Take pride in your body. It carries you around all day. It heals you when it gets sick. It gives you pleasure. Maybe it has brought a child into the world. This body—your body—is an amazing thing.

It helps if you know how to love your own body. I do mean LOVE your body. I mean, masturbate. I'm still shocked at how long it takes women to figure this thing out. We're so embarrassed about our bodies, so "skeeved" about our periods and smells and hair, we can't even bring ourselves to touch ourselves. I've met very few women who learned to masturbate before they had sexual activity with a partner. I didn't. We have to wait for someone else to get us off. Good girls don't. What kind of sexual freedom is that? Meanwhile, boys have been rubbing up against doorposts and sniffing underwear and locking themselves in bathrooms since they were little. Come on, no one ever has to know. You aren't going to get so hooked that you'll never want a partner. And you aren't going to get so used to it that you'll never come with someone else. That's all malarkey so that you won't start thinking that men aren't necessary . . . goodness, it's some sort of femi-Nazi nightmare! I say every girl should get a nice vibrator for her Bat Mitzvah or Sweet Sixteen.

Oh, just plunge into the deep end of the fat pool. Touch it, feel it. It's not easy, but what the hell—you can't hide from it. I know that we think sex is supposed to look like some sort of Soloflex commercial. Forget the strategic lighting and the "I'll keep my bra on, but my panties off," as gravity pulls this up and that down. Just plunge in. Your partner knows that you aren't going to hop into the sack and morph into Halle Berry. Be careful if you fake 'em out too badly with all the control-topping and minimizing. Sure, men have been surprised that my big boobs don't stand up and say hello, because they've mostly seen breast implants instead of real boobs. But not one has ever said, "Your boobs are dipping into your armpits. I'm outta here." They're just like, "Oooh, boobs." They're men. They spend all their time working to get this close to you. Trust me, they're not going to get all choosy when paradise is staring them in the face. Forget the strategically placed T-shirts, the artfully twirled sheets. Stop rushing to be in darkness. This is your body, baby. Show it off. Take some pride. And remember: If you can't trust your partner—man or woman—then it simply isn't worth it.

CHAPTER 13

Shopping and Style

You can't stop my happiness
'Cause I like the way I am
And you just can't stop my knife and fork
When I see a Christmas ham
So if you don't like the way I look
Well, I just don't give a damn!
—"You Can't Stop the Beat,"
from *Hairspray*

Fat Girls have a lot of consumer needs that are not being met. Like knee-high boots, for example. Sure would be nice to find a pair at Bloomingdale's or Macy's that fit over my well-muscled calves. From what I hear, women of all sizes without stick-thin legs are looking for them, too. We've got the cash, we want to spend it, so why isn't Doc Martens or Nine West making them for us?

Speaking of muscles, is it too much to ask for a sporting goods or lingerie store to carry sports bras or exercise clothing in a size 12 or larger? America can't wait to supersize my fries, but when I want to downsize my thighs I have to special order from a catalog or website (www.junonia.com is a great one), but they still don't give me the support or shape I need.

I'd like to buy a bra at Victoria's Secret. But I can barely find a DD, let alone the E that I need. I appreciate that the Gap and Old Navy are now making 16's, 18's, and 20's. But could you order more than one pair per store? Statistics suggest that seven out of ten women buying at the local Gap will be grabbing at that size 12 or larger.

We'd also like to ride in airplane seats that actually accommodate the typical American tushie. If skinny people have a problem with a fat thigh spilling over onto their side of the armrest, then tell the skinny people to buy an extra seat instead of punishing Fat Girls for someone else's prejudice. Southwest Airlines—this means you.

Please Don't Fall into My Giant Vagina

See? Lots of needs for my size market! So you can imagine my delight the first time I saw a commercial for the Always Maximum Protection maxipad. I was pumping up and down on the elliptical trainer at the gym when I first caught it. A big beautiful blond woman cooed about Always Maximum Protection with Flexi-Wings, a maxipad designed especially for women sizes 14 and up. She wondered if I knew that most maxipads are designed for a size 6 or below.

I stopped pumping and started thinking. First: "Cool! Finally a company understands that I belong to a special market with special needs!"

Then: "Do my special needs really include a plus-size maxipad?"

There's no biological connection between the size of my body and the heaviness of my menstrual flow. So I have to think that Always Maximum Protection must not be designed for a heavier flow, but for a wider diameter of protection. In other words, Always is selling me an extra-large pad for my extra-large underwear. Ah.

It definitely looks different than the other pads. You know the Always Maximum Protection when you see it in the drugstore. You'll find the panty liners, and the minipads, and the maxipads, and then you'll wonder why someone left a box of Huggies on the shelf. Hon, those aren't Huggies. That's the Always Maximum Protection maxipads.

Can you say "offensive"? Just because I wear a size 14 or up, I don't run around in a giant pair of granny panties. That lame image has been the punchline of one too many adolescent comedy flicks. I wear sexy, fitted panties in a wide variety of colors and styles. Sure, my skivvies have a wider waistband than that of the size 6 girl, but the strip of cloth that is pad-coverable is pretty much the same minimal width in any pair of panties (except the thong—but that's a different torture for a different day). It doesn't matter if you wear a size 2 or a size 22; the strip is the strip. There ain't a lot of give there.

A press rep at Procter & Gamble, the parent company of Always, assured me that the product was created in response to demand from a plus-size consumer Web site. It has sold so well that other companies are going to knock it off. So maybe there are some of you out there who want or need a wider product like this one. But can you say "uncomfortable"? I felt like I had a throw pillow stuffed down my pants when I walked around wearing the Maximum Protection maxipad in a road test.

I'm curious: If Always assumes that a bigger girl needs a bigger pad, what about petite women? Like Sarah Jessica Parker's size 0 body? Will Always be creating some little Q-tip-looking minipad that she can delicately stick in her ultra-narrow panty strip to accommodate her teeny-weeny va-geeny?

I don't mean to knock the great strides that have been made in panty-liner technology. For example, you can now buy black panty liners. But they are made for black underwear, not for black women.

There's no correlation between dress size/body size and genitalia size. You'd never assume that all plus-size men need plus-size condoms for their plus-size penises—though I'm sure they wouldn't mind if you did.

Putting the general size issue side, I'm insulted by the very creation of this product, because it screams, "Hey, you Fat Girl! Here's a plus-size pad for your plus-size vagina!"

The truth is, while I am a definitely a plus-size woman, I do not have a plus-size vagina. I have a regular-size vagina. I may wear bigger pants than other women do, but our internal organs are all pretty much the same size.

It's not like you gain and lose weight in your vagina. Like, some women carry weight in their thighs, and others carry weight in their butts—and some women carry their weight in their vaginas? No. Do you think Carnie Wilson had some great big Grand Canyon—like vagina and now, after gastric bypass surgery, she's got some itty-bitty little slice of vagina? Nuh-uh.

See, I have enough problems without Procter & Gamble implying that I've got some sort of big, fat, crazy vagina down there that's going to swallow you up if you get too close. Fat Girls have worked too hard to get beautiful, sexy clothes designed to fit our beautiful, sexy bodies. When we dress stylishly, and walk proudly, and speak loudly, we affirm that we wear a bigger size. But sexually, we're just like other women. We have the same parts, pleasures, concerns, and needs.

So please, don't sell me an extra-large spoon, because I don't have an extra-large mouth. Don't invent an extra-thick stick of deodorant, because my armpit acreage is perfectly average. I don't need extra-wide Charmin to wipe my extra-fat ass. And I won't buy an extra-wide maxipad, because I have a perfectly normal vagina. Don't get me wrong, my vagina is fabulous. It does cool stuff. But size-wise, it's just a regular old standard-issue vagina.

Thanks, but no thanks.

Shopping Strategies

One of my favorite girly-girl pastimes—besides group mani-cure/pedicures, or manwatching over mochaccinos—is an all-day shopping spree. Retail therapy cures most of my ills, especially when I have some cash in the old bank account. But lately I've been heading home from the spree empty-handed, or at the most clutching a teeny little bag with a MAC lipstick or a pair of earrings in it. It's always one of my gal pals who winds up juggling a couple of Bloomingdale's Big Brown Bags while trying to catch a cab.

The truth is, as much as I love group shopping, I can't bear one more minute of skulking around the home-décor aisles at Anthropologie. While my friends are trying on tank tops and denim skirts, I'm checking out colorful crystal doorknobs for the eleventh time. There's nothing for me to wear in Anthro-pologie. Or Urban Outfitters. Or J. Crew. Or any of the zillions of mall stores that my friends like the most.

Don't get me wrong—I've got lots of shops on my hit list. But I never drag my friends with me to Lane Bryant. Or make them look at jewelry they won't buy while I'm in the dressing room at

Ashley Stewart or August Max Woman. It's always a solo trip to the top floor at Saks, or the basement at Bloomingdale's, or the aisles of Macy Woman. I'm not embarrassed by my size; it just doesn't occur to me to take a friend to a store where they can't participate in the fun. I'm so good at covering up my shopless malaise that my friends probably don't realize I can't buy clothes at their favorite stores.

I had a memorable shopping experience at a swanky boutique in Beverly Hills. I'd always loved the window displays and poked my head in to . . . well, to look at jewelry. The second I snuck in, an elegant saleswoman whisked me to the back of the store, where she had racks and racks of clothes identical to the ones on the floor, but all size 1X–3X. American Express and I both had quite a little fiesta that day. It didn't occur to me until after I split to ask why my size clothes were quarantined in the backroom. Did the owner want to keep big women out of his aisles? Did the store only cater to a tiny (heh) plus-size clientele?

My dream is to walk into a store where my friend can pull an 8 from the front of the rack and I can pull an 18 from the back. Wait—change that—my dream is a store where I can pull an 18 from the front and she can pull the 8 from the back. It's slowly coming true! I've found some cute stuff at Old Navy and The Gap lately. But the size 18 pants at Old Navy are the equivalent of the 9 1/2 shoe at Nine West: gone in a flash. (You'd think for a store with a "nine" in the name, they'd have a lot more pairs of size 9 or 9 1/2 shoes.) By the way, my friend Martina, who is six feet tall, says that the "long" sizes at The Gap are "a joke." She told me, "The pants are always way too short and any sleeves are even shorter."

We can't just bide our time, daydreaming on an ottoman at Banana Republic while everyone else has fun. We have to be vocal if we're going to see more change. We have to . . . well, I have to put my money where my ass is, and that's in stores and mags that support a tush that's bigger than size 12. So here are a few new strategies to make life a little easier for me and for other Fat Girls.

• Say It with Your Wallet

People may not understand the politics of fat, and they may not understand the complications of gaining and losing it. But one thing that every business and magazine and store understands is the bottom line. There are a helluva lot of Fat Girls out there, and we spend a lot of money. So we have to start funneling it toward brands that support us, and stop giving it to brands that don't.

That means you stop giving *Vogue* all of your attention when there are other mainstream magazines that are opening up to us a bit. *Glamour* and *Marie Claire* have often placed plus-size clothing alternatives in their pages. *Glamour* even included a full-page spread of Mia Tyler seductively lounging in a bikini in a recent issue; readers' letters clamored approval. As I mentioned earlier, I was pretty sure I spotted an airborne pig last spring when I opened up *Vogue* and spotted an editorial spread with Kate Dillon. Sure, they posed her next to a mini-man to emphasize her size, but you and I both know that Anna Wintour never thought she'd see the day. Kate was the first plus-size model to pose in *Vogue*'s 110-year history.

In today's economy, what magazine or designer can resist wanting to make more money? In Great Britain, London's Marks and Spencer made a size 14 (American size 10) their new base size. In South America, Reuters reported, "Argentina's Senate passed a bill on Wednesday night to require clothing manufacturers to make clothes that fit women of all sizes amid complaints that stores stocked apparel only for thin women."

Finally Donna Karan, Tommy Hilfiger, and Ralph Lauren allowed smart business sense to trump possible snobbery and started making clothes for us. Liz Claiborne recently created yet another plus-size line. Keep 'em coming. In 2000, sales of plus-size women's clothes exceeded $32 billion, and from 2000 to 2002 sales of clothing from sizes 10 to 20 increased 18 percent. Lane Bryant alone made over $1 billion in 2002. No wonder the plus-size CEO of Hot Topic, Inc., a retail and Internet clothing outlet that makes $443 million annually, launched Torrid, a size 12–26 clothing line for teen girls that has been a blazing success.

Remember that part of this is actual dollars and sense, and part of it is PR perception. For example, as much as you think every woman except you is sauntering around in a Victoria's Secret demicup, Vicky sells only one third of the lingerie that Hanes does. "The greatest market share of the lingerie business, or intimate apparel as it is known on Seventh Avenue, belongs to Sara Lee, which owns Hanes Her Way; Playtex apparel, maker of the Cross-Your-Heart Bra; and Just My Size, a line of undergarments providing coverage for plus-size women, among other brands devoid of any frisson. Sara Lee's under-garment division has sales roughly triple those of Victoria's Secret." Hanes—not as glamorous, but clearly the bigger, better business. Hanes Just My Size clothing caters to the 12-plus market. So either Vicki can start making me thongs or else I'll swing over to justmysize.com.

Get out there and support designers who make lines speci-fically for you and me. Richard Metzger. Marina Rinaldi. Anna Scholz. Size Appeal. High Class Cho. I.N.C. Donna Ricco.

Encourage straight-size friends to buy at stores with plus-size lines and designers. Oprah once interviewed designer Cynthia Rowley, pressing her to make clothes that real women could wear. Cynthia said that manufacturing issues prevented her from making sizes higher than 12. She promised Oprah that she would try to change, but when was the last time you bought a size 16 Cynthia Rowley peasant blouse?

Don't worry, there are still plenty of designers waving their prejudice flags high enough for everyone to see. Like Arnold Scaasi, for example, who had this recent exchange with the *New York Times*:

"I make couture clothes for very rich and thin ladies," he said.

Why only thin?

"They take care of themselves, they exercise constantly, they have their faces, stomachs, and hips done. And they look great and they are very intelligent."

It seems to us that men can get away with having a distinguishing belly.

"I have never seen a distinguishing belly in my life," Mr. Scaasi said.

Mr. Scaasi has a bit of one.

"I am 65 years old and that is what happens, and life goes on and you drink vodka," Mr. Scaasi said.

What can I say, Fat Girls? Pour the guy another shot!

• Speak Up

When stuck in a straight-size store, I take advantage of my friends' dressing-room time to try something I call "If Not

Now, When?" That's when I ask the store manager, "When will you be getting plus-size clothes in here?" Maybe she can't do much in the moment, but imagine if she hears a chorus of full-bodied voices . . . I go into Victoria's Secret all the time to do this. Anthropologie. J. Crew. Urban Outfitters. C'mon, companies, it's just more cash for you.

• Shop for Fat Clothes with Skinny Friends

Another strategy is called "Equal Time for Different Size." It means saying to my girls, "Hey, can we stop in here a sec?" when we pass by Lane Bryant or Avenue or Torrid. Or inviting them along to one of Manhattan's less-than-central neighborhoods where I find my best 14-plus loot.

Shop Till You Drop

Now that you know how to shop, the big question becomes what to buy. I've finally figured out what clothes work for me. I'm far from being a fashion icon, but I know how to dress to flatter my shape. Great fashionistas are firm believers in getting clothes tailored to fit perfectly. I have a bag of style statements that I keep meaning to take to a seamstress (that is, once I find a seamstress), but somehow that bag never moves out of the bottom of my closet. The legendary style icon Sean Puffy Puff Daddy P. Diddy Combs once said, "Fashion is about leaving on your jacket and tie when other people are too hot to bother." Somehow, my jacket always ends up balled on the floor, and I'm shvitzing anyway. Inspiration versus perspiration, always the great leveler.

Here are some suggestions for style success for those who may think they curve and swerve in all the wrong places.

• Wear Clothes That Fit

There's no reason for a Fat Girl to hide her body when she can flaunt it instead. I can pretty much guarantee that whatever you think is a little too tight on you is more flattering than the dumpy outfit you wear when you have your period. Buy clothes that fit. Hunt down a line of clothing with a "fit model" who is built the way you are. Most labels choose a model as their example size 14, or 16, or 18, and so on. You just need to find the one that has your body type. For example, Lane Bryant has a fit model with an hourglass figure like mine. But Old Navy uses someone who is smaller on top and wider at the hips, because their clothes hang on me at the waist and squeeze me on top. Try stuff on. Bring an honest friend to shop with you. Forget the size on the tag; don't worry about what the label says. If it looks great on you, it looks great. Go for fitted, not tight. There's nothing worse than watching a woman constantly readjust herself. Every once in a while, fine, but to be tugging all day or have seams cutting into you . . . why punish yourself? Buy one size up. That goes for everyone: a hard fit is a hard fit, whether you have a big body or a little one.

• Dress for Success

You will always look better dressed up than down. You will always look smarter in a business suit than a sweatsuit. You will always look sexier in a silk skirt than a denim skirt. Extra effort pays off. When you look good, you feel good; when you feel good, you project confidence . . . you know the drill. Pull a princess move—dress up and bag the prince. Every year I swear that I'll learn to be a lady who wears high heels; then December rolls around, and I'm still clomping around in combat boots. Keep on trying, I guess.

• Don't Buy "Aspirational" Clothes

Nothing annoys me more than a woman who buys clothes that are too small for her in the hope that they will motivate her to lose weight. Never works, girls. Only makes you feel bad. Get rid of that size 8 pencil skirt that you're never going to wear. Why waste the money when you could buy a beautiful outfit that you could wear today? Only buy clothes that fit you NOW. Don't worry about tomorrow, let's just try to get through today.

• If It Works, Buy It in Every Color

If you find a sweater with a great fit at the right price, buy it in every color. If you find a pair of pants that you love, get them in every pattern. I find that each season I find a sort of uniform for myself that looks great on me, then I mix and match. This past winter it was wide-legged cuffed pants from Lane Bryant and a black knit sweater from I.N.C. Found a great pair of boots and wore that look all the time. Always felt confident and looked smashing.

• Develop a Signature Style

Some women are fashion chameleons, but I've always thought there was something cool about a style signature. Sometimes a look is just so perfect that there's no reason to change it. I've been wearing a black bob haircut with blunt bangs and red nail polish and lipstick since I was in high school. I love it. I think I look awesome. Every time someone convinces me to try something new—to go curly, for example, or try nude lip color—I regret it. This hair, these lips, these nails are me.

• Invest

Every time I see a price tag on a $3,000 jacket or a $500 pair of jeans I get sick to my stomach. Who could spend that much money on one piece of clothing? However, there is a reason why designer costs way more than the cheapies at Strawberry. The cut is better, the material is higher quality. It shows in the fit. It is worth investing in a great coat—and it doesn't have to cost thousands of dollars. It is worth investing in a perfect pair of black pants. It is worth hunting down a great black suit that fits you like a dream. You will look fierce. You will wear it forever. You will get a lot of use out of it. Your pleasure in wearing it will be about even with the value of that gorgeous, well-cut, tailored, long-lasting item. At the same time . . .

• Go Cheap

There are some items that are just not worth the money. Basics. Tank tops, jeans, T-shirts. Save your cash for something else. Go to cheap-ass stores that sell cheap-ass clothes that you can wear twice and throw away, like H&M. Get a pair of shoes at Payless to match a one-time outfit. Save your cash for the really good gear.

• No Camouflage

I'm not talking about military gear; I mean the sweater tied over the butt. The cardigan pinned into place. The peripatetic pashmina. Your camouflage ain't working. It's screaming that you don't feel comfortable with a part of your body. Either get something that fits your body the right way, or get rid of it.

• Play Up Your Favorite Features

I have beautiful cleavage. On New Year's Eve, my rack looked so great that even women were coming up to compliment me. Guys kept dropping stuff on the floor, and I was happy to bend over and pick up their cocktail napkins to give them a peek. On the other hand, sometimes I carry what looks like a seven-month pregnancy in my abdomen. So I'll pass on the belly ring. I buy a lot of low-cut clothes, a lot of V-necks. I don't wear a lot of cut-off shirts. I go for what works, and what works always gets noticed way more than what doesn't. If you really, really hate your body, then girl, play up that—don't you know it—pretty face of yours.

• Consider Color

I love black. I own tons of black, and I wear it all the time. But I'll be damned if I don't look good in bright colors, too. Every once in a blue moon, take a chance on a purple shirt or a red dress. Don't fade into the woodwork all the time.

• Build a Foundation

When I had the pleasure of attending the Oscars, I wore the world's most beautiful gown by Richard Metzger. Chocolate brown, beaded, tight. Va-va-voom. Like Morticia Addams, but in brown. Guess what Richard made me layer under there? Foundation garments. Not just control-top panty hose, not just a minimizer bra, but a virtual body armor of Lycra. Where one garment created a roll, he layered another one over it to smooth it out. I could barely move. Forget bending over, forget peeing. But hot damn, I looked so fierce. It was me—I was big and bodacious, but I cut quite the sexy silhouette. This is just to say that the women you see walking down the red carpet don't come by all of it naturally. Their thighs touch, their tummies tumble—unless you're Nicole Kidman. But nine out of ten are wearing foundation garments under the glamour! This tip directly opposes my point about being comfortable, but for a special occasion it's worth it to be you, just sucked in. Even on a daily basis, I love to wear control-top hose (I swear by Berkshire opaques in the winter or Spanx in the summer) just to keep it all together.

• Bone Up on Bra Basics

Okay, Fat Girls need to learn how to wear bras. *All* girls need to learn how to wear bras. It is estimated that 75 percent of all women are wearing the wrong-size bra—which not only looks rotten (double boob, anyone?) but puts us at risk for back and shoulder pain, poor posture, and breathing problems, especially when you've got big plus-size titties. A woman who wears a D cup is carrying fifteen to twenty-three pounds in her over-the-shoulder boulder holder. We put them on wrong. We're spilling out over the top, the back is riding up to our necks, the nips are all puckery and weird. Get thee to a real lingerie store. Not a department store, not Victoria's Secret, but a store with big old ladies with facial hair who get in the dressing room with you and grab you and make you feel uncomfortable. They will put a bra on you that feels too tight. They will put a bra on you that fits. You will walk out of there thinking you look like a Fembot, but that is the right look for you. If you got big boobies, work 'em. If you got tiny teats, show them off. But for goodness sake, wear the right kind of bra. They'll tell you to hand-wash them in Woolite, but I'd like to find a woman alive who actually does that.

• Make a Saleslady Your Friend

If you find a saleswoman who helps you out, who has good taste, who has a good personality . . . pursue her. She will be especially helpful at a department store, and it costs you nothing. Let her know what you like and dislike. Have her keep an eye out for styles that might appeal to you or for sales that might appeal to you even more. Ask for her name. Send her a thank-you note. Tell her manager that she does a great job.

• Pretend

Style is a total mindgame. Here's an example: You can walk in a building with a sign-in list. If you saunter past the counter like you know where you're going and can't be bothered, no one bugs you. But if you sneak in and look like you're clueless, I guarantee that the guard is going to make you sign in. Same with style. If you act gorgeous and confident, all the dummies around you will compute, "She's gorgeous and confident." They don't need to know that your underwear is dirty and your stocking has a hole in it and your skirt is nipped together with a safety pin. You know when you go to a party and a woman walks in who turns your head? She's just vibing away. Maybe she's traditionally gorgeous, maybe she's not, but we project to people what we want them to think about us.

• Season's Greetings

Put away clothes that are out of season. When you bring 'em back out after six months, you'll have forgetten all the stuff you had. It's like finding a whole new wardrobe.

• Stand Up Straight

You've been so embarrassed to be in your big body for so long that you're used to hiding. You try to make yourself look smaller by rolling your shoulders down and leaning and hiding behind tables. Stop that, already. Everyone knows how big you are. *You* know how big you are. No one gives a shit. Stand up straight. Support your back. Look proud. Look entitled. You are.

• Practice Your Walk

I am often shocked to look in a mirror and discover that I am walking like a fat girl! Positively waddling along, feet slapping the pavement! What's that all about? First, I have to think what I want to project when I'm walking down the street. How about "Confident but not thinking about it"? Then I try to translate it into my walk. If I'm in an anonymous area, I'll practice the Sexy Yet Alluring Walk or the Carefree and Fabulous Walk. I'm trying to practice them so much that they become natural.

• Accessorize, Accessorize

Most fat girls have a love affair with shoes, makeup, jewelry, and accessories. I swear by these indulgences. They always fit. They make me feel more me. If your clothes are making you feel crappy, then by all means buy yourself a pretty eye shadow, or a watch, or whatever it takes for you to represent. Spend on facials or grooming. Get those eyebrows done; get a stunning haircut or color. Spend money on manicures and massages; treat your body with luxury and respect. Use beauty treatments and pretty things to enhance your self-worth and confidence. Big diamonds look better on big women.

• **Get Your Smell On**

Helps to smell great. My favorite scent is Opium, by Yves Saint Laurent—an oldie but a goodie. I always think that a Skinny Chick can't carry off a fierce fragrance like that one. It's another way to give your presence a personal signature.

Now, a Note About the Prom

I wore a custom-created two-piece suit that looked hot on me (and would have looked equally hot on Joan Collins) to my high-school prom in 1989. There was no way a Jessica McClintock moment would have flattered me, even if I could find one in my size. I'm happy to say that there is a lot more plus-size formal wear out there now than I had in high school. Why on earth would you want to wear what everyone else is wearing? Be a standout on that dance floor when "Open Arms" starts to play.

And a Note About Bridesmaid Dresses

The only bridesmaid dress that looks good on a fat bridesmaid is . . . no bridesmaid dress. It's 2003. There's no reason for you to look like crap next to a bunch of skinny minnies. Your friend the bride is not going to find an outfit that looks good on you; that's not her job. Her job is to look better than you do. When my friend Emmy asked me to be a bridesmaid, I told her that I would be honored to . . . but there was no way I would go strapless for her. "I love you," I told her, "but on the big day I want to feel happy for you and not embarrassed for myself." Of course, Emmy picked a dress that I would never pick for myself. She also told me to go ahead and wear a shawl over it. She also told me that I could change into my own look for her party. I was so pleased with her generosity on that note. What if your friend, unlike mine, is a big asshole? What if she says, "I don't want you to wear a shawl, I'm afraid you'll look different than everyone else?" Assure her most pointedly that you already do look different than everyone else. A true friend will never make you feel like shit, even on her wedding day.

Finally, a Note About Bridal Gowns

Why is a woman's self-esteem punished when she goes shopping for a wedding gown? Just like Skinny Chicks, Fat Girls would like to try on sample-size wedding dresses that don't cloak them in humiliation. If you wear above a size 10, forget it. Even a size 4 girl has to try on size 8 samples. What's with that? If it's the happiest day of your life, shouldn't it work the opposite way? If the labels are going to be all mucked up, you should be able to try on a size 12 dress that's labeled size 8. Okay, that's next on the agenda.

Luckily, the wedding industry is beginning to recognize that—egads!—men even want to marry fat chicks, and fat chicks are going to need something to wear. Do a little research on the Internet. Find a seamstress who will work from scratch. Don't put yourself through the torture of going to some big bridal store that will make you squeeze into a size 4 sample, then charge you more "because you'll need so much extra material." Don't think that you have to look like every other bride. I don't understand the big poufy princess wedding-dress thing that happens to women. It's the twenty-first century. Chances are you aren't a virgin and don't need to wear white, the least flattering color in the universe. Chances are you don't need to spend thousands of dollars on a dress that you're only going to wear once. You are a special individual; you're getting married because your partner loves YOU for being YOU. So be yourself, not Bridezilla.

FYI, I plan to wear red on my wedding day.

CHAPTER 14

R-e-s-p-e-c-t

We cannot be kind enough or thin enough or generous enough, we cannot be successful enough or attractive enough for those who abuse us to stop abusing us. We cannot make anyone love us. We cannot change anyone. It is not our job to hurt someone who has hurt us, to change someone who is self-destructive, to convince someone who doesn't love us to love us. As long as our well-being and self-worth are dependent on those around us, we are children hanging on our father's affection, waiting for our mothers to call us "darling," our teachers to tell us we are smart, our friends to include us in their clubs, we are waiting, waiting for enough kindness to break open the tight bud of our hearts.

—Geneen Roth, *When Food Is Love*

It's one thing when a nefarious business is making cash off of you. That's great motivation for diet pushers. But what about parents, best friends, spouses, siblings? Those people who are supposed to love us unconditionally? Why can't they love us just the way we are?

It's Only Because I Love You

You generally want the best for your children. Your goal is to raise them into the best possible candidates for good matehood, so that you can continue the race, and your special seed will continue on into eternity. So you try to keep them clean and smart and healthy and, ideally, beautiful. Because you know in this marketplace beauty sells, and a fat little glutton may be your dream child, but that kid is going to go through hell in the fourth grade unless you do something about it. You just want them to be HAPPY.

It is our parents and families and friends who love us most, who have the most invested in us, and who have the strongest desires (objectively and subjectively) to see us succeed in the world. Success means health and happiness; it means financial security; it means creating a family of your own. Unfortunately, parents think that to accomplish a lot of those things, you get a better shot when you're thin and pretty. The constant criticism and commentary about weight is the most painful when it comes from Mom and Dad. If "you only hurt the ones you love," then they are the professionals at bringing the pain. It's always put in a context like this:

- "I just want you to be happy."
- "You'd be happier if you were thinner."
- "I'm worried about your health. You'd be healthier if you lost weight."
- "It's because I care."
- "It's important for your health."
- "I know what's good for you."
- "I lived through this myself, and I know what it's like."
- "You'll be more attractive."

- "I did what I could—I just don't understand this."
- "I'm doing this because you don't seem to be able to do this yourself."
- "What will [fill in the blank] think?"
- "I just want the best for you."
- "I'm doing this because I love you."

It's all so legit, so heartfelt, and usually comes from a true desire to help. But to all those loving parents and brothers and sisters and friends, I ask:

- "Do you think I got fat just to upset you?"
- "Do you think that I can exist as a human being in 2003 and not know about dieting and weight loss and exercise?"
- "Do you honestly think that, given a choice, I would choose this body?"
- "Do you think that if I could change this, I just wouldn't bother?"
- "Do you understand that this is about me and not about you?"

The best possible thing anyone who loves us can do to help us is this: Learn to love and accept us AS WE ARE. We will not change for you. We *cannot* change for you. We don't have to change for you. If you love me, tell me you love me. That's all I need to know.

Conditional Love

I've finally been able to figure out that the people who really love me also really want me to meet someone special, and they probably think I should lose weight to make it happen sooner. I tend to believe that's because they want me to be happy, and they believe that a man will make me happy. But happy is priority number one.

When my friends in the comedy world were starting to get some little gigs here and there, I'd notice the strangest phenomenon: There were some friends who would tell me about some bit of success they'd had, like getting a job or an audition or meeting someone who could be really influential in their careers. I'd feel really, genuinely happy for them. Then there were other people who would tell me the same thing and I'd feel really jealous. It didn't matter if we were in direct competition with each other or not; it was pretty consistent depending on the friend.

I finally realized that the people I was happy for were the same people that would call me to tell me when something bad happened. They'd call me when something good happened that was not related to career. They'd call me to ask what was up in my life. The jealousy perpetrators only called me to trumpet their successes—and then to inquire if I had any similar news to report, which I usually didn't.

It's a two-way street, you see. The ambivalent people were letting me know that they were ahead of me, points-wise. They were insecure; I read into that insecurity and took it upon myself to be jealous. The good guys were rooting for me. I was happy for them because I knew they'd be happy for me. They knew there was room for all of us if we worked hard and had something special to offer.

Now I see that all over the place. If someone rubs me the wrong way, I don't immediately blame myself; I begin to wonder what's up with her. If someone always makes me feel insecure about my body, I ask myself what he or she is projecting. If someone makes me feel like I'm not doing well at work, I ask myself what's happening in his career that he might be dumping onto me. I'm not perfect, I just know I do it to other people, so touché.

Here's a good example. A boss of mine whom I considered a mentor fired me in a really horrible way. My firing had little to do with job performance and a lot to do with bad timing and a money crunch. But when the boss let me go, she went out of her way to demean me. She told me that I had psychological problems and that I'd never find success in my life.

I was devastated. I mean, here she was, total role model, and she was telling me I was doomed to fail. She had to know, right? She was older than me. She was more experienced than I was. What I considered to be passion, she considered to be psychological trauma.

The more I thought about it, the more I realized that IT WASN'T ABOUT ME. This woman went after me because of what I represented—the issues that she had promised to fight for that had been compromised. She had to shut me down because I was echoing the voices she was hearing in her own head, telling her she had done the wrong thing.

So when someone makes me feel shitty, I ask myself how I'm contributing to the shittiness. Why does that girl make me feel bad when another one doesn't? Why does that girl make me feel fat when another one doesn't? Why am I letting her do that? People who love me worry about my weight because they love me. People who don't love me worry about my weight because they worry about themselves. So let them. I can't control their minds or their attitudes. I can only control my own behavior.

As Susie Orbach says in *Fat Is a Feminist Issue*: "To observe an aspect of the self which has been rejected time and time again requires a good deal of self-acceptance. Turning off one's judges—mothers, women's magazines, husbands, lovers, friends, diet doctors, and nutritionists—requires trust in oneself." In other words, I can't control what the judge and jury are going to think of me.

In a way, it really doesn't matter. I am my own best judge and jury. It's a revelation to figure it out. It's like Geneen Roth describes in *When Food Is Love*: "When we experience the body knowledge that no one knows what's better for us than we ourselves do, a seed of autonomy and self-responsibility is planted. Relationships change—with parents, with lovers, with eating buddies, wherever denial and lies were part of the unseen fabric of the connection. Once you experience even the palest glimmer of self-love, it becomes increasingly difficult to feel comfortable in relationships where all that exists is the pretense of love."

If you think someone will love you more if you lose weight, then your weight is not the problem. You have a much bigger problem than your fat belly if you are with someone whose love for you is conditional on the way you look. The problem is not your fat. The problem is your relationship. The problem is your self-esteem. Here's what love isn't: "One [pre-nuptial agreement] stipulated that the wife would pay her husband a sum of money for every pound she gained over a certain weight; she would be reimbursed if she slimmed down again." That is not love. It's a hateful husband who proposes that clause; it's a self-hating wife who signs it. No one will love you more just because there's less of you to love.

You Asked for It

There's only so much you can do to change your attitude about yourself. Then it becomes time to work on everyone else. For example: Why don't people know how to give a compliment? I brace myself for the following example, which I hear with some regularity:

"You look great. Have you lost weight?"

"No, I haven't. But you just made me feel like shit. Congratulations."

"Have you lost weight?" is a slight. It implies that losing weight is what made you look good. It implies that you looked bad before you lost weight and therefore were not deserving of said compliment. It assumes that you are in a constant state of trying to lose weight, which you may not be. We need to disassociate positive compliments with weight loss. When someone says to me, "You look great. Did you lose weight?" I say, "You can just stick with the 'you look great' part, thank you." Or, "No, I did not lose weight, but I do look great. Thanks for noticing." I also like, "No, I did not lose weight, but I look great anyway." FYI, I haven't "lost weight" in eons. But they keep asking, always with a hopeful note in their voices.

There is no need to accept a compliment that's actually a slight. When giving a friend or an acquaintance a compliment, don't talk about weight. Try "You look great." Or "I love your outfit," or "You look really nice today." If your friend begins to fuss, order her to take the compliment. You too must learn how to take a compliment, even if you disagree with it, to help others learn how to give one. If someone has gone through a remarkable physical change—one that I can't help acknowledging—I still avoid saying anything specific. You never know what the hell is going on inside a brain when it comes to a body. I go with the classic, "You look great. How do you *feel*?" Ah, feelings. Beneath the surface. Let them guide you through the conversation.

Some fools go with the eternally obnoxious "Oh my GOD, did you lose a TON of weight?" This is not a compliment. It is downright RUDE. Part of the reason I don't want to lose weight is to avoid this sort of attention. I hate to imagine that in the moment before I walked into the break room, Sherry from Marketing was in there yakking about what an elephant I was before I dropped half my lard load. If Sherry is a real dork, and absolutely deserves it, I suggest you try this response:

"Oh my GOD, did you lose a TON of weight?"

"Yes. Do you think I have cancer?"

I can assure you that your faux-complimentarian will think twice before ever referring to "tonnage" again.

Along these lines, NEVER EVER ask a woman if she is pregnant. Not until she starts pulling out sonograms and showing you her registry on babiesrus.com should you ever assume that a woman is with child. When you're not preggers—just a tub of flub—it's mortifying. After half a dozen embarrassing encounters that began with "When are you due?" I started giving it right back. Now I almost yearn for someone to ask me about my due date. My standard response is as follows:

"When are you due?"

"I'm not pregnant. I'm just fat."

"Oh, I didn't mean . . . uh . . ."

Let the other person be embarrassed. It's not your problem.

My body is not your conversation piece. Sometimes when someone invades my body space by saying something rude to me about my weight, I tell them that fat is contagious—that I used to be a lovely slender girl, then I mocked some chubby chick and woke up fat the next day. Like something out of a Stephen King novel. That shuts 'em up real quick.

You don't have to be cruel to everyone. Some people honestly don't know any better. I was once out at dinner with my friend Matt when an old lady next to me reached over, grabbed my thigh, and said, "You're just a chubbeleh wubbeleh, aren't you?" I thought Matt was going to faint into his pasta. But I laughed it off. "Do you want to know how to lose weight?" she asked me. No, I told her, I'm good, thanks anyways. She and her companion went on to talk about losing weight and kids and so on. Again, all about her, not about me—but not evil, either.

Here's another zinger. When the whole Monica Lewinsky thing went down, even my mother called me to say that I looked just like her. The truth is, I do. I've gone to auditions where I've played Monica. While we have a similar facial structure and a similar smile, and we live in the same city, clearly I'm not Monica. However, I get mistaken for her all the time. I've gotten free drinks in bars; I've gotten free rides in cabs. Saleswomen smile at me when I walk into stores downtown and say, "We haven't seen you here in a while!" Old ladies stop me on the street to assure me, "I don't care what that Bill Clinton says, I think you're a lovely girl." Once at my local supermarket, I had to pull out my driver's license to convince the butcher that I wasn't Monica. Every time I mention this phenomenon, any girl with brown hair who is not rail-thin tells me that she gets it too. I've been told I look like Rosie O'Donnell, Roseanne, Linda Ronstadt, Marie Osmond, Camryn Manheim, Carnie Wilson, Ricki Lake, and the fat chick from Heart. I keep waiting for someone to tell me I look like Queen Latifah. Seen one fat girl, seen 'em all, I guess. It's just a shame that there are so few plus-size women with public stature in our culture. One fat girl represents all of us. So what have I learned to say?

"Are you Monica Lewinsky?"

"No, I'm just a fat Jew."

And that's the end of that.

Speaking of assumptions, here's another common one for fat chicks:

"Are you a lesbian?"

Actually, no, I'm not. Lesbians come in all different shapes and sizes, but most folks imagine they're Pamela Anderson look-alikes or else fat, butch buzz cuts in flannel. I'm not particularly butch, but I am fat, and I'm not a dating machine, ergo I must be gay. If and when this question comes from a lesbian, I take it as a compliment. Women seem to be much more amenable to looking beyond the limitations of what's considered attractive. But from a guy or a straight woman, this question always sounds like wishful thinking.

It's almost easier to have a real confrontation than live with the imaginary fat-attack dialogue that scrolls through my head. For a long time I was incredibly nervous about going through the checkout line at the supermarket. I'd assume that the checkout lady would be silently evaluating my groceries: "She could use more vegetables . . . Is the girl going to eat all of this tonight? . . . She should put the frozen yogurt back and pick the bagels OR the oatmeal." Maybe she is. More likely she's wondering when the hell her shift is over and should she grab some of that cereal on sale to take home to her family. Either way, what I buy is not her concern. She can think whatever she wants.

Same thing in a restaurant. I'd order ranch dressing (on the side, of course), knowing that the waitress thinks that I should stick with oil and vinegar. I finally realized that it's not her job to decide what I should and shouldn't be putting in my mouth—it's just her job to bring it to me. Imagine my horror when I was at a chic restaurant and got this from the waitress:

"I'll have the turkey burger, with French fries on the side."

"Are you sure you wouldn't prefer the salad?"

No, bitch, I wouldn't prefer the salad. Who would? Obviously I'd prefer FRENCH FRIES, or else I wouldn't have ordered them. I couldn't flare up in a joint like that, though, so I made do with the simple "That's okay, I want the fries." But if I'm ever put in that position again . . . and if *you're* ever in that position, you stick to your guns, hear me? Don't you dare leave a tip on the table for that waitress. Believe me, she'll get the message.

More Ways to Demand Respect

Once you start, you can't stop. Conversations become learning examples, and then the respect starts to seep into the rest of your life. Here are more ways to demand respect. After all, Aretha is fat, and she got some.

• Write a Letter

When you see something that pisses your big fat self off, fight back with a letter. That includes a misleading ad or an offensive article. Here's one I wrote that *Time Out New York* published in response to an article called "Why America Is Fat and New York Is Skinny":

I'm a stylish, outgoing, high-income white woman living in Manhattan, and I'm fat. Sure, spotting me is like having a Sasquatch sighting on the Upper West Side, but fat people are all over New York. So don't worry, TONY, I won't let our city miss out on the next big thing.

Let's check back in on the Monica tip for a minute. Just goes to show you that when the most powerful man in the world is attracted to a fat chick, the fat resistance is so strong that it turns him into a laughingstock rather than raising fat status. Her body became a bigger issue than her political scandal, tarring her and Linda Tripp for life. The press was merciless. Headlines in the *Post* included EATING UP A STORM, MADISON AVENUE BINGE AS TRIAL KICKS OFF, SEXGATE SIREN MONICA LEWINSKY TRIED TO CHEER UP WITH A CHOCOHOLIC CHOW-DOWN, and MONICA'S LOSING THE BATTLE OF THE BULGE. When the *Post* ran these two headlines in the same day: BLIMPY MONICA BLOWS HER COVER and TV'S VANISHING ACT—STARS CRACK UNDER STEADY DIET OF PRESSURE, I'd had enough. I wrote a letter to the *Post* that was published:

> You question why Hollywood actresses like those on *Ally McBeal* feel driven to become "painfully" and "shock-ingly" thin. Maybe it's because of the piece in the same issue of the *Post* on Monica Lewinsky. If the choice for women in the public eye is to be rewarded with concern by your paper if they are too thin, but taunted like hated children in a schoolyard if they are too heavy, no wonder they prefer anorexia over appetite.

You should also applaud work well done. When you see a magazine that features plus-size silhouettes, give them a shout out. When a business supports plus-size shoppers, buy there.

When a nice salesperson helps you out, be sure to tell her manager. I also can't emphasize the power of snail mail over the power of e-mail. It's nice to point and click, but nothing competes with the power of the tangible written word.

• **Question Yourself**

If you decide to pursue thinness, that's fine and dandy, but don't do it the same way you've always done it before. Don't let your diet consume you. Let a diet be a temporary element, not "a lifestyle change to fulfill a lifelong goal" and blah blah blah. Step on the scale just once a day or week or month, not twelve times a day. Eat a clean lunch and don't obsess about dinner. Or try to cut back on your body-image obsession in general. If you have to rip on yourself, go for broke for two minutes straight, but then cut it out of the rest of your day. There are more worthwhile things that deserve your all-consuming attention.

And remember, YOU DO NOT HAVE TO SPEND MONEY TO LOSE WEIGHT. Walking is free. Nutrition information is available online or at a library. You can make a piece of chicken or you can buy a frozen Lean Cuisine dinner. If you want to diet, do it for free.

• **Join In**

There are plenty of organizations and lists that would love you to join them, or at least pursue information on their behalf. These are just a few you can look into for information or insight:

National Association for Fat Acceptance (NAAFA)
(www.naafa.org)

National Eating Disorders Association (NEDA)/
    Eating Disorders Awareness and Prevention (EDAP)
    (www.edap.org)
Big Fat Blog: A Fat Acceptance Weblog
    (www.bigfatblog.com)
Pound: I'm Not the New Me (www.poundy.com)
Adios Barbie (www.adiosbarbie.com)
About-Face (www.about-face.org)
Love Your Body (www.loveyourbody.org)
Fat! So? (www.fatso.com)
Jennifer Weiner's Weblog (www.jenniferweiner.com)
American Obesity Association (www.obesity.org)
International Size Acceptance Association (www.isaa.org)
Dads and Daughters (www.dadsanddaughters.org)

Question the System

That's what this whole book is about, really. You don't have to answer the question, just ask. Does this weight-loss thing make sense? Are we supposed to be so skinny? Isn't it weird to spend so much money on stuff that doesn't work? Just putting the idea out there makes a difference.

Ask Out Loud

Take it a step further. Put a body-image question out there in conversation: "Doesn't it seem strange to you that school kids are fat but they put Coke machines in schools?" Shed light on your creepy personal private fear that you thought was just about you: "I have eaten leftovers out of my garbage can." Listen as nine out of ten people shriek, "Really?!? I thought I was the only one!" When you're not alone, your issues can seem a lot less scary. You know that communal feeling when a bunch of women get together to air out their emotional dirty laundry? What a release! Back in the day it was called consciousness raising. I'd like to raise some more consciousness.

Find New Sources of Inspiration

It's time to stop calling on old-time images of big beauty and find some new ones of our own. I'm not telling you to run out and buy Botero prints—that size drama always freaked me out. But you can look for art exhibits like "Feast, Famine and the Female Form," which gives an opportunity to see how the idealized female form has evolved over time. Photographer Ellen Fisher Turk takes photos of women with eating disorders, helping them make peace with their bodies in a process she calls Photo Therapy (www.efturk.com).

We can look to women of physical power for different role models. Lynne Cox is a pro athlete who uses her body fat to survive cold temperatures in Arctic swims. Like it is with Venus and Serena Williams, it's a pleasure to see atheletes take up space with muscles, to use their bodies for strength and not just display them for vanity. Or Cheryl Haworth, a twenty-year-old Olympic bronze medalist who set two U.S. records and won three gold medals at the Goodwill Games in Brisbane, Australia, in 2001. She may be the strongest woman in the world: She weighs about 300 pounds and can lift about 341. Her sisters are atheletes also; one sister wants to be a Supreme Court justice. Her agent "wants her to cash in on her body's power to explode assumptions about female strength, and the challenge she poses, willingly or not, to our one-size-fits-all culture."

Check out the Real Women Project at www.RealWomenProject.org, a multimedia Web site that "uses sculpture, poetry, video, music, and storytelling to inspire dialogue and self-awareness, to broaden our definition of beauty, and to deepen our understanding of well-being." Or Go Girls! at www.goldinc.com/gogirls, a project started by the non-profit Eating Disorders Awareness and Prevention (EDAP) to let teen girls voice their opinions to advertisers. Full of Ourselves is a similar program started by the Harvard Eating Disorders Center (www.hedc.org).

Alexandra Beller proves that there's more than one kind of body built for modern dance. Irving Penn recently photographed her for a New York City exhibit. The *New York Times Magazine* said, "Beller projects an exuberant confidence, making her solidity work for her." Lynda Raino runs Big Dance, a dance studio for big and beautiful dancers in Victoria, British Columbia, Canada, where each dancer weighs between 220 and 300 pounds. Be sure to catch a show by the Glamazons, a group of hot 'n' sexy, big burlesque babes. Check them out at www.glamazongirls.com.

Nope, none of this is very Hollywood. None of it is very cool. But it's much, much healthier.

Keep the Drama on the Down Low

Now this tip runs contrary to everything else I've said so far. But there's one situation in which Fat Girls need to keep a lid on it: no more public kvetchings of "Oh, I'm so fat." No more "I'm so disgusting." No more refusing compliments and making faces in the mirror. Stop putting yourself down in public, or in front of your kids. Say it to me. Say it to your best friend. Fill page after page of your journal with it. But you cannot take yourself down in front of other people. When a skinny girl complains about how fat she looks, she just seems silly. When a Fat Girl does it, it's pathetic. Let's fake it till we make it.

CHAPTER 15

The Other F-Word

Feminism argues that being fat represents an attempt to break free of society's sex stereotypes. Getting fat can thus be understood as a definite and purposeful act; it is a directed, conscious, or unconscious, challenge to sex-role stereotyping and culturally defined experience of woman-hood.

—Susie Orbach, *Fat Is a Feminist Issue*

If you haven't read Susie Orbach's groundbreaking book *Fat Is a Feminist Issue,* get cracking. It's a goodie. Written in 1978, it basically connects the rise of the women's movement with the change in the way women view their own bodies. Orbach sees fat as a kind of triumph. "Fat is a way of saying 'no' to powerlessness and self-denial, to limiting sexual expression which demands that females look and act a certain way, and to an image of womanhood that defines a specific social role. Fat offends Western ideals of female beauty and, as such, every 'overweight' woman creates a crack in the popular culture's ability to make us mere products." The only problem for this triumph? We pay the emotional cost for it. In 1978, Susie Orbach told us that we started a war against society and our own bodies. Twenty-six years later, we're still fighting.

Fat Is Still a Feminist Issue

"Feminism" is the only f-word as scary as or scarier than the word "fat." I know a lot of bright young women, and bright old women, and bright young men, who don't consider themselves feminists. They say things like, "Of course I think men and women should be paid the same thing for the same work. But I'm not a feminist." Or, "Of course I think that women should be able to own land, but I'm not a feminist." To those people, and to you, I give this simple "Are You a Feminist?" test. It goes like this:

"Do you think that men and women deserve equal rights?"

Unless you're some sort of Neanderthal or self-hating woman, you say, "Yes."

Then I say, "Congratulations, you're a feminist."

Feminism is about equal rights, about women being protected by the laws of our country the same way that men are. It doesn't matter if you and I agree about abortion or voting or health care. I think we both agree that our gender shouldn't make us less human. So we are both feminists. And fat, my friends, is still a feminist issue.

How does fat connect to feminism? Well, as Orbach explains, the rise of our current body-image drama really coincides with the rise of the women's movement. Not that women didn't diet or weren't body-conscious before 1970, but the whole thing didn't go into overdrive until women started to make some noise about other issues.

Part of this body backlash is our own fault. When we started a sexual revolution, we naturally started thinking about our bodies in a different way. After all, if for the first time sex outside of marriage becomes socially acceptable, then we are going to evaluate ourselves sexually. Instead of saying "Any body is a good enough body," we became hard on ourselves and critical. We decided that we needed improvement.

Once you can improve something, you can sell something. Advertisers noticed a whole new audience to pitch to—young, single, unmarried women—and started to play into that insecurity, creating an unattainable image of female sexuality and success that we still can't live up to today. An exercise craze starts, we buy running suits and Jane Fonda tapes, Jane gets anorexia, we get fat, and hallelujah, we got an obesity crisis on our hands.

Of course, we feel guilty our about failures of body and spirit, so we start to eat, then we feel bad for eating, so we diet, and the circle of fat begins anew. It becomes easier and easier to focus on the fat instead of the personal issues that cause us so much concern. Madison Avenue feeds right in. Eventually the fat becomes the personal issue. We're gluttons, we're sinners, we have to be punished. The system plays perfectly into the hands of angry spinmeisters in the media on Capitol Hill who don't like uppity women one bit. Beauty becomes our Achilles' heel, a way to keep us in our place, an American burka.

At each significant moment in our female lives, we are confronted with challenges by and about our bodies. We go through physical evolutions; we face self-criticism; we are appraised by others. Rites of passage that should be celebrated as victories are often another notch on an ever-widening belt, another loss in the struggle between feminism and fat.

Girl, You'll Be a Woman Soon: Puberty

The first time I remember thinking negatively about my appearance, I was thirteen and dressing for my bat mitzvah party. I put on the spangly sweater and velvet knickers I had bought six months earlier. When I looked in the mirror, I did not like the shape I saw. I looked all puffy in the middle, like a Weeble or an egg. I wished I hadn't worn my stylin' hot-pink jacket to a different bat mitzvah the previous weekend; it would have covered up my brand-new belly. Ugh. Too late. So I put on my turquoise eyeliner and went to my party and still hate looking at the pictures. I think about looking in the mirror at my thirteen-year-old self, surprised that the body that slid into velvet knickers and a spangly sweater just a few months before was suddenly . . . not right. I was all . . . round. Like an apple. In Michigan recently, I saw a twelve-year-old girl who had been an absolute stick as a kid. When she was little, I noted to myself how pleased her parents must be that their little girl hadn't inherited their fat genes. Now, there she was, in *my* bat mitzvah body! A little golden apple! Puberty strikes again!

I didn't know it at the time, but it was puberty that changed my body. They skipped that when they taught us about menstruation and sex in the fifth grade. I didn't have a name to put on it or an association for it, couldn't connect it to anything else that was going on. Even now, I can't track all of the adolescent changes my body went through. I have completely wiped those memories about my body away. I went from a flat chest to big boobs. When did that happen? Now I can see the moment puberty hits in other little girls. Research indicates that it's happening earlier and earlier, as adulthood awareness trickles down to younger ages. And good nutrition helps girls come to fruition that much sooner.

Is it any wonder that 42 percent of first-through-third-grade girls want to be thinner, that 81 percent of ten-year-old girls are afraid of getting fat, and 51 percent of nine- and ten-year-old girls feel better about themselves if they are on a diet? These are third and fourth and fifth graders. The latest headline? GIRLS AS YOUNG AS 6 ARE UNHAPPY WITH THEIR BODIES AND WANT TO BE THINNER, AN ALARMING NEW STUDY REVEALS. Why exactly are we evaluating little girls on their beauty, anyway? Just when we're developing adult personalities, checking out boys, being evaluated on how pretty we are, we couldn't feel uglier. I wonder, is that little girl in Michigan getting the kind of support she needs, or is she being told she needs to go on a diet? I mean, in her mind there's no way she's gonna go from this body to a Barbie body. (By the way, I love Barbie as much as the next postfeminist chick does, but there's obviously a connection between this doll and negative body image. Barbie was a German sex doll, discovered by Ruth Handler and repackaged and sold to little girls in the U.S. There's a reason nine out of ten strippers and porn stars look like Barbie. Maybe the original intention wasn't to corrupt our sense of self, but then again, even the bomb was invented for self-defense.)

The skills that we need to slog through grown-up fat anxiety are the same ones we lose right when we hit that ugly phase—when we puff up and break out and our hair looks weird and our clothes don't fit and we smell funny and boys start to mock us (because, remember, they're running a couple of years behind). Right when we need to get sassy and smart and talk back and speak up and get angry and ask questions and demand answers, we are taught to behave. To be good. To shrink, to fit in. To act like nice girls. To act like ladies. To shut up. Just like the therapist told me to do at Duke. Like my boss told me to do at work. Shut your mouth, girls. Don't eat. Don't speak. And above all else, don't talk with your mind full.

That longing to hear our own voices, to make our own noise, is its own kind of passion, its own kind of hunger. It's all oral, baby. In her book *Breaking Free from Compulsive Eating,* Geneen Roth describes it as "the hunger that demands release. The hunger that roams in the caves of our bodies. The hunger, not just for food, but also for intimacy, for comfort, for sex, for satisfying work, for setting limits, for self-expression. The hunger that was squelched years ago, before we could fight back, before we could wonder why. The messages received about ourselves and our bodies, about our hungers: that we were intrusive, that we demanded too much, that if we ate what we wanted, we'd be fat, sick, unhealthy. And if we did what we wanted, we'd do nothing, be worthless, destroy ourselves."

Those messages we received were wrong. They made us sick. Now it's time for a little mouth-to-mind resuscitation.

The Booty Myth: Young Adulthood

As we transition into adulthood, women need to take owner-ship of our bodies, not only for our own health and well-being, but also for the message that we send to the world. If we keep showing men that we have a fundamental lack of respect for our bodies—that we are too fat/thin/old/ugly—then what do we expect them to learn from us? Right now we give them front-and-center seats to our show of self-loathing and self-disgust. Our priority is to change our bodies, because we are so ashamed of the ones we were born with. So we diet and exercise and Botox our way to more failure. This cultivates a society where disrespect of the female form is acceptable. Where every ad features naked women. Where hooting and hollering is something you just have to deal with. Where women aren't safe in their homes. Where daughters aren't safe in their beds.

It's quite common for people who have issues around food—whether it's eating too much of it or too little—to have some experience with sexual abuse, especially as a child or an adolescent. Therapists love to talk about fat being both a physical and an emotional barrier against sexuality. Fat literally covers the body, and it serves as an instant turnoff or excuse when it comes to sexual contact. For some of us there's validity to that theory. Writer Karen Durbin explained it best in an incredibly personal and brave essay in *Elle* magazine:

> By getting fat, I was punishing myself, but if I hadn't been, the world would have done it for me . . . Like the uncle who trapped me in my grandmother's kitchen and tried to use my body as a masturbation object? The "cool" boys in seventh grade who liked to decide when a girl had gotten too popular and launch a hate campaign to cut her down to size? The guys in my Midwestern high school who cajoled their girlfriends into sex and then brayed about what sluts they were if the girls dared break up with them? The would-be date-rapists I encountered in college and after, years before I met the one I allowed into my home? The New York City body snatchers who murmured obscenities—or performed them—as they passed me on the street or crowded me on the subway? In a sense I was getting revenge on all those men. I think of them as the enforcers. They're the ones who see to it that sex is a

burden for a woman as well as a pleasure, that pleasure itself comes at a price, sometimes too steep to pay—even simple pleasure in one's body, the way it feels, the way it looks.

There has been no definitive study done on the connection between women and food and sexual dysfunction. But I know a lot of women with a lot of sexual problems and a lot of food issues. The skinny girls are terrified, the fat girls are terrified. If it's not a threat from an outside force, it's an inner fear of exterior change. In response to that, women act out by eating too much or too little.

I've rarely met a woman who hasn't experienced sexual harassment of one form or another. Maybe it was adolescent teasing about her body, maybe it was sexual abuse by a friend or relative, but few of us escape unscathed. I've also met few women who don't feel obsessed with eating and weight or self-loathing about their bodies. There is a connection between the two, and we act out sexual dissatisfaction by punishing the body that did us wrong. One valid point the therapist at Duke made was that even if you haven't experienced direct molestation, being sexually ignored in your life—as many fat women are—can be its own kind of sexual abuse, and worthy of discussion. What's most important to remember is that your story is yours, and it's as valid to you as anyone's.

Bony Bride Disease

The fight against common sense, genetics, time, and what our bodies tell us starts young. Our eventual goal is to find a mate; to get married, to stay married. So the wedding day becomes the most significant day in our lives. Think of all the brides who are so determined to lose weight for their weddings and end up catching Bony Bride Disease. They want to look their "best"—in other words, their "skinniest." This is their photo spread, their shot at *Vogue,* their greatest moment as a woman. So they (and their moms, and their mothers-in-law, and their brides-maids) starve themselves and work out like crazy and hire personal trainers to hone their biceps and triceps and shoulders. Please notice, by the way, that it's only since the 1990s that brides have revealed so much skin in their wedding gowns. It used to be the princess look that was so in demand—high necks, puffed sleeves, billowing skirts. I think the new sleeveless looks are a big step forward for style, but a big blow to our self-esteem.

The problem is that few of us can maintain that low betrothal weight forever. The second they're on the honeymoon, newly-wed brides begin to feed themselves again. They're hungry, you see. Their bodies and brains are calling out for good, delicious food and some emotional nurturing. They eventually climb back to a weight that their bodies can sustain. Then they have a wedding portrait to look at and sigh, thinking, "I used to be so skinny. How did I get so fat?" And of course, their husbands are thinking, "Gee, she was so skinny at our wedding. How did she pork up like that?"

We need a vaccine for Bony Bride Disease.

Big Mama: Pregnancy

Next on the traditional female timeline: Brides become wives, who become mothers. That means pregnancy. And pregnancy means fat. Fat and pregnancy have a similar side profile, but a pregnant woman does not want to look fat or be thought of as fat. We're supposed to be pregnant and sexy, and even though you can't have procreative sex with us for nine months or more we're going to keep up the allure. So we diet during pregnancies. We wear maternity thongs (oh yes, they exist—I couldn't make that up). We find exercise programs and clothes that make us look slimmer and hipper. Weight-loss programs jump right in—Weight Watchers even offers a special program for nursing mothers.

Celebrity moms make sure that the only fat gained on their bodies is in that handy carrying case where you and I have the pouch. And that pregnancy gain is GONE the second the baby is outta there. They Pilates and squat and crunch their way back to that pre-pregnancy profile. Easy enough for Elizabeth Hurley and Elle Macpherson and Sarah Jessica Parker, who didn't have to work for their bodies in the first place—SJP has actually publicly apologized for her warp-speed metabolism—but it seems a lot harder for normal folks like you and me. As writer Michelle Malkin acknowledged, a long line of female celebrities have "sent a dubious cultural message that any and all physical traces of motherhood are shameful legacies that should be worked off, shed immediately, surgically removed or lasered away."

Not everyone is down with the public pregnant profile. I had to include this letter that I found from a *Vogue* reader, because I thought it was absolutely hilarious: "Up to now, I have refrained from commenting on pregnant women, both clothed and unclothed, who have been featured in *Vogue* over the last year or so. I can no longer remain silent. Despite what you and other sentimentalists would have us believe, the pregnant body is not attractive. Beauty and fashion are about cleanness of line and elegance, two things the pregnant body is lacking. Louise E. Wright, Philadelphia, PA." Sing out, Louise!

I'm not saying that pregnancy should be an excuse to binge yourself silly on the world's most fattening foods. As in non-pregnant life, there are healthy weight gains and unhealthy weight gains. I just wish we didn't give ourselves the same kind of scrutiny during pregnancy that we do every other day of our womanhood. When our bodies change and our hormones shift and we gain weight after pregnancy, as our bodies are built to do, we curse ourselves. Enough, already. Our bodies are built to birth babies and get fat. Why be ashamed of a "postbaby body"? Shouldn't we grab our loosey-goosey stomachs, point to our stretch marks, and say, "Do you know what caused this? Birth! My incredible body gave birth to a child! It grew inside me, then I gave birth to it, and I can even sustain its life by feeding it with milk from my own body!" Why would you want to erase the map of your life that is written in your skin? Your life is different after you give birth to a child, so why expect your body to stay the same?

Motherhood

Poor moms. As *New York* magazine recently stated, "If you wanted to stay thin back in our parents' era, you smoked a couple of packs a day. And if you had a secret thing for Oreos and ballooned to a size 14, you had lots of company at PTA meetings. But these days, moms (particularly in the [wealthiest] zip codes) are expected to look like ABT dancers. 'The pressure to be thin; it's just brutal,' says one Upper East Side mom. Another says that now that she's not working full time—she has an interior-design business—she finds herself in greater spiritual alignment with her abs. Asked the biggest difference between her days as a working stiff and today, she doesn't have to think hard before offering an answer: 'I had a much bigger ass.' " The *New York Times* concurred on the model motherhood trend: "Fitness has become the ambition and the opiate of so many women populating the country's affluent suburbs today ... They've subjected their bodies to an almost round-the-clock schedule of yoga, running, Pilates and weight training. It's often the women who gave up the most high-powered careers ... who fuel the most energy into working out."

Forget the competition among mothers to see who can gain the least weight during pregnancy. Forget the fact that the first statistic you hear about a newborn baby is how much it weighs. Forget that a woman was telling me that she makes her two-year-old son lift weights. "He has nice muscle tone," she said proudly. "I don't want him to get fat like his teenage girl cousins. I told them it's what's inside that counts, but we know that's not true, right?" She winked at me as if she DIDN'T NOTICE THAT I'M FAT, THANK YOU, and then lit up another cigarette.

Moms are putting more and more pressure on themselves to mother, to work, to play, to look model-riffic. As moms try to make themselves smaller and smaller, I wonder if they are actually trying to become like children themselves. Maybe their extreme control of their bodies, besides being a cry to the world that they are still sexually attractive human beings, also signifies some frustration at all the control they need to exert, all the planning they need to do. Maybe we're just longing to be taken care of, to have decisions made for us, to be little kids once again. Often when our frustrations with our own bodies' limitations grow too large, we put the pressure on our kids.

I'm so grateful that I didn't grow up as a fat kid. A boy called me "Butterball" in the fifth grade—I wasn't even fat then, but I knew how awful it was, and the undeserved epithet scarred me for years. Listen to this report from the *Washington Post*: "The quality of life for severely obese children and adolescents is roughly equivalent to that of pediatric cancer patients undergoing chemotherapy, according to a new study. The research compared very overweight children to ones who were healthy and others who had cancer, and found that obesity colored nearly the entire spectrum of physical, social and emotional activities. Most very overweight children have at least one medical complication and miss four times as much school as normal-weight children. They're also more likely to report feeling socially isolated even though they aren't clinically depressed or anxious, which most of them aren't." You mean to tell me that a fat kid feels as sad and socially ostracized as a kid with cancer? To me that indicates less about childhood health and more about the need for other kids to leave the fat kids alone. Instead of parents torturing their fat kids for being fat, why don't the skinny bullies' parents torture the skinny kids for being assholes?

Do you really want your children to feel as badly as you've always felt, to go through the same suffering you went through? The best thing you can do for your kids is be a role model for them. Find beauty in your appearance. Find strength in your body. Be honest about your struggle. Then join them as they eat their veggies and go outside and play.

Having It All—or At Least Having Some

At some point we look around at what we've got so far, be it careers, families, homes. Inevitably we're not satisfied. We tend to get scared when we have it too good. We like to make trouble for ourselves. We like to create drama. We do it when we set up our best friend with the guy we have a crush on. We do it when we share gossip with someone we know can't keep a secret. We do it when we buy something we know we can't afford. We do it when we give the best of ourselves to cruel men. I watch women now as we struggle with the bounty that feminism has given us: the right to vote, a voice in the government, a place in the workforce, money. But we complain that we can't manage our time. We make ourselves feel guilty about working and feel guilty about staying at home. We forget that "having it all" wasn't a command—it was an option we wanted to give ourselves. It was a choice that we wanted to make for ourselves.

Author Peggy Orenstein studied this conundrum in *Flux: Women on Sex, Work, Love, Kids, and Life in a Half-Changed World*: "Women's lives have become a complex web of economic, psychological, and social contradictions, with opportunities so intimately linked to constraints that a choice in one realm can have unexpected consequences (or benefits) ten years later in another." As lawyer (and diet guru) Susan Estrich says in her book *Sex & Power*: "If America's most powerful women are of at least two minds about their power, reluctant to even admit that they have it, much less that they like it, should it surprise anyone that the rest of us are unwilling to do what it takes to get it? If nice guys finish last, should it shock us when nice girls don't even get in the game?"

A friend of mine who struggles with the motherhood/work dilemma told me what a paradigm shift she had when she met a very powerful female executive who had adopted two kids. The exec gave a speech in which she said that she loved her work, but her family would always come first. That's the right answer, in case you're wondering. Not to say you shouldn't work hard, or put every bit of attention that you can on your career, but your family always wins. So take that struggle off your plate.

Instead of saying "I am grateful that I live in a culture where I can have a job," we complain that we have to choose between work and family. Instead of saying "I am grateful that I have food to eat," we complain that we are too fat. We need to cultivate our minds in the same way that we cultivate our bodies. We need to honor our bodies in order to cultivate our minds.

A lot of frustrated dieters mention that Victorian women had much different bodies than modern-day women. They note that a full figure indicated a woman of wealth and stature, sexuality and desirability. They forget that in the Victorian age, a woman wasn't evaluated by her body alone. As author Joan Jacobs Brumberg points out in *The Body Project,* a woman was evaluated by the good deeds she did for the community, for the attention she paid to her family. Appearance was important, but not the priority. Experts today suggest that "improving self-acceptance and self-esteem, not achieving 'the right kind of body,' is what makes us feel more attractive, confident, and comfortable with ourselves and others. They suggest that people consciously change their response to the beauty culture and focus instead on their 'minds and hearts, skills and talents' to find fulfillment."

The drive to Have It All, like the drive to be thin, isn't one that we created. It's one that we let get out of hand. It's one whose parameters have been defined by forces outside ourselves. Now, as we do with the word "fat," it's time to redefine "having it all." As Cynthia Gorney writes looking back on her experience and the experience of women of her generation:

> We got nowhere close to Having It All. But here's what I think . . . we had an awful lot of it. I'm not an economist or a policy analyst, but I know there is an abundance of reading out there to support the position that what my friends and I are passing on to younger women is a giant mess of colliding opportunities and sacrifices from which the only real outlet is Either/Or—as though the word has gone out, among women who might be the smaller sisters trotting along behind me: It's too hard, what they tried to do. It can't be done . . . My point is simply that [this] turned out to be the very life I wanted: not my mother's life, not my husband's life, but a patched-up-some-of-both model that I worry is in danger of being cast aside as unworkable by people who have listened to too many women like me despair over what we were missing. We didn't make enough noise celebrating the great parts, did we?

No—but now is a good time to start.

*Results Not Typical

We can destroy ourselves and our spirits in a pursuit of youth and beauty that we didn't ask for in the first place. Elizabeth

Gilbert writes of a yoga vacation she takes at a Far East spa after her body suffers a physical meltdown. Her realization at the end of the trip moved me to tears:

> I for one start bawling my damn eyes out. Which doesn't feel so inappropriate, at all, actually, even though I am experiencing the most transformatively blissful moment of my life. I'm not crying out of sadness or confusion—not like all my other tears this year. I am crying out of release and understanding. I am crying out of compassion for myself and for these other American women whom I've come to love so much over the last two weeks. I'm crying for all the hard times we've ever had, for all the effort we've put forth into holding our ground in our barren modern culture, for all the mistakes we've ever made, for all the hours we've ever struggled, but mostly for this: I am crying out for all the hateful things we've ever said or thought about ourselves. How could we have treated ourselves so poorly? Why had we not been more sweet to ourselves?

It's easy to hate women and hate women's bodies when we don't do very much to fight back. We have to step into the skin we're in. Your body isn't perfect? Well, neither is mine. Neither is anyone's. It's time to redefine "perfect" or drop the expectation. It's time to feed ourselves with compassion instead of grief. Compassion instead of starvation. Compassion instead of food.

I have put myself on a steady diet of compassion that touches every element of my life, from my relationships to my career to my body. I do not judge myself on any standards but those I set for myself. At some point I had to stop relying on the traditional medical stats, like BMI and pounds versus inches, and set my own markers for body balance. I see my doctor regularly. I research new drugs on the market. I investigate alternative health sources. I pay a lot of attention to my blood pressure, blood sugar, and cholesterol levels. I ask myself a lot of questions:

- Am I eating 'cause I'm hungry or 'cause I'm emotional? (Not that I stop, but at least I ask.)
- Am I eating in secret?
- Am I eating a lot of fake crap (i.e., pre-packaged foods), or real food (fruit, veggies, protein, bread, etc.)?
- Am I reaching my goal heart rate when I exercise?
- Do I feel flexible and strong?
- Do I feel comfortable in my clothes?
- Am I sleeping well?
- Am I setting decent goals?
- Am I using common sense?
- Am I being honest with myself?
- Am I acknowledging my gratitude for the goodness in my life?
- Am I finding balance?

I may not score an A-plus, but at least I'm giving myself an essay test instead of a fill-in-the-blanks. So how'd I do today? Well, my hamstrings are still tight from yesterday's yoga class. My watch slides up and down my arm in a way that it didn't a few months ago. If I poke around in my upper arms, I can feel muscles in there that no one will ever be able to see unless I get a surgical arm tuck someday. I'm not ruling it out. I'm a fierce Fat

Girl, but I still can't wear a tank top without feeling a certain lack of confidence. It's my Achilles' heel (my Achilles' upper arm?).

I power-walked on a busy street for thirty-five minutes this morning. My shirt was too long, and it kept twisting around my butt and slowing me down and annoying me as I walked, but I feared tucking it in, because what if someone I knew drove by and saw my ass hanging out, and then I decided I was being ridiculous so I tucked in my shirt and continued walking and so far it hasn't been reported in the papers and all is well in the world.

I don't expect to meet the man of my dreams today, but if I do, then I guess if he's really the man of my dreams he won't reject me when he sees the pudge around my knees.

As far as I know, Gwyneth Paltrow has not compared herself to me today, so I've decided that I will not compare myself to her.

No dieting today. Why diet if that means eating a dry salad at lunch, then sneaking Doritos from my desk drawer all afternoon? Been there, done that. What's the point? I know how my body works better than anyone. I know that croissants have more calories than broccoli, and that I will lose weight if I work out and gain weight if I sit on my ass. Part of feeling good about my body is accepting its limitations and taking responsibility for my choices. One day I may find a way to get a little lighter, but I will never be skinny, and that's okay.

The idea is to be who you are, not who you're not. I've spent my life inside this body trying to be someone I'm not. The truth is, like cobbling together the right food and exercise and attitude and image and style, I'm cobbling together the right life, the best way I can. In the meantime, let's give ourselves a break. Let's take a minute out of each day in which we are not allowed to talk trash about ourselves, to think about pounds and calories and carbs, or to dream that life would be so much better if you were Julia Roberts instead of you.

You can choose to be a mom or an executive or both. You can choose to be happy or healthy or none of the above. You can choose to be fat or you can choose to be thin or you can choose to be in the body you're in today. It's not about what you choose, it's about the fact that you have a choice. So make one. Choose to be yourself. And may the results never be typical.

Notes

INTRODUCTION
p. 4 68 PERCENT OF THE U.S. Census Bureau

CHAPTER 1
p. 7 WENDY IS A *Friends*, NBC, December 12, 2002

p. 10 FERGIE RECENTLY CAME Jill Serjeant, "Once-reviled Fergie reinvents self in U.S.," *Reuters/Variety*, January 10, 2003

p. 14 BUT AT 5′4″ AND 152 POUNDS *Shape*, November 2002

CHAPTER 2
p. 19 CAN'T YOU SEE *Big Eden,* Chaiken Films © 2001

p. 26 FAT IS DEPRESSION Fay Weldon, "Is Thin Better?" *Allure*, January, 1994

CHAPTER 3
p. 35 I HAVE LIVED Camryn Manheim, *Wake Up, I'm Fat!* © Broadway Books 2000

p. 41 BMI IS A MEASURE "Surgeon General's Healthy Weight Advice for Consumers," www.surgeongeneral.gov

p. 42 SOMEWHAT ARBITRARY "Guidelines on Overweight and Obesity: Prevalence and Time Trends," www.nhlbi.nih.gov

p. 42 SEVERAL MUSCULAR HOLLYWOOD HUNKS Betsy McKay, "Who You Calling Fat? Government's Standard Lumps Hunks, Athletes with Truly Obese," *Wall Street Journal*, July 23, 2002

p. 44 AMERICANS NEED TO EXERCISE Jane Brody, "Panel Urges Hour of Exercise a Day," *New York Times*, September 9, 2002

p. 44 61 PERCENT OF US "Overweight and Obesity: At a Glance," www.surgeongeneral.gov

p. 44 THOSE NUMBERS, BASED McKay, "Who You Calling Fat?"

p. 45 FUNDED BY CORPORATE PARTNERS American Obesity Organization, www.obesity.org

p. 46 RAISING MEAT IN AMERICA Michael Specter, "The Extremist," *New Yorker*, April 14, 2003

p. 46 THE ROUTINE USE OF ANTIBIOTICS Editorial, "Fast Food, Not Fast Antibiotics," *New York Times*, June 22, 2003

p. 46 AMERICANS SPEND $35 BILLION Douglas Martin, "Dr. Robert C. Atkins, Author of Controversial but Best Selling Diet Books, Is Dead at 72," *New York Times*, April 18, 2003

p. 47 WEIGHT WATCHERS TOTAL SALES Mui Poopoksakul, "Weight Watchers Beefs Up Attendance," *Fashion Wire Daily*, February 20, 2002

p. 47 THE WEIGHT LOSS INDUSTRY Patricia Winters Lauro, "The Media Business: As Waistlines Expand, So Does Advertising for a Range of Weight Loss Programs and Products," *New York Times*, January 13, 2003

p. 47 JENNY CRAIG SPENDS ibid.

p. 47 MCDONALD'S SPENDS Nat Ives, "You Want Fries with That Salad?" *New York Times*, May 5, 2003

p. 47 TWENTY MILLION AMERICANS Specter, "The Extremist"

p. 48 IF I HABITUALLY "CNN in the Money," June 21, 2003

p. 51 PLANS TO TAKE Susan Flockhart, "The Big Issue," *Sunday Herald*, September 15, 2002

p. 51 ONLY SIX POUNDS Alison McCook, "Study Looks at Pounds Shed with Weight Watchers," *Reuters Health*, April 8, 2003

p. 52 THE WEIGHT WATCHERS PROGRAM Weight Watchers print advertisement, May 2003.

CHAPTER 4

p. 55 THE YEAR I LOST Wendy Wasserstein, "New Year New Outlook," *Harper's Bazaar*, January 2003

p. 55 GIANT PORTIONS Erica Goode, "The Gorge-Yourself Environment," *New York Times*, July 22, 2003

p. 62 A TWELVE-WEEK PROGRAM Alexandra Lange, "The Gospel Truth: Slimming the Other Cheek," *New York*, August 4, 1997

p. 62 GERMAN DESIGNER Joelle Diderich, "Shrink-To-Fit Takes on new Meaning at Chanel," Reuters, October 8, 2002

p. 64 NEW YORK MAGAZINE Beth Landman, "Too Good to Be True," *New York*, May 30, 1994

p. 64 IN LATE 2002 Marian Burros, "Fewer Calories Than Ice Cream, but More Than You Think," *New York Times*, November 2, 2002

p. 65 ON JULY 9 David Barboza, "Food Makers Trim Fat as Lawsuits and Regulations Loom," *New York Times*, July 10, 2003

p. 65 KRAFT FOODS Bruce Horovitz, "Under Fire, Food Giants Switch to Healthier Fare," *USA Today*, July 1, 2003

p. 66 VITAMIN-PACKED Lauran Neergaard, "Cancer Concern at the Breakfast Table," Associated Press, February 25, 2003

p. 66 [A] LAB FOUND Maggie Farley, "Mom Calls 'Booty' Breakfast Cereal on Its Contents," *Los Angeles Times*, May 20, 2002

p. 68 IN HIS ESSAY Greg Critser, "Let Them Eat Fat: The Heavy Truths About American Obesity," *Harper's*, March 2000.

CHAPTER 5

p. 69 I HAVE NOT BECOME FAT Jane Stern, "The Big Fat Lie," *Allure*, September 1993

p. 71 RECENT STUDIES EVEN SUGGEST "Hooked on Hamburgers," *Sunday Times* (London), July 13, 2003

p. 72 ALTHOUGH MEDICAL LITERATURE Ginia Bellafante, "When Midlife Seems Just An Empty Plate," *New York Times*, March 9, 2003

p. 73 EVEN AFRICAN-AMERICAN WOMEN Mary Duenwald, "One Size Definitely Does Not Fit All," *New York Times*, June 22, 2003

p. 75 [ORBACH] BELIEVES Susan Flockhart, "The Big Issue," *Scotland Sunday Herald*, September 15, 2002

CHAPTER 7

p. 107 OUR BELIEF THAT Paul Campos, "The Weighting Game: What the Diet Industry Won't Tell You," *New Republic*, January 13, 2003

p. 108 I CONSOLED MYSELF Jason Epstein, "Carbo Loading," *New York Times Magazine*, June 1, 2003

p. 109 AS WOMEN DEVOTED Daniel Akst, "On the Contrary: Belt-Loosening in the Work Force," *New York Times*, March 2, 2003

p. 109 MOTHERS TODAY SPEND Kathleen Gerson, "Work Without Worry," *New York Times*, May 11, 2003

p. 110 PEOPLE USED TO BE PAID Randy Kennedy, "Tunnel Vision: $15 An Hour, and Trains to Dodge," *New York Times*, November 26, 2002

p. 111 RESEARCHERS HAVE IDENTIFIED Jeanie Davis, "Fat Gene: It Really Exists," Web MD, October 30, 2002

p. 111 SCIENTISTS HAVE IDENTIFIED Denise Grady, "Hormone That Causes Full Feeling Is Found," *New York Times*, August 8, 2002

p. 111 A RECENT STUDY REPORTED "Study Links Binge Eating to Mutation in a Gene," *New York Times*, March 20, 2003

p. 111 RESEARCHERS WHO HAVE BEEN "Scientists Question Whether Fast Food Is Addictive," Yahoo News, January 31, 2003

p. 111 A NEW STUDY SUGGESTS Jennifer Warner, "Eating Disorders Linked to Immune System," Web MD, December 11, 2002

p. 112 AMERICANS ARE BEING THREATENED Pamela J. Johnson, "Obesity Is America's Greatest Threat, the Surgeon General Says," *Orlando Sentinel*, January 23, 2003

p. 115 SOME PEOPLE ARE QUITE HEAVY Elizabeth Fernandez, "Pursuing Fat Chances in a Slim World," *San Francisco Chronicle*, March 18, 2002

p. 115 RECENT STUDIES DOCUMENT Patricia Leigh Brown, "Jazzercise Relents to Plus-Size Pressure," *New York Times*, May 8, 2002

p. 115 ABOUT TWO DOZEN STUDIES Kevin Helliker, "Physicians Start to Turn Focus to Fitness, Not Body Weight," *Wall Street Journal*, July 23, 2002

p. 115 THE FEDERAL TRADE COMMISSION Linda Stasi, "Living and Eating High on the Hog," *New York Post*, September 22, 2002

p. 116 A STUDY OF 692 Michael Singer, "Fat of the Land," *New York Times Magazine*, March 4, 2001

p. 116 A RECENT STUDY MSNBC, January 14, 2002

p. 116 EXPERTS BELIEVE *Glamour*, July 2003

p. 117 I'M NOT SAYING "He Ain't Heavy: Fat But Fit?" *People*, December 2, 2002

p. 118 LOSING WEIGHT COULD PREVENT "Study Hailed as Convincing in Tying Fat to Cancers," Associated Press, April 24, 2003

p. 118 THE SOCIETY SAID Ira Dreyfuss, "American Cancer Society Takes On Fat," Associated Press, February 17, 2003

p. 119 AS THE AUTHORS Jane E. Brody, "Major Study Erases Doubt on Link Between Excess Weight and Cancer," *New York Times*, May 6, 2003

p. 120 NOW CONSIDER Paul Campos, "Fat-Cancer Link Hysteria," *Rocky Mountain News*, April 29, 2003

p. 121 NEW YORK YANKEES George King, "I Was Flat-Line," *New York Post*, February 22, 2003

p. 121 NO OTHER DIETARY SUPPLEMENT Gina Kolata, Walt Bogdanich, "Despite the Danger Warnings, Ephedra Still Sells," *New York Times*, February 20, 2003

p. 121 THIS YEAR, 60,000 AMERICANS Denise Grady, "Why We Eat (and Eat and Eat)," *New York Times*, November 26, 2002

p. 121 "DUMPING" SYNDROME Johns Hopkins Bayview Medical Center, "Nutritional Guidelines After Gastric Bypass Surgery," (http://www.jhbmc.jhu.edu/NUTRI/gastricsurg.html)

p. 122 REGAIN WEIGHT DESPITE Atul Gawande, "The Man Who Couldn't Stop Eating," *New Yorker*, July 9, 2001

p. 122 THE DEATH RATE Michelle Tauber, Mark Dagostino, "100 & Counting," *People*, November 18, 2002

p. 122 A 1993 NATIONAL Gawande, "The Man Who Couldn't Stop Eating"

p. 123 PEOPLE CAN'T STOP EATING Denise Grady, "Why We Eat (and Eat and Eat)," *New York Times*, November 26, 2002

p. 124 HERE IS WHAT WE KNOW Gina Kolata, "What We Don't Know About Obesity," *New York Times*, June 22, 2003

CHAPTER 8

p. 127 HOW DARE ANYBODY *Real Women Have Curves*, © HBO films, Newmarket Films, 2002

p. 130 THE UNFIT LEAN Kevin Helliker, "Physicians Start to Turn Focus to Fitness, Not Body Weight," *Wall Street Journal*, July 23, 2002

p. 131 A POUND OF MUSCLE Rebecca Mead, "Burn Rate," *Vogue*, April 2001

p. 131 THE REASON IS Gina Kolata, "Weight Builds Muscles, but Not the Manly Kind," *New York Times*, August 19, 2002

CHAPTER 9

p. 143 FEMINISTS MAY FROWN Ellen Tien, "The Doctor Is In," *Harper's Bazaar*, August 2001

p. 144 DAYS OF OUR LIVES Alison Sweeney, "How I Dropped 30 Pounds," *Us Weekly*, May 19, 2003

p. 144 THESE DAYS Larissa Phillips, "Get With the Program," *Allure*, July 1997

p. 147 THE AVERAGE MODEL Kate Betts, "The Tyranny of the Skinny," *New York Times*, March 3, 2002

p. 147 NEXT TO THESE GIRLS Bill Hoffman, "Twiggy's Lament," *New York Post*, September 30, 2002

p. 147 THE AVERAGE AMERICAN WOMAN *Shape*, November 2002

p. 147 THE AVERAGE AMERICAN MODEL National Eating Disorders Association

Notes

p. 148 REPRESENTS A WOMAN Kristen Harrison, "Television Viewers' Ideal Body Proportions: The Case of the Curvaceously Thin Woman," Plenum Publishing Corporation, 2003

p. 149 DURING THE TWO WEEKS Jennifer Tung, "Model Boot Camp," *Allure*, May 2001

p. 149 WHEN THE ARTICLE Jennifer Tung, "The Bod Squad," *Vogue Australia*, January 2003

p. 150 I WENT ON A FAST Tisha Campbell-Martin, "How I Got My Life Back," *Us Weekly*, April 21, 2003

p. 152 DURING PUBERTY Geoffrey Cowley, "The Biology of Beauty: What Science Has Discovered About Sex Appeal," *Newsweek*, May 3, 1996

p. 152 SEVEN CANDIDATES Jennifer Tung, "A Leg Up," *Allure*, January, 2001

p. 153 PORTRAYED WITH A Alex Kucynski, "Victoria's Secret on TV: Another First for Women," *New York Times*, November 18, 2001

p. 153 SO, ALONG COMES Joe Soucheron, "Lingerie Models Look Like Real Women Should," *Pioneer Press*, November 22, 2002

p. 155 ARE THESE REALLY WOMEN Farrah Weinstein, "Life in the Fat Lane: N.Y. Men Size Up Fashion Show's Sex Appeal," *New York Post*, February 6, 2003

p. 155 MS. MONROE Mary Duenwald, "One Size Definitely Does Not Fit All," *New York Times*, June 22, 2003

p. 155 THE EVOLUTIONARY ARGUMENT JD Heyman, "The Science of Sexy," *US Weekly*, April 1999.

p. 156 THOSE TIGHT AND TRENDY Aly Sujo, "Hip-Hug Health Hazard," *New York Post*, January 9, 2003

p. 157 THE SYMBOLIC NATURE Ginia Bellafante, "At Gender's Last Frontier," *New York Times*, June 8, 2003

p. 158 IN A RECENT POLL Drew Mackenzie, "The Body Beautiful: Most Wanted List," *Daily Mirror*, February 16, 2002

p. 158 JENNIFER ANISTON'S HAIR Rita Delfiner, "The Perfect Woman," *New York Post*, August 12, 2001

p. 158 IT WOULD COST YOU Johanna Huden, "Britney's $100,000 Body—That's How Much It'll Cost a New Yorker to Buy Her Curves," *New York Post*, December 4, 2001

p. 159 CALLED VISADERA Deborah Schoeneman, "The Current Rage," *New York Post*, November 19, 2002

p. 159 NEARLY 6.6 MILLION Aly Sujo, "Sagging Economy," *New York Post*, April 17, 2003

p. 159 TO PUT IT IN PERSPECTIVE Richard Jerome, "A Body to Die For," *People*, October 30, 2000

p. 160 THE NEW BOTTOM LINE Alev Aktar, "The New Bottom Line," *New York Daily News*, July 10, 2003

p. 160 WHATEVER NEEDS Susannah Breslin, "Designer Vaginas," *Harper's Bazaar*, November 1998

p. 160 IT IS MEN Alex Kucynski, "Why Are So Few Plastic Surgeons Women?" *New York Times*, July 12, 1998

p. 161 I FULLY TAKE ON BOARD Anna Wintour, "Letter from the Editor," *Vogue*, April 2002

p. 161 I COULDN'T HELP BUT Anna Wintour, "Letter from the Editor," *Vogue*, April 2003

p. 162 SHE SHARED HER DELIGHT Bob Morris, "Blithe Spirit," *New York*, May 3, 1999

p. 162 OVER A YEAR AGO Kate Betts, "The Tyranny of the Skinny," *New York Times*, March 3, 2002

p. 163 THIS IS NOT Lisa Schwarzbaum, "Britty Woman," *Entertainment Weekly*, April 20, 2001

p. 163 I DO NOT LOOK Ting Yu et al., "Scoop," *People*, January 27, 2003

p. 163 THE EVIDENCE THAT Ginia Bellafante, "Young and Chubby: What's Heavy About That?" *New York Times*, January 6, 2003

p. 164 BEAUTY MAKES US Linda Wells, "Letter from the Editor," *Allure*, August 1997

p. 165 A WAVE OF OBESITY Seth Mydans, "Clustering in Cities, Asians Are Becoming Obese," *New York Times*, March 13, 2003

p 165 IT IS NOT ONLY FAST FOOD Reuters, March 24, 2003

p. 165 GET THEIR CHEEKBONES Claudine Ko, "A Woman's Ugliness Cannot Be Forgiven," *Jane*, August 2002

p. 165 A DOCTOR CUT Craig Z. Smith, "Risking Limbs for Height, and Success, in China," *New York Times*, May 5, 2002

p. 166 JUST A FEW YEARS Erica Goode, "Study Finds TV Trims Fiji Girls' Body Image and Eating Habits," *New York Times*, May 20, 1999

p. 166 IN IRAN Elaine Sciolino, "Iran's Well-Covered Women Remodel a Part That Shows," *New York Times*, September 22, 2000

p. 166 FACE OF AFRICA Ian Fisher, "Rating Beauty with a Tape Measure, Inch by Inch," *New York Times*, May 22, 2001

p. 166 LOOK THE LEAST UGANDAN Erica Goode, "The Face of Uganda Can't Look Ugandan," *New York Times*, May 5, 2001

p. 166 IN A CULTURE Norimitsu Onishi, "Globalization of Beauty Makes Slimness Trendy," *New York Times*, October 3, 2002

p. 167 IN SOUTHERN NIGER Alex Duval Smith, "Where Men Love Big Women," *Marie Claire*, September, 2001

p. 167 IN NIGER Norimitsu Onishi, "Maradi Journal: On the Scale of Beauty, Weight Weighs Heavily," *New York Times*, February 12, 2001

p. 168 I'VE CHANGED MY PSYCHE Alex Witchel, "At Lunch with Emme: Size 14, 190 Pounds: A Model Figure," *New York Times*, March 12, 1997

CHAPTER 10

p. 171 IT'S NOT MY JOB Julie Burchill, "I'm Fat, So What?" *Guardian* (Manchester), February 22, 2003

p. 172 THIS PRACTICE Alison Anders, "Weighty Matters," www.ew.com, November 14, 2001

p. 172 ACTUALLY THE FUNNY Evgenia Peretz, "Let's Try It Ben's Way," *Vanity Fair*, October 1999

p. 174 I'M 110 Nancy Collins, "Cherry Poppin' Mama," *Rolling Stone*, March 4, 1999

p. 174 SURE THEY'RE RICH *People* cover, August 27, 2001

CHAPTER 11

p. 175 SIZE 4 IS FAT JD Heyman, "Hollywood's Obsession with Weight," *US Weekly*, March 19, 2001

p. 175 THERE'S A REALITY *More*, September 2002

p. 179 ON A NEW ABC SITCOM Alessandra Stanley, "Prime Time Gets Real with a Plump Heroine," *New York Times*, October 8, 2002

Notes

p. 180 YOU DON'T HAVE TO BE Jeremy Helligar and Lori Majewski, "Kelly!" *Us Weekly*, May 12, 2003

p. 180 IF HARVEY WEINSTEIN Liz Smith, syndicated column, *New York Post*, December 16, 2002

p. 183 ABOVE ALL Richard Klein, *Eat Fat*, © DIANE Publishing Co., 1996

p. 185 THE REAL REASON John Waters, "Finally, Footlights on the Fat Girls," *New York Times*, August 11, 2002

p. 192 IT'S ALWAYS Nancy Franklin, "The Time of Her Life," *The New Yorker*, April 14, 1997

CHAPTER 12

p. 197 OUR GENERATION Madonna, "What It Feels Like for a Girl," *Interview*, March 2001

p. 200 LOOKING BACK AT THE TAPE "Overweight and Alone: Teen's Video Diaries Show Despair and Loneliness," ABC News *Primetime*, November 21, 2002

p. 205 THINNESS IS NEVER Rita Delfiner, "Good Sex Worth the Weight: Fat Women Enjoy It More, Top Doc Says," *New York Post*, July 4, 2000

CHAPTER 13

p. 211 YOU CAN'T STOP "You Can't Stop the Beat," from *Hairspray*. Music by Marc Shaiman, lyrics by Marc Shaiman and Scott Wittman. Copyright © 2001 by Winding Brook Way Music and Walli Woo Entertainment. All Rights Reserved. Used by Permission.

p. 217 IN GREAT BRITAIN John Arlidge, "Sizing Up the British Market," www.just-style.com, July 10, 2000

p. 218 ARGENTINA'S SENATE "Argentine Senate Backs 'Real' Clothes Sizes," www.CNN.com/Reuters, June 22, 2000

p. 218 SALES OF PLUS-SIZE "Full Figures Can't Be Ignored," www.CBSNEWS.com, September 19, 2002

p. 218 LANE BRYANT Russell Scott Smith, "Living Large and Loving It," *US Weekly*, April 22, 2002

p. 218 NO WONDER Galina Espinoza, Amy Baumgartner, "Next Big Thing," *People*, May 26, 2003

p. 218 THE GREATEST MARKET SHARE Ginia Bellafante, "The Skinny on In, Out, Under and Over," *New York Times*, November 1, 2002

p. 219 I MAKE COUTURE Joyce Wadler, "Boldface Names," *New York Times*, May 13, 2003

p. 220 FASHION IS ABOUT *New Yorker*, September 9, 2002

p. 225 A WOMAN WHO WEARS "Wearing Wrong Bra Size Affects Health," www.newsnet5.com, March 14, 2003

CHAPTER 14

p. 231 WE CANNOT BE KIND Geneen Roth, *When Food Is Love*, © Plume, 1993

p. 236 ONE [PRE-NUPTIAL AGREEMENT] Larissa MacFarquhar, "So You Want a Divorce," *New Yorker*, April 23, 2001

p. 241 I'M A STYLISH Wendy Shanker, "Large and In Charge," *Time Out New York*, March 20–27, 2003

p. 242 EATING UP A STORM *New York Post*, January 15, 1999

p. 242 MADISON AVENUE BINGE *New York Post*, January 15, 1999

p. 242 SEXGATE SIREN Bill Hoffman, "Blimpy Monica Blows Her Cover," *New York Post*, March 3, 2000

p. 242 BLIMPY MONICA Bill Hoffman, "Blimpy Monica Blows Her Cover," *New York Post*, March 3, 2000

p. 242 TV'S VANISHING ACT Bill Hoffman, "Calista: Pound for Pound, I'm Just Like Monica & Linda," *New York Post*, March 8, 2000

p. 245 WANTS HER TO CASH IN Pagan Kennedy, "Wonder Woman: The Strongest Woman in the World," *New York Times Magazine*, July 28, 2002

p. 246 BELLER PROJECTS Susan Chumsky, "Amazing Grace," *New York Times Magazine*, April 28, 2002

p. 246 LYNDA RAINO Julie K. L. Dam, Vivian Smith, "Fly Girls," *People*, September 10, 2001

CHAPTER 15

p. 247 FEMINISM ARGUES, *Fat Is a Feminist Issue*, © Berkley Publishing Group, 1978

p. 251 AND GOOD NUTRITION Sue Johanson, "The Late Show with David Letterman," CBS, April 30, 2003

p. 251 42 PERCENT OF FIRST National Eating Disorders Association

p. 251 GIRLS AS YOUNG Bill Hoffman, "Girls Start Hating Their Bodies at 6," *New York Post*, May 9, 2003

p. 253 BY GETTING FAT Karen Durbin, "Size Matters," *Elle*, September, 2000

p. 256 SENT A DUBIOUS Michelle Malkin, "The True Shape of Motherhood," *New York Post*, May 11, 2003

p. 256 UP TO NOW *Vogue*, October 2002

p. 257 IF YOU WANTED TO STAY THIN Ralph Gardner, "Mom Vs. Mom," *New York*, October 21, 2002

p. 258 FITNESS HAS BECOME Ginia Bellafante, "Stepping Out in Stepford Style," *New York Times*, October 20, 2002

p. 259 THE QUALITY OF LIFE David Brown, "Study Cites Pervasive Effects of Obesity in Children," *Washington Post*, April 9, 2003

p. 260 IF AMERICA'S MOST POWERFUL Susan Estrich, *Sex and Power*, Riverhead Books, © 2001

p. 261 IMPROVING SELF-ACCEPTANCE Jane Brody, "Adding Some Heft to the Ideal Feminine Form," *New York Times*, November 19, 2002

p. 262 WE GOT NOWHERE CLOSE Cynthia Gorney, "Having It All," *Harper's Bazaar*, August 2001

p. 263 I FOR ONE Elizabeth Gilbert, "The Road to Rapture," *Allure*, February 2003

ACKNOWLEDGMENTS

I am so grateful for the following:

The love I have received from my friends and family, especially Mom, Dad, & Josh;

Wonderful insight and advice from Carrie Ansell, Nancy Gell, Tracy Ginsberg, Lynn Harris, Marjorie Ingall, Kimberly Kleid, Emmy Laybourne Podunovich, Marta Ravin, Deborah Grayson Riegel, and Samantha Saturn;

Generous support from Ceslie, Kevin, Susan, & the staff at *Grace Woman*; Sue Shapiro & the Tuesday night writing group; Susan Swan, Eve Ensler, & V-Day; Marcelle Karp & BUST; the TRL team; Jennifer Baumgardner & Amy Richards, Emme, Ophira Edut, Diane Landau, Karen Robinovitz, Alix Strauss, Jennifer Weiner, and Michele Weston;

The hard work of the staff at Bloomsbury USA, including Lara Carrigan, Dena Rosenberg, Yelena Gitlin, Greg Villepique, and especially my editor, Colin Dickerman;

The motivation of my agent, Peter Steinberg, and his wife, Lisa Shapiro. This book would not have happened without them;

The thoughtful and inspiring words of the female writers I have quoted in these pages;

And the efforts of all Girls, Fat and Thin, who have paved the way.

A NOTE ON THE AUTHOR

Wendy Shanker is one of *Us Weekly*'s Fashion Police and was the resident humor columnist for *Grace Woman* magazine. She has appeared on Lifetime, VH1, MSNBC, and *The Ricki Lake Show*, and hosted a style and shopping show on the Oxygen network. A contributor to *The Bust Guide to the New Girl Order* and *Body Outlaws: Young Women Write About Body Image and Identity*, Wendy has also written for *Glamour, Cosmopolitan, Marie-Claire, Seventeen,* and MTV. This is her first book.

A NOTE ON THE TYPE

The text of this book is set in Linotype Sabon, named after the type founder, Jacques Sabon. It was designed by Jan Tschichold and jointly developed by Linotype, Monotype, and Stempel, in response to a need for a typeface to be available in identical form for mechanical hot metal composition and hand composition using foundry type.

Tschichold based his design for Sabon roman on a font engraved by Garamond, and Sabon italic on a font by Granjon. It was first used in 1966 and has proved an enduring modern classic.